MAKING IT

The Business of Film and Television Production In Canada

D0721157

MAKING IT

The Business of Film and Television Production In Canada

Barbara Hehner
and Andra Sheffer, Editors

The Academy of Canadian
Cinema and Television

Doubleday Canada Limited

Canadian Cataloguing in Publication Data
Main entry under title:
Making it: the business of film and television production in
Canada
Rev., updated ed.
Includes bibliographical references and index.
ISBN 0-385-25514-4
1. Motion picture industry – Canada. 2. Motion picture
industry – Canada – Finance. 3. Television broadcasting –
Canada. 4. Television broadcasting – Canada – Finance.
I. Hehner, Barbara

PN1993.5.C2M25 1995 384'.83'0971 C95-930996-9

Cover illustration by Pol Turgeon
Cover design by Avril Orloff
Text design by Heidy Lawrance Associates
Printed and bound in the USA on acid-free paper

Published in Canada by
Doubleday Canada Limited
105 Bond Street
Toronto, Ontario
M5B 1Y3

Contents

PREFACE

There's nothing like a hit — and then its sequel. The first edition of *MAKING IT: The Business of Film and Television in Canada* (1987) has gone through three reprints and remains the Canadian film and television industry's "bible," taking the mystery (or at least some of it) out of this incredibly complex business, and providing the basic "how to's" for all those who are determined to see their ideas on the screen.

But after eight years, skimming through the book, we were amazed to see how much has changed. It was no longer justifiable to go through another reprint. Our industry has undergone enormous changes. The Canadian film and television industry's leadership internationally in co-productions, exports, and financial deal making, for example, has gone far beyond its early experience of 1987. Clearly, it is time for a new edition to reflect the complexity and sophistication of the industry today.

The Academy of Canadian Cinema and Television has played a key role in the past decade in developing and undertaking unique training programs for our industry. Our success in professional development activities has been an important Academy accomplishment. With the sales record of *Making It*, we proved that there is a demand for knowledge about how this industry works. Our publishers, Doubleday Canada, encouraged us not only to do it again, but also to create a new partner publication, *Selling It*, which together with this book will be invaluable resources for all who produce in Canada. Special thanks to Doubleday's Maggie Reeves and her team for their support, patience, and advice.

An Academy advisory committee planned this new edition: Alexandra Raffé, Seaton McLean, Andra Sheffer, and I took on the challenge — deciding its general scope and direction and recommending the new writer-experts for this edition — a stellar new team of authors. We are all indebted to these industry specialists who have so generously shared the secrets of the trade that they have accumulated through many years of experience. Andra Sheffer, my former colleague and Academy executive director, nursed into existence the first edition of *Making It*, and couldn't resist the temptation to co-ordinate our revised edition. And Barbara Hehner, the editor of *Making It*, with her combined editorial experience and knowledge of the industry, was once again the only logical choice. My thanks and sincere appreciation to them all.

There is no question that the world of film and television will continue to undergo even more dramatic changes in the next decade. The traditional approaches to the business will be questioned and challenged, with vast new opportunities opening up for us all. New technologies will drive multi-media and interactive production for which new forms of "screen software" will be required. This is an exciting era for film and television producers. We hope that with the basic know-how found in *Making It* the future will provide undreamed of possibilities — Best of luck to all!

Maria Topalovich
Executive Director
Academy of Canadian Cinema and Television

A Note from the Editors

It has been almost ten years since we began work on the first edition of *Making It*. In those ten years, we kept in touch and hoped that the chance would come to work together again. When the opportunity to revise the book finally arrived, we found we were looking at an industry that, like us, had matured in ways that none of us had predicted in 1986. Both our personal lives and *Making It* had reached points where spin-offs were appropriate — both of us now have six-year-old daughters, and *Making It* has a new, much-needed companion volume, *Selling It*.

The second edition of *Making It* came together much more quickly and smoothly than the first, for several reasons. The most important is that a successful model already existed, and for this, our sincere thanks to the pioneering authors of the first edition: Ronald Cohen, Peter O'Brien, Jack Darcus, Richard Neilson, Douglas Leiterman, David Patterson, Michael MacMillan, Martin Harbury, Bob Wertheimer, Daniel Weinzweig, Ralph C. Ellis, Jan Rofekamp, David Novek, and Louis Applebaum. They created practical, generously detailed accounts of the aspects of the business they knew best. Our present team of authors was able to draw upon their work for inspiration.

In addition, computer technology made an enormous difference to the speed at which this book could be written, edited, and revised. In 1986, only one author submitted his chapter on a computer disk; in 1995, of course, they all did. Nevertheless, a blank screen can be every bit as intimidating as a blank page, and we sincerely thank our new author team for stealing time from their formidably scheduled lives to write lively, informative chapters reflecting the current complexity and sophistication of the industry.

Finally, our personal thanks to Maria Topalovich for remembering how much we cared about this book, and for persisting in finding the resources to produce an updated version of which we all can be proud.

Barbara Hehner and Andra Sheffer

1

So You Want to Be a Producer

by Alexandra Raffé

In June of 1994, Alexandra Raffé was appointed the chief executive officer of the Ontario Film Development Corporation. Before that, Raffé was president of Riff Raff Films Inc., an independent production company concentrating on the development and production of theatrical feature films.

From June of 1993 to August of 1994 she served as co-chair of the Advisory Committee for a Cultural Industries Strategy, an industry-led partnership with labour and government, to develop an industrial strategy for the cultural industries of Ontario.

Raffé is also known for her work as executive producer on three recently released Canadian feature films: David Wellington's I Love A Man In Uniform, Peggy Thompson's Lotus Eaters, and John Greyson's Zero Patience. Raffé produced two features in collaboration with filmmaker Patricia Rozema: 1990's White Room, and the 1987 critical and commercial success, I've Heard The Mermaids Singing.

Prior to her career as a producer, Raffé worked for Xerox Corporation in a variety of positions both in England and Canada.

But Don't You Really Want To Direct?

It sometimes seems that everyone is an expert on show business. There has never been an industry so closely followed by the public, or so interesting to talk about. Everyone knows the importance of a star to a picture, and many can also speak knowledgeably about this or that director's work. Ultimately, this extended gossip is a form of the prized "word of mouth" — it creates public interest in going to see films or watching television programs featuring actors and directors known to the public.

Only a handful of Hollywood and European producers (count them on your fingers and toes) have this kind of public recognition. When did you last go to a movie because so-and-so produced it? Face it, being a producer is unlikely to get you featured on the front cover of *People* magazine. In this job, your recognition will come from within the industry — from your investors, distributors, cast and crew, and so on — and your rewards will come from the critical and commercial success of the project itself. The value of a successful producer's name does not derive from being in the public eye, but rather from having the credibility to enable a production to be made at all.

Much to my bewilderment, I am often quizzed at cocktail parties or during interviews about whether I would really like to be a director. The unspoken implication seems to be, "now that you are a success as a producer, you could probably get a chance to cross over to the really interesting job." The assumption that producing is somehow a less interesting job quite baffles me. Quite the contrary. My secret fear has always been that "they" will discover how rewarding this producing thing is and give the job to someone more qualified!

I firmly believe that producing is the most marvellous job in the world. You are captain of the ship; never mind that you are navigating tricky waters. There are many good ideas for film or television projects, but without the producer, they remain just that: good ideas. Yours is the position that takes a concept and coaxes it onto the screen.

What Exactly Is It That You Do?

Flushed with the success of my first film, and working hard in pre-production on my second, I visited my parents in England. My mother, thrilled to be reading about the success of my project in the local newspapers, beamed at me over her glasses and said: "We are really proud of you darling. But what exactly is it that you do?"

Good question, Mum. And ten years later, it is still a tough question. What a producer does varies as much as the personality of the producer in question. Some producers very much drive the project: they come up with the story, hire writer and director, raise the money, and supervise the line production, final campaign, and ultimate marketing. Some producers team up with writers or writer/directors and jointly develop the property, working closely in partnership with their creative alter egos. Some producers hire line producers and don't involve themselves overmuch in the day-to-day management of the production. Others run big corporations, and delegate much of the detailed decision making to creative and production personnel within them. It really depends on both your personality and skills, as well as on the demands of the production itself and the size of the organization at your disposal.

Just to confuse things a little further, in your search for a job description you will also have to sort among the various producer titles: executive producer, producer, co-producer, line producer, associate producer, and so on. Again, precise job descriptions for these roles are as varied as the individuals who fulfil them. However, here is a rough guide to the usual distinctions.

EXECUTIVE PRODUCER

Executive producer is the title often given to an individual without whom the film would not have achieved some critical element of the production, such as a major star, the sales or distribution deals required to raise finance, or sometimes a large portion of the finance itself. Increasingly this appelation is awarded as a vanity title to major stars or directors, who, in lending their names to the project, have helped ensure that it happens at all. Or sometimes the stars or directors have developed the project and wish to keep some element of control over the production by retaining a producer-related function for themselves.

On low-budget films, the executive producer is often a more experienced producer who is committed to helping a less seasoned producer initiate her or his first large project. The executive producer's presence provides assurance to the distributors and investors that the production won't spiral out of control, financially or artistically.

CO-PRODUCER

Co-producer credits are usually used when a team of producers is taking shared responsibility for the entire production. This term can describe a team within one country, or can be used when mounting a joint venture or treaty co-production between countries. (For more on co-productions, see Chapter 8.)

LINE PRODUCER

The *line producer* is usually the individual hired to manage day-to-day production. Many producers share line producing functions with their production managers without hiring an individual for this role. If one is hired, the line producer will be brought on well before production starts, and will hand over to the producer at some time after the production wraps, perhaps well into the final editing phases.

ASSOCIATE PRODUCER

Associate producers are often individuals who have performed some producer functions, but without the clear responsibilities associated with executive and line positions. The term usually connotes a position that does not have final say in the producing of the project, but has, instead, responsibility for specific elements under the control of the producer. This can also be a title awarded to a producer who has developed a project but, for whatever reason, is unable to move forward to mount it. When this person hands over the rights to the project to someone else, an associate producer credit is often negotiated in recognition of the work already completed.

Our business is very credit-conscious, and wars have been fought over exact titles and ultimate placement on the finished production. The credit wording and placement, together with the expected job duties, must be clearly detailed in contracts at the outset of the relationship. Sometimes, it must be said, credits are used as bargaining chips in a way that makes nonsense of the rough outline detailed above.

THE PRODUCER — A JOB DESCRIPTION

The title *producer* is reserved for that individual who has primary responsibility for ensuring that all the previously described functions come together on the project. On smaller productions, this is often the only producer credit, and the job will include all the elements sometimes hived off to other producer functions. All these elements are part of the producer job description, whether or not additional people carry out some of the duties. There are also a score of other responsibilities, large and small. But the essence of the job, as outlined earlier, is to turn a story into a filmed entertainment, whether for film or small screen.

The producer is generally perceived as the person who

raises the financing for the production. Whatever else might be delegated to another producer function, there is no doubt that this is an essential part of the duties. However, the job usually begins several years before the cameras roll and finishes several years later. Producing includes all aspects of the production: securing the story rights, developing the property, financing the production, hiring cast and crew, supervising the production itself (together with post-production), developing the campaign elements in conjunction with the distributor or sales agent, strategizing the best launch or broadcast timing, following up on sales and disbursement of investors' returns, and so on. Don Haig, one of Canada's foremost producers, once remarked that each feature film becomes a tenth of the workload of an independent producer for life. He was right. Quarterly reports to investors, following up distributors, generating corporate and GST returns for single-purpose film production companies, maintaining books and records — these requirements continue long after the applause from the premiere has faded.

In short, the producer is responsible for *everything*. It is certainly true that if the film is a great success, the press and public reaction will ascribe this fact to the director, or to a magical performance by an actor, or to the brilliance of the screenplay. Nevertheless, the producer has been responsible for commissioning the screenplay and deciding that it is ready to go into production; the producer has hired the director; and the producer has approved the choice of key cast.

If the cinematography is poetic, the sets are stunning; the costumes are incredible; the special effects stupendous; and the music a runaway soundtrack hit; you are still the person who hired the DOP, the production designer, the costume designer, the F/X wizard, and the composer. If the production comes in on time and on budget, you are the person who hired the production manager, the assistant directors, and the accountant. If the marketing campaign is brilliant, you are the person who decided that the distributor was the right one for this production. And so on.

The reverse is also true. If your production is a critical failure, it is the poor director or writer or actors who will be held responsible in the public eye, but it will still be you who commissioned all the elements of the production, and the greatest failure is actually yours. Even if the production is a critical success, described as a "sumptuous entertainment, deftly executed, powerfully acted, gorgeously staged" but you made it for several times more than it earns, you have failed in your obligation to the investors.

It is a much-beloved staple of production lore that the producer and director are continually at loggerheads over the direction of the production. Somehow, the director's vision is being compromised by the tightfistedness of a producer who wouldn't know "creative" if he or she fell over it. Just as often, you hear of the director who ran amuck, spending thousands of dollars on a whimsical shot, incapable of keeping to production schedules, and generally costing the production a fortune in cost overruns for the sake of a personal "vision." Stories of out-of-control productions or feuds on set make good books and great gossip items in the press. However, the truth is more prosaic.

Producer and Director

It is incredibly hard to make a good film or television program. The key relationship on the entire set is that of the producer and the director. The producer, responsible to the financiers and the distributors, has an overriding obligation to deliver a production substantially in line with their expectations, and capable of being exploited to recoup their investment. The director, in charge of all creative aspects of the production, has the responsibility to make the best possible production from the raw materials of script, cast, and material to hand. In the best of all possible worlds, the producer's and the director's objectives will be in harmony. Within the constraints of production size, the budget should permit the director to fully exploit the potential of the material. This, in turn, requires the producer to understand exactly what emphasis the director needs to place where in the telling of the story, and exactly where scarce resources need to be allocated to facilitate the production.

Developing the Property

Producers become involved in a property in a variety of ways. Sometimes you acquire a script from a writer. Sometimes a writer or director will approach you with an idea, or a treatment or outline. Sometimes you will commission a writer to develop an idea you yourself have generated. You can adapt a stage play, a book, or a short story. You can develop a story from newspaper stories or magazine articles. Whatever the source, the producer's responsibility is to secure the rights to the property, raise development financing to pay the writer (and potentially attach a director), guide the story development, and reach a point where the project is sufficiently developed for the producer to set about securing sales and raising production financing. (This is covered in more detail in Chapter 2.)

STRATEGY

This is also the critical stage in developing the strategy for the production. The producer will have to research the potential market for the production, which will in turn determine how the story develops, as well as the size of the production budget. Remember, your potential investors will require that the size of the budget (and their investment) relate to the potential market returns. The producer will also have to determine what elements — such as key cast or soundtrack music — will be needed to reach that market. Based on these factors, the producer can then develop a sales and financing strategy.

At this time, too, the producer begins to work on a preliminary marketing strategy. This is the document in which you lay out precisely who it is that you think will be interested in seeing your finished production, and precisely how you intend to make sure that they not only know about your production, but also want, nay crave, to pay good money to see it.

Unfortunately, a sound marketing strategy is rare in independent Canadian film, and often runs something like this: "We will finish the film; it will be invited to premiere at Cannes/Berlin/Sundance (select one) where it will be a smash/critical/popular (select one) hit, and will sell to multiple territories overnight. Following the festival success, the film will be launched domestically to capitalize on the attention received at Cannes/Berlin/Sundance (as appropriate). The drawbacks to this plan are that (*a*) you might not get invited to the festival; (*b*) your film might not be a smash hit; and (*c*) even if it does and it is, it might not sell to more than half-a-dozen territories. Unfortunately, if this is indeed the case, you now have no plan to get your film in front of an audience. The marketing strategy should not be dependent for its fundamentals on elements as risky as these, but rather on a sound strategy for selling the production. Extra heights that can be scaled through festival success should be a bonus, not the foundation.

The Budget

To determine the financing you will need, you obviously have to develop a budget. This sometimes involves raising further development money to pay an experienced production manager to do this for you, but low-budget producers often have to develop these skills themselves. Before preparing the budget, you will have to determine the length and complexity of the production, which requires completion of a preliminary schedule or production board. This is done by breaking down the script into its component shooting parts, identifying cast and equipment needs (all of which carry a price tag), to say nothing of estimating how long you need in order to shoot, edit, and so on. (See Chapter 5 for considerably more detail on the components and methodology used to prepare the board.)

Once the board has been established, a budget can be developed that includes all the necessary elements. The preferred start to budgeting is to develop a "best of all possible worlds" budget. The bad new is, it will almost inevitably be too high. This is where you start to relate the budget back to the script, rewriting as necessary to reduce locations, remove the car crashes, eliminate cast and special effects, and so on. However, as you cut and carve to fit your situation, you are *knowingly* making compromises and cutting for available budget, rather than simply not budgeting for items with no regard as to whether or not you will need them. The script and budget move in lock step from this point onwards — script changes affect the budget; budget will constrain the script. The script and budget have to be two seamless parts of a whole. (For more on the budget, see Chapter 3.)

RAISING THE MONEY
There are a variety of potential sources of finance for production. Television programming requires pre-sales to broadcasters, sometimes (although rarely) for the full amount of production, but usually from a patchwork of licence fees, supplemented by overseas sales or government financing.

Theatrical productions need a combination of pre-sales over-seas, a domestic distributor, and usually government financing as well. Private funds can be raised through tax shelters, tax credits, and private offerings, but this type of money is hard to find. (The potential sources and their ease of access is fully detailed in Chapter 4.)

Essentially, film and television are highly competitive mar-kets, with an enormous amount of indigenous and foreign production competing for broadcast slots and film theatres. The better you have done your market research, and the more clearly articulated the potential market for your production is, the more likely you are to raise finance for the production.

Every bit as important as identifying your potential market place and your target audience is knowing the factors that might induce any given investor to look favourably on your production. While overseas pre-sales are possible, they are very hard indeed to secure with unknown cast and director. Some territories have had good experience with Canadian produc-tion of one sort or another, and these may prove profitable opportunities for pre-sales or joint ventures. Do your home-work to identify clearly whether or not your production is eligible for government financing, at either the federal or provincial levels. Each has specific mandates and eligibility requirements, and it is pointless and frustrating to hope for finance from a source for which you do not have prerequisite elements. Potential use of tax shelters or investment tax credits means your production will have to qualify in regard to items of Canadian content, and provincial or labour expenditure lev-els. Ensure that your production qualifies before you go to the trouble of preparing the voluminous paperwork needed to apply for such financing breaks. Research your distributors to discover which players have released which kinds of films in the past. This will help you discover who may be interested in your particular project. The same research is needed in seeking a broadcaster for a television program — what types of production will suit which player? (Chapters 6 and 7 explore the subject of distribution.)

Many forms of pre-sale or licence are not payable until the production is complete and delivered to the end user. During this phase, the producer will have to develop cash-flow forecasts and secure interim financing as necessary to keep the production going. There are huge up-front costs associated with cast, equipment, locations, film stock, and so on; and the weekly carrying costs during production are immense. Any inability to meet your commitments will shut down your production faster than you can blink.

Also around this time, the producer will need to negotiate insurance and completion bonds to satisfy investors that they won't incur huge liability for accidents or overruns during the production, and that there will be a completed production at the end from which they hope to recoup their investment.

Production

Most productions are made through single-purpose companies. These are production companies set up for the purpose of making a single production, and are essentially shut down when it is completed. The producer will need to work with his or her lawyer to set up the production company, establish books, hire an accountant, and so on. (Chapter 10 goes into more detail on this subject.)

There are a number of production components on which the investors and distributors of the project will require final approval, including cast, final budget, key members of the production crew (DOP, production designer, editor, production manager, unit publicist), as well as the final script. Securing these approvals, often at the last minute as script and budget change to accommodate locations and other factors, can be nerve wracking. Also ulcer-precipitating is the process of closing the financing with the distributors and investors, all of whom require completed documentation from the other investors before any of them will flow funds to the production. All this takes place against a backdrop of military operation proportions. Securing the production office and production staff, finalizing cast and crew choices, installing phones, setting up systems, scouting locations, ordering equipment and transportation, arranging meals, costumes — all of these are the overall responsibility of the producer, in concert with the line producer or production manager. At the same time, you will be negotiating with unions, performers' and directors' guilds, and musicians' unions, to say nothing of spending hours in meetings with various departments vying for additional budgets, schedule changes, extra equipment, or additional crew.

STAYING ORGANIZED

Clear communications within your production team are vital. Your director might be out on a location scout with the DOP and production designer, your camera team doing camera tests downtown, your props and sets people out scrounging suitable artifacts, and your costume designer rushing around collecting a dress here, looking at a suit there. Meanwhile, you and your production staff have had to change the schedule around to suit a cast member. You must devise a system whereby each of those key people will receive this schedule-change information immediately. Five hours later, when everyone is somewhere else, the information will change again. As crew go off and prepare their part of the production based on schedule, script, and similar information, all these hourly and daily changes need to be communicated with top speed. The amount of paperwork on a production is staggering: schedules, scripts, budgets, breakdowns, day-out-of-days, cast lists, crew lists, contact lists, vehicle lists, location lists, and so on. All must be colour-coded to show quickly that a change has taken place from the previous version, which you received two hours or two days before.

Each production will have a few scheduled production meetings, at which all the key crew members are gathered together to go over production details. This will include a read-through of the script, and often a read-through of the schedule once you are nearing production. These are often marathon meetings lasting several hours with upwards of 25 people in the room, but they are an invaluable means of clarifying production responsibilities.

The final stages of pre-production are the most exhausting part of a production. This is not just a question of hours of the day on your feet, since production itself chews up just as many of your waking hours (and many that should be spent sleeping as well). Rather, it is that all the major decisions that will affect the eventual outcome of the production are being made, one by one, during prep. Each decision that is made reduces your options for later decisions, so the pressure to get it right is immense. This pressure affects most of the senior crew, as well as, needless to say, the director. Tempers are often frayed, and the producer needs to stay clear and calm, because productions, like most enterprises, take their tone from the top.

THE PRODUCER'S ROLE DURING THE SHOOT

The production phase is usually when the producer stops having time to do his or her laundry. Unless you have a loving or understanding significant other, the end of production is usually celebrated by the arrival of the producer (and rest of the crew) on set in clean clothes!

All during production, the producer smooths ruffled cast

and directorial feathers, soothes tired and angry crew, pacifies
investors with cost reports and production information, makes
a million decisions affecting cost and schedule, and generally
does whatever is necessary to keep everyone in this huge and
fractious and overtired family performing at peak ability. There
is not, unfortunately, a position of producer pacifier on the
production, so keeping your cool and your sense of judgement
is essential.

How much time a producer will spend on the set itself
depends on the individual and the production. Some producers like to spend a great deal of time on set, even if details are
being taken care of by the line producer or production manager. Some prefer to stay back in the production office unless
there is a set disaster which necessitates their presence.
Obviously, if things are going poorly, there is a much greater
need for the producer to be involved in re-scheduling, re-bud-
geting or other brushfire issues.

There is also plenty to do back at the production office.
The task of the production staff at this point is to arrange for
all the logistical elements of the upcoming shoot days: flying
in cast; securing locations; renting equipment; arranging for
special insurance; generating the call sheets for the next day's
shoot as well as doing production, film stock and other reports
for the previous day's shoot; and somehow making time to
respond to frantic calls from the set to do this or do that
immediately if not sooner. Production accounting also continues at full tilt, paying bills; generating payroll; approving cash
advances for sets, props, and production assistants; generating
cost reports; and generally ensuring that the production is fis-
cally on track. The producer gets to supervise all of this.

THE WRAP

Once production is over, everyone seems to disappear. Sixty or more cast and crew melt off to work on their next job, take a much needed break, or simply collapse in a heap for a few days. The producer, with the production manager and accountant, will attend to the final details of wrap: getting the equipment back, returning the props, selling production inventory, generating end-of-production cost reports for investors, and paying the final production bills — after which even the production manager and staff depart. The huge machine is now reduced to the director and the editing team, occasionally with a post-production supervisor to help with the day-to-day detail management.

Finishing the Film

CUTTING THE FILM

Post-production has some similarities to the development phase of a production, in that, once again, you are shaping story elements. Picture cutting will usually start at the same time as production. The editing team will assemble the daily footage, synchronize the sound with the picture for the screening of rushes, and as more footage accumulates, begin to assemble the picture into rough order for the director to view on completion of production. Although the director and editor are primarily responsible for shaping the finished picture, the producer is also generally closely involved, particularly as the picture nears completion.

Screenings of the picture have to be arranged for investors and distributors, often as a pre-condition for the next instalment of financing. Their comments need to be taken into consideration on the final edit, until you arrive at a cut that the director, editor, investors, and distributors are all happy with. Approval of final picture cut by investors and distributors/broadcasters is also often a pre-condition of continued financing.

SOUND

As the picture cut nears completion, the producer hires the sound team. There are usually two elements to the team. The dialogue cutters clean up the dialogue tracks, going back to the original 1/4-inch masters to replace tracks that have become chewed up during the picture-cutting process. They also supervise the additional dialogue recording, when actors go to a sound studio to replace muddy or garbled dialogue lines by repeating their lines to match the picture. The sound effects team lays in numerous tracks to build up texture in the soundtrack, adding room tones, car horns, windows and doors closing, telephones ringing, and so on. The Foley artists then work in the sound studios to record the small noises that accompany every action on the picture, such as footsteps and clothes rustling.

MUSIC

During the latter stages of the picture cut, the composer has started working closely with the director on the music cues for the film. All of these sound elements come together in the final sound mix. This is the point where the dialogue, effects, and music are blended into the finished film. The producer then oversees the final processing of the negative cut, answer printing, creating of duplicate negatives and optical sound tracks, and all the other final details that lead up to delivering the finished production to the distributors/broadcaster.

PREPARING THE CAMPAIGN

The list of delivery items can be extensive, relating not only to the film elements but also to stills, both black and white and colour, text for the press kit, credit lists, biographies, a synopsis of the film, production anecdotes, and all kinds of other materials that may be useful in the marketing or selling of the film.

One of the many vital producer responsibilities during production is to ensure that appropriate photographic stills have been captured by the stills photographer. For many years, Canadian films routinely suffered from a paucity of usable production photographs. This, in turn, left the distributors with few images to sell the film. It is surprising how often a production will fail to have a photo of all the key cast together, or only have photos of them out of costume. Unfortunately, hundreds of shots of the grip doing something hilarious to the second electrician are only useful as souvenirs for the crew, not for selling the film. If you are lucky, you will need dozens of excellent photos of cast and director, together with any major scenes, for magazines to use as exclusives, as well as the dozen or so photos that will routinely come to be associated with the production during its release.

Also during production, the producer will often supervise the creation of an electronic press kit, or EPK. This requires a team to conduct behind-the-scenes interviews with the stars, as well as the director, production designer, cinematographer, and producer. The EPK will be used, together with clips, at markets and as promotional materials in support of the launch of the production or in anticipation of its airdate.

During the post period, the producer will sort the production stills and, working with the distributors/broadcasters, select the ones that will be used in promoting the production. At this time all the final elements of the campaign creation take place, from commissioning the poster or one-sheet to preparing the press kit. The producer will work closely with the distributor to develop an appropriate launch strategy, which ranges from determining which festivals will best showcase the film to planning the advertising campaign and public presentation of the production. If the production is made for television, the producer will work with the broadcaster to secure the most advantageous time slot for the initial screening, and to try to ensure that appropriate advance publicity creates public awareness. (For more of the creation of effective publicity campaigns, see Chapter 9.)

Marketing and Selling

Film and television production is a global industry. The cost of making productions is so high that it is seldom possible to recover the cost of the budgets from domestic sales alone. To a greater and greater extent, productions rely on foreign sales to recoup production costs. The international market is tremendously competitive, and requires enormous expertise and deep pockets to navigate with any success. We have all heard stories of credit card productions, where the plucky producer/filmmaker has hitched his or her way to a major festival or market and struck lucky, but these Cinderella stories are few and far between. (See Chapter 6 and 7 for considerably more detail about the pressing realities of marketing and selling in the current environment.)

Much more likely is a scenario that requires the producer to cede the international exploitation rights to a production in order to raise the financing to make it at all. The rights can be held by a sales agent or distributor, who in turn sells to international territories. Ultimately, that sales agent or distributor determines the markets, campaign elements, sales strategies, and so on, for the exploitation of the film or television production overseas. The producer's role is to influence, as effectively as possible, the sales and marketing strategy to ensure that the production gets the optimum handling overseas.

The closer your relationship with the distributor/sales agent, the more you can influence the outcome, and the more you learn about the international marketplace. If the rights to your production are held by a third party, it may be tempting to you, as a novice producer, to deliver the film, attend the premiere, and move on to your next project. This is extremely short-sighted, because the insights and knowledge gained from staying close to the distributor during the international sales and local territory releases of your production provide an invaluable data bank of information on which you can build as you are putting together your next production. You will learn how much films like yours will fetch in the marketplace, what types of film suit which markets, who is buying what for which country, and so on.

Your investors also expect detailed reports on the progress of the production — both critical reviews and commercial success — along with your regular disbursement to them of production revenues. Thorough and responsible follow-up with your investors will go some distance towards creating a favourable response to your quest for funding for your next production.

After the Show

As mentioned earlier, the paperwork for the production seems to go on for years. Most investors require quarterly reports for the first couple of years, with six monthly reports thereafter. Your reports should include detailed analysis of the press and sales generated by the film, together with box office and television sales information by territory, where available.

Distributors sometimes fail to report, or fail to report honestly. It is your job to push for an accounting when it is due, and to push for collection of revenues from territories sold. Sometimes the information is suspect, and it will be the producer's responsibility to perform an audit or take legal action to ensure the investor's revenues are safeguarded.

You will have to maintain the production entity in good standing, keep bank accounts, disburse revenues, pay ongoing expenses (for stills, rights renewals for performers or musicians, lab transfer costs to make videos, printing up press materials) and so on, to say nothing of filing corporate returns and keeping the books. Being a producer is *not* a short-term commitment.

How To Begin

There is no clear path to gaining the experience to become a producer, no accepted and traditional way to graduate to the role. Some producers start by working in the production office, going from production manager to line producer to producer, although just as many producers have no prior production experience at all. Some people move to producing from the fields of entertainment law or accounting, some from distribution, some from screenwriting or directing, some from completely out of the blue. For a job best described as "jack-of-all-trades," all kinds of experience can be useful.

Although every other film and television craft field has long been taught in film schools, producing was not the subject of many curriculums, until recently. The Canadian Film Centre has a comprehensive producing workshop, although for many, the best training ground continues to be on the job. Emerging producers often fall into the business by joining forces with emerging filmmakers, figuring out together how to finance, manage, and sell a production.

In summary, it is hard to find a job description for a producer that any two producers would agree on, hard to find a training program that will teach you how to do the job once defined, and hard to measure your progress other than by the success or failure of your production, that success or failure in turn depending on a hundred factors outside your direct control. That said, it is also hard to find an occupation as all-consuming and exhilarating as being a producer.

2

Developing
A Property

by Laël McCall with Richard Craven

Laël McCall is vice-president, Film Development, at Alliance Productions, responsible for shaping the company's feature projects, and was co-producer and executive producer of the Alliance movies Turning April *and* On My Own, *both Canada-Australia co-productions. Before joining Alliance, she was producer resident at the Canadian Film Centre. Prior to that, Laël McCall was creative affairs executive at London's United British Artists Developments, involved in developing projects for West End theatre, as well as television and feature films, including* The Lonely Passion of Judith Hearne, *starring Maggie Smith, and* Windprints, *starring John Hurt. Before joining UBAD, she was editor of AIP & CO., the monthly magazine of Britain's Association of Independent Producers.*

Introduction

The process of film development is similar to generating an architect's blueprint or making a prototype for a car. More often than not, the people who generate the original idea become exasperated by the sheer number of collaborators who have contributions to make before the project finally goes into

production. Development is a time-consuming, labour-inten-
sive, collaborative endeavour that, by the time a property
reaches the market place, has drawn upon a wide range of individuals, sources, and disciplines.

While you as the producer hold ultimate control, your
vision of the property will be redefined many times during the
life of a project, with input from writers, directors, actors, studio development personnel, distributors, broadcasters, marketing personnel, and financiers, all of whom will have certain
rights of approval over everything from the script to production financing. It isn't a process suited to bad communicators
or loners. Outside of the core team, consultants will be
brought in to check for accuracy and authenticity; lawyers will
make sure the story doesn't misrepresent a real-life situation;
and marketing and publicity experts will try to ensure that this
"blueprint" has enough "hooks" to reach an audience.

The *auteur* lives in fear of working in such an environment,
where art becomes a commodity, where pictures can be deal-
driven, and where returns are more important than the film's
intrinsic quality. Such directors sometimes choose to work
with low budgets, often writing their own material in an
attempt to retain control, so that financiers feel they know
what they're getting and financial risk is minimal. Even the
auteurs, however, do not entirely escape the rigours of the
development process.

The primary people who work in development are producers, writers, distributors (theatrical releasing companies or
television broadcasters), and often directors and performers.
Producers and distributors usually refer to the prototype as a
property. Writers and directors more often call it a *screenplay*: a
dramatic text of visual images and dialogue that is rarely
understood by more than three people — the producer,
director, and the writer — and sometimes even *they* have

differing interpretations. Unlike the blueprint of a building or the prototype of a car, with a film you never know exactly what you're getting. Who knows how the casting of the leads might change the film, or what the director will do when he or she begins a visual interpretation of the written words that make up a script?

All of these factors make the process of development a rocky road. Out of the hundreds of producers who begin with an idea, a treatment, or even a draft script, only a couple of dozen will succeed in placing their property with a film distributor or broadcaster. And of those, only a few will go into production, even with considerable talent behind them.

Not surprisingly, independent financiers in the private sector often look at film and television development proposals with horror, not only because putting money into projects at an early stage is a very high-risk R&D process, but also because they cannot determine how to quantify the value of something they rarely understand, which is often being developed by unpredictable creative people with strong points of view. This private-sector timidity is one reason why many film industries around the world have persuaded their governments to set up agencies to make substantial investments in film and television script development. For, at the end of the day, and whatever you may be encouraged to think, one thing the industry does understand is that, with rare exception, a good film is only as good as its script.

Property development, therefore, is not for the faint-hearted or for lunchtime dreamers of overnight success. It is a rigorous and emotionally exhausting process, which demands courage, astute judgement, endurance, a talent for communicating, and a temperament that enjoys vicissitude and attention to detail in what is a very complicated artistic endeavour.

Properties and Copyright

In Canadian law, a concept or story is just an idea, and until it is written down in some material form it is not protected by copyright. By writing down a specific idea, as only he or she can tell it, an author takes possession of it. Only in its written form can an idea by copyrighted.

At any one time, the chances are good that there are people with an idea similar to your own, breathing the same "creative ether." After all, if the idea occurred to you, it might occur to someone else. Certain ideas, even if written down, are very difficult to copyright: for instance, a proposal for a film on a public figure. What *is* protected by copyright is the author's written expression of the idea.

WHO OWNS THE COPYRIGHT?

The owner of the copyright in a work is the author, *the person who has written it down*, unless it was produced as part of the duties of an employee, in which case the copyright owner would be the employer. A producer must acquire the right from a copyright holder to reproduce, adapt, publish, perform, or broadcast all, or even a substantial part, of any work that has not been created by the producer.

Many stories are the inspired creation of a writer, who writes an *original script*. Other stories come from books, plays, or short stories that serve as the basis for a screenplay and are, therefore, *adapted from another medium*. Projects based on previously published or performed material are sometimes appealing, because they have already proven that the stories can attract attention. Adaptations are generally considered less risky than original screenplays. In Canada, however, most films have been based on original scripts created by writer/directors with distinctive points of view.

If the source material is a novel, a short story, or another work previously written down, or is based on true events, the story is already largely defined and you, as a producer, must secure the rights to adapt it. Even if you only plan to base your property loosely on another work, you should still get a legal opinion as to whether it is necessary to acquire underlying rights. It is usually sensible for you to write down on paper your own ideas for the adaptation. This process will help a lawyer to discern similarities and differences from the original, and to determine whether or not underlying rights need to be obtained.

PUBLIC DOMAIN

In Canada, the period of copyright lasts 50 years from the death of the author, after which it normally enters the public domain. If the property is based on existing material that is in the public domain, it means the work is unprotected by copyright and a producer can benefit by not having to pay for rights. However, because there are no rights to secure, you also have no protection against the same property being developed by other producers at the same time. Again, setting down your ideas for adapting or interpreting work that is in the public domain will serve to protect the development process, because it demonstrates the particular, idiosyncratic direction you wish to pursue.

GETTING YOUR IDEAS ON PAPER

If the written work is based on your own original idea, then expressing it on paper is crucial to making it your own. To distinguish original ideas from other properties, the written text should contain as many details as possible that illustrate how it is unique. This includes writing descriptions of characters, plot, mood, and any other supporting elements that show how it is different from other stories past and present.

Getting the written description of a story is as important as owning a piece of land before you build a house. Frequent disputes arise over copyrighted ideas that have been stolen. If this happens to you, you will have to fight for your right to the property in court. If all you have is a written description, the more specific and detailed it is, the better your chances of success.

Where Do Properties Come From?

Projects arrive on a producer's desk in a variety of ways. A writer, director, or agent may submit an idea, treatment, or even a completed script; or you might read a book or article, or see a play or television interview that you think would make a good screen story.

Wherever the idea comes from, producers are essentially property seekers and creators, because everything they do depends on owning a property. You aren't in business until you have a property, and development can't begin until the property is sufficiently developed to attract both money and talent. Even if it's based on the producer's own idea, a producer will normally commission a writer to flesh it out.

The producing function begins with choosing a tale to be told and deciding that it deserves to be filmed. On this decision rests the potential for future success or failure, defined in terms of both art and business. A property represents a goal to be accomplished and a contract to be kept, and the producer controls the ability to do so on behalf of all concerned. Your worth as a producer lies in the ownership of a good property that can be exploited in the marketplace for profit.

Assessing Good Stories

Generally speaking, good stories are about people. They often feature diverse characters and have protagonists who overcome opposition to a goal and go through dramatic change during a series of events (plot twists). They are told with control, energy, and sensory cues that are intended to produce an emotional reaction in an audience. A script is likely to be commercial if it produces an emotional response in the reader. A good story always has high stakes — it makes people *care*. One way to test whether a story can provoke a strong, interested response from an audience, is by whether or not an audience member can retell the story in a few sentences.

You should identify the selling points of your property early on, and know the audience for whom the project is being developed. You should know what you want to say about the subject and the style in which you want to do it. A producer's ability to define and communicate these things greatly smooths the development process by allowing everyone involved to understand the nature of the goal.

Rights

A producer needs to be very careful about securing all possible rights in both the option and purchase of a property. If at all possible, you should clear rights for maximum use: everything from music to merchandising. This allows you a degree of *control* in the market place. For example, all media rights should be granted at the same time.

Being granted both film and TV rights also gives a varied number of options for exploiting the property. For example, a property originally envisioned as a theatrical movie might, because of a changing marketplace or financing opportunities, eventually be developed as a cable or network movie-of-the-week, or as a pilot for a television series. You should therefore ensure that your rights in the purchase agreement cover prequel, sequel, TV series, remake rights, and so on.

Ideally, exclusive rights should be acquired to ensure that no one else can make the same story. Since a producer must always contemplate hiring other writers, the agreement with the original writer must allow for the possibility of revisions by another.

Having secured the rights to a property, you then control it (in the case of an option, for a fixed period of time) and can seek investment towards its further development. This usually means finding partners. When acquiring partners, it's important that you continue to own or control underlying rights, even though those who may participate in financing during development will have certain rights to revenues derived from their eventual exploitation.

REPAYMENTS

If, during the development process, a studio or financing party no longer wishes to pursue the project, you will find yourself in a *turnaround* situation where you may need to seek a new group of financiers or partners. It is important for you to have ensured that there is only a limited requirement for you to return any development money that has been advanced. As a rule, turnaround provisions require only that the producer return third-party financing, plus reasonable interest, *if and when* the project is made with another group of financiers.

It is not an unusual practice that, if a producer eventually abandons a property, rights will revert to the author after a set period of time. This allows the copyright holder to either resell the rights or personally develop the property. Again, it is normal industry standard that, if the property is made by another party, some of the originating producer's and financier's costs (say, to develop the script) are repaid.

PROTECTING YOUR PROPERTY

If an idea in written form is your own, you need evidence that enables you to prove that you are the creator. The property can be registered with the Copyright Office, which is not expensive. A simple way to create evidence is by mailing yourself a registered letter with the property inside it. Don't open the envelope when it arrives. In this way, the date of its creation will be established by the postmark on the sealed envelope. Alternatively, you can send a copy of the property to your lawyer or bank manager for safekeeping. You should have the recipient send you written acknowledgement of the fact that your letter has been received, providing evidence of the date of its receipt by a third party and verifying its contents, before placing your letter in a vault.

You can also, as a copyright holder, register a script, treatment, or specific outline with the Writers Guild of Canada Registry Service (for members, $10; for non-members, $20).

Agreements

While developing a property, producers will potentially work with four types of agreements.

OPTION AGREEMENT

This is a written agreement that allows a producer the right to acquire specified rights in written material for a specific fee and for a specific period of time.

An option agreement will specify the option price, and a purchase price if the option is exercised; the precise nature of the rights that the producer has the right to acquire; the length of time (with specified allowable renewals) that the producer has to develop the property; and the specifications of the *exercise event*: that is, the things that need to happen to make the purchase price payable. An option payment is generally a comparatively small amount of money, or "down payment," made in return for being granted the exclusive right to purchase rights at a later time. It is often 10 per cent of the amount payable for purchasing the rights, in return for a one-year option, with the option price being applicable to the purchase price.

If you are short on cash, and just want to test an idea in the marketplace, you may wish to secure an option for a very brief time. In the case of a script, an option of one month or less is completely negotiable between a producer and writer and is not subject to all the normal provisions of the Writers Guild of Canada Agreement.

Generally, for feature projects, 18 months is the bare minimum for an option, to give you time to commission and develop a script and test the marketplace. Given how long the development and financing process can take, an initial option for a year is hardly worth the money and effort. In television, however, 6 and 12 month options are more normal. Option agreements usually provide that, after the initial option period has lapsed, producers may renew their option for one or two further periods of time (for a total of three years) and for a further fee, which, typically, will once again be 10 per cent of the purchase price per year. Following the first 18 months, however, this further fee will not generally be applicable against the purchase price for the rights.

LITERARY PURCHASE AGREEMENT

This agreement specifies the terms of payment a producer is obliged to make to the rights holder in order to "own" a licence to exploit the property. An outright purchase of rights can free a producer from further co-operative obligations with an original creator but, in a very high-risk business, it's an expensive route that requires considerable experience and knowledge of the marketplace.

SCREENWRITER'S AGREEMENT

Once you, as the producer, have secured an option, you are free to commission a script (or a rewrite of the script, if the material you've optioned is already in screenplay form). An agreement with a writer will specify the ownership of the rights, what has been licensed, and for what period of time. It will also contain the amounts to be paid for the rights licence, the total fee to be paid for the script, and the date by which it is to be delivered. A screenwriter's agreement will also specify credits, the rights of both parties to modify the script, and whether (if you're hiring two writers) they're working as a team.

If a producer or a writer is a Writers Guild of Canada signatory or member, the rights agreement must conform to the WGC Agreement. All aspiring producers should immerse themselves in the WGC Agreement to determine their obligations and rights.

The agreements outlined in the preceding pages are fundamental to a producer having a *clear chain of title*. Before you can finance the development of your property, you will have to produce evidence of there being a clear chain of title, which precisely identifies each change in ownership of the property and the rights that are held. (For more on this subject, see Chapter 10.)

DEAL MEMOS

These are short-form contracts which are legally binding documents setting out the basic terms that the negotiating parties have agreed upon. A producer might use a deal memo to secure a director to work with a writer during development of the screenplay. The deal memo would provide for a consultancy fee for the director and specify the terms and conditions upon which the director would be hired when and if the project became financed. A deal memo is generally followed by a longer form agreement at a later date, once financing for the project has been secured.

LAWYERS

Any deals a producer enters into should be clearly understandable in layperson's language before being written as legalese. While producers often wish to do their own negotiating, it is *essential* that they have an entertainment lawyer go over contracts before they are finalized. Good lawyers are expensive, but they're indispensable. They play an important role in the fate of a project by providing full protection of the producer's interests. As they are relatively impartial, they also often help to provide the necessary edge to close a deal.

Development Financing

Once the idea has been identified, a producer will have to arrange for development financing: funds for the acquisition of rights, and for supporting the development of a screenplay and for other expenses involved in getting property from basic idea to the point at which it can receive production financing. (See Chapters 3 and 4 for more on this tricky stage and how to budget for it.)

Producers generally try to avoid investing their own money in developing a property. Producers should minimize their risk by negotiating modest options and seeking writers who are prepared to work at WGC scale. This is particularly important with low-budget, first-time productions.

Other than arts councils, no third-party funding bodies will enter into business with an individual producer. You should be prepared to incorporate the moment a third party agrees to contribute money to develop your property. Your lawyer can usually obtain an "off-the-shelf" numbered company or set up a new company.

THE BUSINESS PLAN

It is important for a producer to create a realistic business plan for the development of a property that is based on a estimated schedule. The budget should cover all phases of development from idea to final script. Areas of expertise often omitted or underestimated in development budgets are legal and accounting fees, as well as consultants and researchers (even if you end up doing the research yourself, an allocation for time and expenses should be included). Having made a careful development budget and schedule, you will know your cash-flow needs and thereby avoid amassing unexpected overheads and expense.

The role of a producer is half-creative and half-businessperson. If it is only the creative aspects of producing that appeal to you, you should consider working with or within larger companies that have a centralized business structure, because more than 50 per cent of an independent producer's time is spent on business while developing a property.

It may take a year to get your idea into development with a writer, another year to develop a script and begin to package it, and a further year to take your project into the marketplace. Producers must take account of this scale when negotiating rights and making a business plan. It's important to keep your investment (both time and money) to a minimum until you get a development deal and ensure a proportion of costs are being borne by third parties. Bear in mind that if you finance development yourself, you won't necessarily be able to pass on all historic costs to third-party financiers (government agencies in particular) later on.

If development financiers turn a project down, it is the producer's job to ask why. Is everyone else wrong, or is there a problem with the property that needs correcting? Putting up one's own money is unlikely to be a solution. Furthermore, the odds are enormous against any one property actually getting made. No one likes to take too huge a risk, and producers should feel uneasy about spending large sums of money before they've had a chance to test the marketplace.

WHAT WILL IT COST?

Below is a sample development budget for a low-budget feature film (first time producer) that has a projected production budget of $1.5 million Canadian.

Category	Treatment	First Draft	Second Draft	Total
STORY/RIGHTS (Two 12-month options on novel with a purchase price of $40,000)	$4,000		$4,000	$8,000
WRITER (WGC Scale: $36,386, payable 35% for Treatment, 50% for First Draft, 15% for Second Draft)	$12,735	$18,193	$5,458	$36,386
FRINGE BENEFITS (13%: 9% Actra, 2% WGC, 2% CFTPA, each up to $1,500)	$1,656	$2,365	$710	$4,731
RESEARCH Writer	$500			$500
TRAVEL Writer (Toronto/Thunder Bay/Toronto)	$300			$300
LIVING Writer (Scale per diem — 5 days × $67; Hotel – 5 days × $100)	$835			$835
DIRECTOR Retainer		$5,000	$5,000	$10,000
TRAVEL Director (Vancouver/Toronto/Vancouver)		$600	$600	$1,200
LIVING Director (Scale per diem – 5 days × $100; Hotel – 5 days × $100)		$1,000	$1,000	$2,000

LEGAL (Option, writer's agreement, director's deal)	$5,000	$2,000		$7,000
PRODUCTION BOARD/BUDGET			$2,500	$2,500
Development Costs **Less Fees and Overhead:**	$25,026	$29,158	$19,268	$73,452
Overhead Fees (Per Telefilm: 15% of dev. costs):	$3,754	$4,374	$2,890	$11,018
Producer Fees (Per Telefilm: 15% of dev. costs):	$3,754	$4,374	$2,890	$11,018
Total **Development Costs:**	**$32,534**	**$37,906**	**$25,048**	**$95,488**

In Canada, the federal and provincial development funding agencies generally accept a blanket 15 per cent development producer and overhead fee (calculated on the amount of the development budget less these two fees). The overhead fee is to cover telephone, office, secretarial expenses, equipment, printing, couriers, mail, and support materials. It is also possible, rather than taking a blanket overhead fee, to break down exact costs, but this can be time-consuming and difficult to estimate in advance.

If a producer chooses to involve a director in the development process, his or her consultancy fee is strictly a matter of negotiation, unlike the fees that are payable to a writer, which must be according to the Writers Guild of Canada minimums. Every picture is different in terms of its needs. It is your job, as the producer, to determine what they are for the story you have chosen.

Sources of Development Financing

All sectors of the Canadian film and television industry have come to recognize the critical importance of developing good properties.

Development financing can be requested from the sources outlined in the following pages. (This is not necessarily an exhaustive list and all sources are subject to frequent change.) All accept proposals at different times of the year (some monthly, some bi-annually) and have guidelines that normally require a producer to submit an application form and proposal. If a producer is unknown to them, they may require a meeting, possibly with the proposed writer as well. They may also warn a neophyte producer that they will expect him or her to partner with an experienced executive producer at some point during the development process. All of these funds require that a producer be a Canadian citizen or landed immigrant and, in some instances, be a resident in a particular province in order to be eligible. Most of these organizations grant development financing in the form of interest-free loans that are only repayable if and when production financing is raised.

NATIONAL SOURCES OF DEVELOPMENT AND CORPORATE FINANCING:

- *The Canada Council* has several programs offering development assistance. They contribute, through grants, to the development of Canadian productions that are usually non-commercial and experimental in nature.
- *The Canadian Independent Film and Video Fund* is aimed at the non-theatrical market and is geared to educational, business, health, and special-interest groups. They can normally finance development of a project to a maximum of $10,000.
- *The COGECO Program Development Fund* is administered by the Maclean Hunter Television Fund and provides devel-

opment financing loans for Canadian dramatic television series, treatments, first draft or final draft scripts, in English or French. The writer must be Canadian, and a letter of intent from a Canadian broadcaster is required in order to be eligible for funding.

- *CIDA's Film and Video Co-production Program* is administered by the Canadian International Development Agency and encourages productions relating to international development issues. Development funding to a ceiling of $14,000 is available.

- *The Cultural Industries Development Fund* was established several years ago to provide financing and management consulting services in order to strengthen the financial base of Canadian business in the cultural sector. The CIDF provides loans ranging from $20,000 to $250,000 to companies that have been in business for at least two years. The CIDF will also pay up to half (to a maximum of $10,000) of the costs of professional management consultation.

- *The Department of External Affairs and International Trade* runs a program to promote the marketing and export of Canadian film and video products. Depending on availability of funds, the department can cover a portion of international travel expenses, or costs related to promotion. Although this program is a bit of a stretch for general development purposes, a producer might be able to persuade the program that a trip to a country or region of economic or trading priority to Canada (for example, Southeast Asia or Chile) would be of benefit if the producer is seriously developing a viable co-production.

- *The Export Development Corporation* is a financial institution that has a number of financing and insurance packages for Canadian companies exporting product.

- *The Foundation to Underwrite New Drama for Pay Television*

(FUND) supports feature film script development with an annual budget of $1 million. Projects high in Canadian content and talent are given priority. In exchange for financing, they have a first right of refusal to further develop/produce the project.

* *Owl Communications* has a fund called *The Family Channel/Owl Program Development Fund*, which provides development financing for joint ventures with producers to make quality family entertainment.

* *Radio-Québec/TVOntario* is a program development fund established in 1994, encompassing a wide range of educational programming. They have $500,000 to spend over three years.

* *The Telefilm Canada Canadian Broadcast Program Development Fund* was established about ten years ago to help independent producers develop television programming. The fund may, in certain circumstances, finance up to 50 per cent of a development budget, in the form of a non-interest-bearing advance, repayable on the first day of principal photography to a cap of $100,000 per project. Once initial stages of development have occurred, broadcaster commitment may be required before further funding is advanced.

* *The Telefilm Canada Concept Development for Television Series Program* is a fund to support experienced producers develop initial concepts before approaching broadcasters. Maximum investment is $10,000.

* *The Telefilm Canada Cross-Over Writers Program* is designed to give experienced writers in other fields an opportunity to work on a feature film script. Playwrights and writers from Western and Atlantic provinces are eligible to apply for a maximum investment of $10,000.

* *The Telefilm Canada Feature Film Fund* was created in 1986 to stimulate investment in Canadian features destined for

theatrical release. The fund may, in certain circumstances, finance up to 50 per cent of a development budget, to a ceiling of $100,000 per project. The funding comes in the form of a non-interest-bearing advance, repayable on the first day of principal photography. Once initial stages of development have occurred, distributor commitment may be required before further funding is advanced.

- *The Telefilm Canada Scriptwriting Assistance Program* has a maximum allowance of $10,000 to assist experienced screenwriters in developing detailed treatments.
- *Bravo!/City* will support development of features, television movies (City TV) and performing arts programs (Bravo!) with up-front funding repayable only if the project is produced.
- *New Initiatives in Film* assists Aboriginal women and women of colour by providing professional development and film-making opportunities. Established by the NFB's Studio D, this $300,000 initiative provides some development funding to experienced filmmakers by means of an internship.
- *Superchannel Development Fund* provides development loans ranging from $5000 to $30,000 for features, television movies, series and children's programming. Funding can be accessed at any stage of development.

PROVINCIAL SOURCES OF DEVELOPMENT AND CORPORATE FINANCING

- B.C. *Equity Capital Program (Venture Capital Corporations)* is a tax credit program whereby investors can acquire up to 50 per cent of a company to a total of $5 million.
- B.C. *Film Fund* finances up to 40 per cent of a development budget, to a maximum of $20,000 for features and $40,000 for television series.
- *Kick Start* is a competitive program offering assistance to first-time filmmakers. It is administered by the Directors

Guild of Canada B.C. District Council. The competition awards up to $10,000 per short film or video project, with a budget no higher than $20,000, and is restricted to western Canadians. This program, at time of writing, is under review.

- *The Alberta Motion Picture Development Corporation* funds up to 60 per cent of development budgets (to a maximum of $15,000) and up to 60 per cent of pre-production budgets (to a ceiling of $200,000 excluding producer fees).
- *The Saskatchewan Communication Network (SCN)*, the province's educational broadcaster, has no set program, but participates in developing material with a local spin, in return for which they like to have a first broadcast window.
- SASKFILM *(Saskatchewan Film and Video Development Corporation)* has three phases of development interest-free loans: up to 60 per cent of a development budget to a maximum of $5,000 for an outline or treatment; up to 40 per cent to a maximum of $15,000 (TV) and $20,000 (film) for a first draft screenplay; and up to 30 per cent to a maximum of $15,000 (TV) and $25,000 (film) for a final draft screenplay, to a total cap per project of $35,000.
- *The Saskatchewan Television Network Development Fund* is a Baton Broadcasting fund designed to foster local development and production. Average development loans are between $4,000 and $5,000, in return for which the station has first right of refusal to participate in further development and/or production.
- *The Manitoba Cultural Industries Development Office (CIDO)* makes interest-free development loans up to 50 per cent of a budget to a maximum of $25,000 per project.
- *Horizon*, administered by Telefilm Canada, is an initiative available for directors who are working on their first or second feature and are residents of Alberta, Saskatchewan, or

Manitoba. A producer or distributor need not be in place for candidates to apply for development funding. AMPDC, SASKFILM, and CIDO may also participate.

- *The Ontario Arts Council (and other provincial and local arts councils)*, while not specifically geared to development, do have small Film, Video, and First Project grants, ranging from $5,000 to $40,000, that may prove valuable to producers as part of overall financing on projects with budgets ranging from $75,000 for first-time directors to $500,000 for more experienced filmmakers.

- *The Ontario Film Development Corporation (OFDC)* finances the development of feature films and documentary television programs. Ontario producers are eligible for interest-free loans to a cumulative maximum of $35,000; in exceptional cases, the maximum for feature films may be increased to $50,000. Additionally, development funds are available for New Media projects up to a cumulative maximum of $35,000 over two phases. In exceptional cases, the maximum for New Media development may be increased to $50,000.

- *BBS Ontario Inc./CJOH-TV Development Fund* was established by Baton Broadcasting and makes television development loans of up to $5,000 to applicants resident in the Ottawa area. In exchange for these funds, CJOH has first right of refusal to further develop/produce the project.

- *MCTV Fund*, established by Baton Broadcasting, provides $100,000 per year to go towards the production of 13 half-hour pilots for primetime broadcast by MCTV. Interest-free loans ranging from $1,500 to $7,000 per project are administered through the *MCTV Development Fund* and are repayable on commencement of principal photography.

- *Racial Equity Fund* provides development grants of up to

$3,000 for filmmakers from the Aboriginal, African, Asian, Black, Caribbean, Central and South American communities of Ontario. The program's main source of funding is the OFDC.

- SPEQ *(Société des placements dans l'entreprise québecoise)* provides a mechanism whereby companies can raise funds from the private sector. Investors acquire minority interests in small-to-midsized companies and receive a tax deduction that equals 125 per cent of the SPEQ investment. The maximum investment through SPEQ in any one company is $2.5 million.

- SODEC *(Société de développement des entreprises culturelles du Québec)* has approximately $1 million allocated annually to support optioning, scriptwriting, and rewriting (script-related costs only). SODEC will support up to 50 per cent of a development budget.

- *The Nova Scotia Film Development Corporation* will invest up to $25,000 per project in interest-fee development loans for features, series, miniseries, TV specials, documentaries, and non-theatrical programs.

- *Fundy Cable* contributes $50,000 per year in development and/or production financing to New Brunswick projects in all TV genres as well as short films.

- CBC, CTV, Baton, Western International Communications, Global, YTV, and the Family Channel also provide financing for developing programs they eventually hope to broadcast.

The Treatment

Preparing to meet a financier or applying to one of the agencies for financing is a little like going to court. A producer is in the business of providing evidence that must establish an overall picture with no contradictions. The "jury" must believe in the producer, and not lose confidence at any step along the way. The evidence a producer chooses to present (for instance, a fine treatment) is crucial.

WRITING A TREATMENT

A treatment is a narrative, scene-by-scene, description of a story or "map" for a screenplay. For feature films, treatments are generally 25 to 40 pages long, and will include descriptions of characters, the story plot, and possibly dialogue or key scenes. The creation of a treatment allows a producer/director and a writer an opportunity to determine exactly what they want their story to be.

Treatments aren't, however, easy to write. The art of writing a good treatment is nothing like that of writing a fine script. It's a little like comparing a trailer to a completed film, except treatments need to tell a whole story in just the manner you want it to be told. They should not include highly condensed detail that reads flatly, nor should they be so slight that a reader cannot imagine the project will run for its intended duration. Treatments need to provoke the interest of a reader (possible financiers) to see your story made into a film.

Whether you choose to include a scene from the film (inadvisable unless it's very strong), or support material such as magazine articles or director's notes, depends very much on your judgement and the nature of the story (these kinds of materials can help to make your treatment package more diverse and interesting).

FINDING A WRITER

Suggestions for writers can come from friends in the business, story editors, directories, agents, development personnel, agencies, and financiers such as broadcasters. It's a producer's business to know who's who, to read copiously, and to meet writers, in order to determine what a particular writer will bring to a project. Does your shortlisted writer have a love and knowledge of the subject in question? Does he or she have the screenwriting skills to pull it off? This is something you can determine only by reading that person's previous work. Can you (and your director) communicate easily with the writer? Recognizing good chemistry is an important producer skill, and applies just as much to choosing your director, cast, and heads of department as it does to choosing your writer. Once you've identified a writer who is interested in scripting your property, deal with the writer's agent or lawyer.

Developing a Script

Syd Field describes a script as "a story told with pictures, with a beginning, middle, and end." Broadly speaking, a script is a detailed story narrative, including dialogue, descriptions of characters, settings, action, and sound effects. It is an interwoven, layered piece of writing that is a bridge between a literary form and a visual one (without describing its visuals in detail) that makes full use of the medium to make fresh connections.

Long-form scripts can be anywhere from 90 to 130 pages in length. Action scripts are generally shorter than the norm. A page of script is approximately equal to a minute of projected film — a 98-page script takes about 98 minutes to view. Screenplays differ from stage plays in that they play around with time and locations in a way not possible in reality. Use of a single location, for example, will make a script feel like a stage play. Good scripts don't remain static or move in a straight line. The motifs established in the early scenes should gain richer meaning by the end of the script.

Most important, a script should involve the audience in the life of the protagonist. Elements that break the thread of emotion or the empathy the audience feels for the protagonist are disruptive. Generally speaking, a script should not fool around with the point of view.

The Producer's Role

Producing a project is a little like playing a good game of chess. At every move, producers must re-evaluate their plan. Producers exercise authority at the earliest and final stages in the life of a property. The buck always stops on their desk. No matter what their background, their position is one of innovation, leadership, and control. While a key producer task is to watch the property's bottom line, a good producer is a creative ideas person, salesperson, self-promoter, entertainer, opportunist, *and* someone who had diverse knowledge of all aspects of film production, sales, and marketing.

The climate for independent producers in Canada is changing rapidly as broadcasters, government agencies, and distributors redefine their terms of trade. While we cannot say there has never been a better time for Canadian producers, a changing landscape means there are always new opportunities for those who have their ear to the ground.

When Is a Property Ready for Marketing?

The marketing process for feature films usually begins in earnest when a producer has a fully developed script. It's easier to secure interest from talent, distributors, investors, bankers, and agents if the producer is also able to talk about potential directors and "packaging" with some authority.

A fully developed property will have the following preproduction delivery materials in order: rights/chain of title; script; director (feature films are director-driven, television less so); possible cast (whether committed or a wish list, they can help bring a property to life in the minds of readers); a production schedule (outlining the work to be done, the time needed to deliver the property, and the style of the production); a production budget (reveals standards, the priorities, and the marketing intentions of the producer); financing and marketing plans (answers the question of whether the film can be made and reach an audience); and key art (establishes the audience to whom the finished product will appeal).

DO THEY REALLY LIKE IT?

The Canadian marketplace is small, with few companies who can help advance a property toward production. Producers will eventually need commitments from distributors or broadcasters, and should discuss their ideas and test the marketplace before getting in too deep. Producers can only benefit by knowing how much people like their idea, and whether they are prepared to help pay for it (a telling indication of whether they *really* like it). By doing so, producers can determine how much work and money is needed to get the property to a stage where production funds can be secured.

Producers should only back a project for as long as it takes to test the marketplace properly. This means asking tough, direct questions, without fearing the answer will be negative from a potential investor. Chances are, if a producer feels an answer might be negative, it always will be. Why spend time developing something that is doomed? Always bear in mind that *sympathetic* responses from agencies, broadcasters, and development executives do not mean they are necessarily expressing real interest.

Discussions with directors and actors tell a producer whether they like the project and are willing to have their names associated with it or not. Many producers, once they have attracted a director, will have a closed reading of the script with actors before working on final script revisions and submitting the property to financiers.

If particular talents are of importance to your property, it is advisable to get their expressed interest in writing, although it must be borne in mind that such interest is rarely binding. Never suggest that someone is committed to your property without his or her permission. Although it can be a boost to involve "named" talent in a project, it can also kill it dead if, for instance, a broadcast executive or distributor doesn't share your taste.

APPROACHING DISTRIBUTORS AND BROADCASTERS

The initial approach to distributors and broadcasters can be done by telephone or letter to establish whether a particular company is interested in receiving more material. In broadcasting, in particular, commissioning is cyclical, and producers need to know when broadcast executives are open to "pitches" and new proposals, and what program slots they are trying to fill. In television, development tends to mean having the marketplace — a broadcaster or end user — buy in at the beginning of the development process.

Program ideas should be presented clearly in a one- or two-page outline. If the broadcast executive is interested in further discussion, a producer may be asked for a "pitch" meeting, very often with a writer, before beginning to prepare a treatment. A pitch is a verbal trailer meant to hook those who are being told the story.

Broadcast, agency, and distributor responses vary. They will often need nudging. If a producer hasn't received an initial response within a month, it is reasonable to drop a line or telephone to follow up. Once interest has been expressed, producers should feel free to press for a response.

Producers should be cautious about presenting any *written* material prematurely — an idea is fresh only once. You've only got one shot with written materials, so make it count.

Generally, distributors and agencies log every submission received. The material is read, evaluated, and written up in synopsis form ("coverage"). Reader's comments are carefully registered and filed away. If you resubmit your script, chances are it won't be looked at again, because nobody likes to read the same material twice, has the time, or wishes to spend money on readers for a script that wasn't well received the first time around.

Finally...

A strong, independent, indigenous production industry depends on producers with the passion and judgement required to develop good properties based on innovative themes and ideas. National cinema and television industries are, in many ways, like individuals. Our health and well-being depends on understanding who we are and what sets us apart from the rest. It's not that we must make *Canadian* films and television where Canada is central to everything. That would be like meeting someone who only talks about himself. Whatever the problems of Hollywood, Americans don't wonder how they can make an *American* film. Our concern must be to tell a story that compels an audience, *that is told from our unique point of view.* It is the role of the producer to develop universal stories written with a very clear understanding of who we are: Canadians. On this, everything depends.

This chapter was written with the generous assistance of Richard Craven, who established the Toronto office of Eureka Location Management in 1987. His location work has included the miniseries "JFK — The Reckless Years", and the "Robocop" TV series.

3

The Budget

by Charles Zamaria

Charles Zamaria has had a diverse career in the television and movie industry. He has performed the roles of executive producer, line producer, production manager and production accountant on many independent productions, including: "Dudley the Dragon," "Groundling Marsh," "The Big Comfy Couch," "The Elephant Show," "The Last Winter," "Sweating Bullets," and many variety specials, documentaries, and "one-off" productions. Previously, he worked for CTV and YTV in management capacities, for the CBC as a film editor, and for Telefilm Canada as assistant manager of Business Affairs. He also has experience as a video editor and sound recordist. Currently, along with operating his own consulting and service production company, Professor Zamaria is a full-time faculty member of Ryerson Polytechnic University's School of Radio and Television Arts where he has been teaching since 1991. He also serves as the co-ordinator of its Continuing Education program.

Overview

WHAT IS A BUDGET?

A budget is more than just a collection of numeric values indicating how much it will cost to create a product (a completed movie or television program). It is also more than a record of the costs of negotiated contracts and agreements for material and human resources. A budget is *definitely* much more than a series of calculations to determine how much a producer wants to spend.

A budget, in essence, is all of the above. When prepared properly, it is the master business plan for the television program or movie you intend to produce! It will reveal every production parameter. It will show in detail how you have decided to produce your production. For example, one could "break down" a script and prepare a budget for $500,000. The same script, however, could also result in a budget of well over $5,000,000.

The budget is a revealing portrait of how much money will be paid to every cast and crew member. It is also a testament to how good a negotiator its author is, since it will contain the cost of all "deals," for such things as equipment rentals and supplies.

Many of those who will invest in your production will be more concerned with reviewing and analyzing your budget than any other document you submit for their approval. It should contain every single bit of information they might want to know about how your production will be "produced." Aside from the creative aspects of your production — the script, and the "packaging" of cast, director, marketing plan, and so forth — the budget is the most essential element required in order to obtain financing for your project. It is also the map used to navigate your project through all stages of production.

What follows is a summary of some of the most important aspects to consider when preparing a budget for the television and movie industry. It discusses not only what is expected, but what you can include to help individuals read and understand your "plan."

WHY IS THERE A BUDGET?

To understand why a budget exists, you need an awareness of the entire production process, including how projects are financed and what the financiers or "investors" will want in return for their contribution. Seldom will you have the financial resources necessary to produce a movie or television project on your own, unless you are independently wealthy and foolish enough to spend your own money on a film or television project! Therefore, you must find other sources of funding to help you finance and complete the production.

The television and movie industry is funded from a diverse variety of sources: government agencies, private individuals, corporations, and so on. As in any other industry, before providing this funding, these investors need to know what they will be investing in. In our industry, this is usually conveyed to the investors by a script. After reading the script, the next thing investors want to know is how much it will cost to produce and a detailed justification and explanation for this cost. This is the information the budget must convey.

By reviewing and analyzing the budget, investors can determine if it is likely that the product can be produced for the cost that has been budgeted (and they will want to satisfy themselves that it could not be produced for less, thus decreasing their financial risk); second, they will want to ascertain whether there is a reasonable expectation that their investment will be returned and a profit will be reaped once the product is sold in the market.

In summary, *budgets are prepared to indicate to potential investors how the production will be produced, how much it will cost, and why it will cost that much.*

But the budget isn't only for investors. It also enables you, as the producer, to set up a cost reporting system that helps you determine how you are progressing financially. Financing is finite in the television and movie industry; you cannot keep returning to the cash well if your production begins to exceed your estimates. Once a budget has been set — or "locked in" — it rarely changes. Investors do not provide producers with a continual line of credit. That is why it is necessary to estimate all production costs before proceeding to production.

Once you are in the heat of production and costs begin to fluctuate, the budget provides you with a summary of projected expenses that you can compare to your actual expenditures, thus determining *variances* of costs compared to budget estimates. If there is an under-budget variance in one category, you can apply the "savings" to an over-budget variance in another. In the end, the most important objective is to complete the production within the overall or bottom-line estimates you originally provided, thereby honouring your commitment to your investors and securing your reputation as a brilliant prognosticator and able manager of finances! Investors will not only desire this, they will insist on it. As the old adage suggests, "you are only as good as your last *successful (completed on budget)* production."

WHO PREPARES THE BUDGET?

Producers are ultimately responsible for the creation and execution of the budget; their time is more often consumed by raising the funding than working out in detail how much the production will cost. Producers always know how much they want to spend, often based on how much money they think they can raise. They generally have a grasp of the overall budget and the percentage of costs that should be apportioned to the various budget categories and subcategories. However, for the most part, they do not have the acumen to prepare a detailed budget thoroughly and accurately. This onerous task, more often than not, is reserved for the individual who is specifically trained in these skills: the *production manager.*

Production managers are a shrewd and intelligent lot, who have spent much of their careers finding out how much everything used on a production costs, and how to obtain these things even *less* expensively. They are well versed in commerce and fiscal responsibility, but also are thought of as "artists" for their ability to creatively budget productions and see them through to completion within these estimates. Generally speaking, if a production manager is hired in the "development" or "pre-production" phases, this professional will remain until the production is completed.

Production managers possess a wealth of experience — they have a remarkable ability to anticipate the many things that could go wrong with a production, and they budget accordingly. They are well aware of all current union and non-union pay rates and the terms and conditions of collective agreements. Production managers are also familiar with what specific deal points might be negotiable and what must be recognized as an expense in the budget.

They have a very strong and supportive network of both key crew personnel, and equipment and facility suppliers who can assist them in the breakdown of specific cost details. Well informed about all the needs of the various production departments, they know how much to budget for each one. Ideally, they consult with a colleague regarding the budget breakdown for a specific department when advice is needed, and they do not resist hiring or consulting with a department head to prepare a department budget. They maintain a library of various government and private publications and rate cards summarizing up-to-date costs of all production exigencies. But, most important, they worship detail and know how to add, multiply, divide, and, of course, subtract! In conclusion, though virtually anyone could prepare a budget for a movie or television program, production managers most often are the best ones that do it.

WHO READS THE BUDGET?

The budget, being a very revealing document, is closely guarded. Indiscreet disclosure of its contents to the wrong party could undermine a producer's competitive edge or create acrimony on the set. Therefore, the budget and its specific categories are disclosed only on a "need to know" basis, and then only after careful consideration.

Obviously, investors and broadcasters must be able to study the budget. It is their money that is helping you to produce the movie or television program and they have every right to know how their money will be spent. Rest assured that after they review the budget, they will let you know how they think you can spend less.

Department heads in the production unit are generally provided with budgeted amounts for categories within their jurisdiction. For example, an art director has to know the total amounts available for art supplies, locations, set dressing, props, wardrobe, and so on, to determine the scope and size of his or her department's creations. The more money the art director has to spend, the more sophisticated and creative the look of the production; the less money, the more thrifty and adaptable the art director will have to be. A production manager will sometimes hold back disclosure of the full budgeted amount to a department head, to provide some "padding" to offer the department later.

Regardless of what you have budgeted for, department heads will always demand more, even if they were the people who originally provided the budget breakdowns for their departments. The process of disclosure is often more painful than creation of the budget itself! However, once the department heads have received the financial information, they become responsible, in part, for tracking their expenditures against the original estimates. The producer and the production manager then have a tangible way of judging the department's needs, expenditures, and fiscal responsibility.

Many crew members, performers, and equipment suppliers want to see the budget contents, but are seldom allowed to do so. Occasionally, crew members will do their utmost to obtain a copy of the budget, even by unscrupulous means. Some insist the lack of full disclosure means that the producer and production manager are hiding something. Perhaps more money was actually budgeted for their services or for their supplies than they have received, due to the brutal negotiating skills of the production manager. In some situations this is true, because a good production manager will always attempt to pare down the original cost estimates, thereby providing more money for other categories in the budget. For anyone to suggest this is a sinister plot is inaccurate. As long as the production manager has negotiated fairly, it simply represents fine business skills and common sense.

Your production accountant will also require access to the budget, tracking actual expenses and comparing them with the estimated costs in order to produce a weekly report known as a *cost report*. (Refer to p. 106 for more on this vital document.) This is the most important document produced during production. It represents an audit of how closely expenses are following projected estimates in the budget. All investors, broadcasters, and guarantors will insist on seeing this report regularly.

Insurance brokers will need to see the budget to determine what should be included and excluded from coverage, and the amount of premium to be assessed. Your lawyer will also need the detailed budget information when preparing contracts and draw downs. The completion guarantor (the quasi insurance company that ensures that the producer will complete the production on budget) will approve the budget prior to production; use the budget to determine the amount of their premium, usually based on a percentage of the budget; and monitor expenses compared to the initial cost estimates.

Some unions and guilds will want to see at least a copy of the budget summary to ensure that their members and fringes have been properly budgeted for; as well, they will need to see it in order to determine the amount of the refundable "bond" they will ask the producer to provide. This is money that the union or guild will hold in escrow until your production is complete and all its members have been paid. It is important to note that "bonds" are not part of the budget since they are refundable and do not constitute an expense. Nevertheless, it is necessary to account for this money from a "cash flow" standpoint.

Preparation of the Overall Budget

When we discuss preparation of the "overall" budget, we mean evaluating and reviewing all the elements that are required for a particular production, before itemizing and calculating the details of a budget. This is an important process that will enable you to establish the scope of the production as well as make calculating details much easier.

HOW MUCH TO BUDGET

One question that is often asked at this stage is: Do we "budget for production" or "produce for budget"? That is, do we budget with the assumption that money is no object? Or are we limited in our budgeting to a finite amount that will require certain compromises?

In Canada, we "produce for budget," because budgeting must reflect how much financing the producer is able to raise. The majority of production in Canada is "deficit financed," meaning that, as a producer, you have to finance your production with funding from other investors, who will not recoup or have their investment returned to them immediately after completion of the production. The production begins, in essence, in a deficit situation.

In the television sector, for example, producers sell their productions to broadcasters and obtain a licence fee in return. The maximum licence fee one can obtain from a broadcaster in Canada is approximately 30 to 35 per cent of budgeted costs. That is an insufficient amount to return the original investment to all equity investors. As well, the broadcaster's licence fee is often used as part of the financing for the budget. In other words, there is not enough revenue earned to cover the cost of production or to clear the deficit.

If the producer is successful in earning revenues through international sales of the program and other ancillary markets to pay back the investor's original investment, the producer will then attempt to sell the production to earn a profit for the investor. However, "recoupment," let alone profit, is seldom seen in the Canadian movie and television industry. The financial status of any Canadian production usually will continue as a deficit.

There are many reasons, both cultural and economic, that account for investment in movie and television programs despite the financial drawbacks. Most notable are the tax incentives, government agencies mandated with cultural agendas, and private funds set up to contribute a portion of profits from successful media enterprises back to the production community. We have a limited market compared to countries like the United States, where initial licence fees may be large enough to pay for the entire budget.

Producers generally know before they even commission a script how much the budget will be. They base this on how much financing they will be able to raise for a particular project. It is quite common for a producer to hire a production manager and tell him or her: "This is a $500,000 production," or "You have $2.2 million to work with," regardless of the production demands of the script. If you want to be a producer in Canada, you have to be realistic about how much financing can be raised. And you must discover very inventive and creative ways to spend your limited financial resources.

There are many ways you can control your cost projections in the budgeting process. We will discuss some of them shortly. As well, keep in mind that each script and production does have a bottom line of absolute minimum financing necessary to achieve a reasonable finished production. Perhaps you have inadequate financing to complete even the most bare-bones budget. This is when you learn the difference between a budget challenge and an impossible budget. Experience and thorough planning will help you determine which one you are facing.

BUDGET FORMATS AND TEMPLATES

Before sharpening your pencil and putting figures to paper, you must determine how to organize your hundreds of different cost estimates in a coherent and presentable manner. A budget may be as specific or general as you choose. Financial information can be sorted into as many discrete categories as you believe necessary. However, if you want to obtain financing from a recognized government agency or private investor, the manner in which you break down and summarize the costs is crucial.

It is extremely important to decide upon the most appropriate budget format or *template* to use in presenting your cost estimates. "Most appropriate" usually means the format the investor is accustomed to seeing, and does not necessarily refer to the most appropriate manner to break down costs for your specific production. Various financing agencies and investors review hundreds of budgets annually, and it would become very time-consuming for them if on each budget they sat down to analyze, the cost estimates were presented in a different manner. Therefore, standard budget templates have been created to ease the evaluation and analysis of budget information.

A standard budget form also helps those who adjudicate your budget to compare your estimates with other budgets submitted for different projects. This will greatly assist the budget reviewers in determining how reasonable they think your cost estimates are.

You might decide that a budget format you have invented is far clearer than the standard form. However, resist the temptation to use it. You will only make it more difficult for the individuals and agencies who will scrutinize your budget to read and understand it — and you will irritate them, which is clearly *not* in your best interests.

In Canada, for most mainstream independent film and television productions, the budget template that the agencies and investors are most accustomed to reviewing is called the *Telefilm* or DGC budget format. You can obtain a blank copy of this "template" from Telefilm Canada and most other recognized funding agencies. It is almost 60 pages long and contains over 64 categories (and many more subcategories) for every type of expense you might incur on a movie or television production. Everything you could imagine as an expense or exigency for your production can find a place in one of these subcategories. Don't be concerned about the length of the budget format, it won't take months to prepare and complete! You will need to provide cost estimates only in the categories required for your production.

Keep in mind that if you are planning to apply for funding and produce your project elsewhere, other budget formats exist that you would be expected to use. In the United States, most major production studios have their own customized budget formats that you would use if you were producing your movie or television program in conjunction with them. Television networks also have their own templates for summarizing costs. If you find that you are applying to several different investors, each using a different budget format, you might have to prepare different versions of your budget, even though they all add up to the same amount. Generally speaking, if you are able to chose one form or another, use the budget template for the investor who will potentially be providing most of the funding.

Generally, the differences you will find in budget formats reflect the accounting needs of the investor. Almost always, the discrete numeric codes used to distinguish among different categories and subcategories in your budget are the same codes that the accounting department will use for the ledger accounts of expenses and for preparation of cost reports.

In Canada, a distinguishing feature of our budget format is that we separate labour and material expenses. For example, the wardrobe department would have a separate category for labour costs and for the cost of supplies and rentals. In the United States, for the most part, labour and material costs of the wardrobe department would be placed in one category. Whatever the case may be, remember: "When in Rome, do what the Romans do." Use the budget format that the funders want you to.

There exist several computer programs specifically designed for television and movie budgeting. Most are able to offer any budget format. Some are so sophisticated that they are able to "read" information from an adjunct script breakdown program and serve as the template for a cost reporting and accounting package. Standard administrative software packages such as Lotus and Excel are also excellent programs for budgeting purposes. With the many revisions that a budget will go through, some sort of computer software program that enables you to change cost estimates readily and often is indispensable. To obtain the best computer budgeting program for your needs, you should consult with a production manager or a computer software facility specializing in film and televison production applications.

Budget Versions: Preliminary, Fine Tuning, and Locked-in

A budget goes through many revisions before it is finally set or "*locked in.*" The locked-in version is the one that everyone has agreed to before commencing principal photography. This includes the investors and broadcasters, and all key crew personnel and department heads, who must indicate acceptance by signing off their portion of the budget. Completion guarantors and investors will insist on this type of audit control.

The locked-in budget is the definitive and final version, so that investors know exactly what they are getting in return for what they are contributing. If there are variances between actual expenses and your original budget estimates after this budget is prepared, this will be indicated on the weekly cost report. There is nothing wrong with a variance, as long as the overall cost of the production remains on budget. Production managers, no matter how talented, will always have to allow for balancing "overages" in one category against "underages" in another.

Before you finalize your budget, it will proceed through several stages of development. The first version or *preliminary budget* is generally accomplished without much information as to how the project will be produced. At this stage, the producer (or the producer's delegate, the production manager) will normally prepare an overall estimate based only on the script and its breakdown, as well as a few of the essential parameters — who the director is, how many stars there will be, locations, union versus non-union crew, and so on. The preliminary budget will provide answers to many of these questions and, above all, offer a plan as to how the project will be produced. Even though this budget is simply a rough draft of your business plan, it is the version that will most likely be shown to potential investors. The closer it is to reality, the more credible you will appear and therefore the more likely it is that you will gain the confidence of your investors.

Fine tuning the budget is the process of determining more and more precisely the scope of your production, and acquiring accurate quotations and estimates for actual costs. By this stage, certain fundamentals are known: studio versus location shoot, size of crew, period or present-day setting, and video versus film stock. As well, many of the key crew members, talent, and director(s) have already been chosen. Fine tuning your budget is the process of listening to their version of how they would like the project to be produced and balancing this against how much money you, as the producer, can raise.

Creative personnel — the art director, the director of photography, the director — always want the most and the best for your production, which inevitably costs more money than you have. As producer you too will want the best, but must be more concerned about spending as little as possible, since there is only so much funding that can be raised. The production manager's ability will be tested as he or she finds ways to keep both the creative and financial partners of the production content.

Another important aspect of fine tuning the budget is obtaining quotations from suppliers for rentals or material costs. Many experienced production managers know how much various items required for the production will cost. They can prepare a preliminary budget without much external consultation. However, no matter how experienced and knowledgable the production manager is, nothing instils more confidence in the investors than actual written quotations and estimates from suppliers. Once these are spelled out, it is difficult to argue against them.

HOW MANY DRAFTS?

How many drafts of a budget do you prepare? It could be as little as two, as many as ten. The number of revisions is dependent on many different factors: you keep revising the estimate of how much money you can raise for the production; the art director demands more and more money for the department, since the director is increasingly ambitious with the script; the production manager wants to compare the costs of union and non-union crews; the music director keeps changing views on whether to acquire previously composed music or hire a composer to score the entire production; and the stars keep demanding more money. Be patient through the process of budgeting and be as thorough and accurate as possible. The more crucial decisions made at this juncture, the more research and preparation done, the more actual quotations and cost estimates you are able to obtain, the smoother and more successful your production will be. Remember that the more information you can provide for your cost estimates, the better your chances will be to obtain funding, and the more likely you will be to complete your production on budget.

Parameters

"Parameters" are general factors that will have a significant effect on how you produce your project and how you budget for the production. Before moving on to complete the detailed breakdown of cost estimates, it is important to decide on several of the main production parameters. You should always prepare a summary of these factors (keep it to one page, preferably in point form), which will provide everyone who reads and analyses your budget with a guide to the inherent assumptions of your cost estimates. Some of these parameters are:

- length of the program or individual episodes
- single-camera versus multi-camera production techniques
- location versus studio
- film stock versus video
- shooting ratio
- approach to production: for example, how many directors/assistant directors, and how will they will be used in your schedule (for production of a series of programs)
- cast and talent: number of "stars" versus principal performers, actors and extras; child performers
- decision to use ACTRA (talent association) and/or WGC (writer's guild)
- crew labour: union versus non-union technical and craft personnel, or a combination of both; "flats" or hourly payment
- time budgeted for an average shooting day (cast and crew implications); prep and wrap periods budgeted for individual departments (average)
- travel and living exigencies if shooting on remote locations; time of year when shooting; geography of location
- art department overall particulars: for example, set construction versus location; period versus contemporary time frame
- special equipment needs or requirements
- special effects; stunts
- existing suppliers and rental facilities
- music considerations
- post-production parameters: for example, to be edited on film or video; an explanation of the schedule and process used
- any publicity factors of note

• any other important details or limitations that the producer has determined.

Along with the brief statement describing these factors, you
should prepare an overall schedule for pre-production, production, and post-production. For example, how much prep,
shoot, and wrap time should be provided to different crew
members? This will help you to determine the amount of time
to estimate in various budget categories and help to establish
budget credibility. This will also assist any budget reviewers in
determining the credibility of the budget.

Finally, always prepare a *top sheet* for a budget, containing
the following: key personnel being used on the production;
important dates with regard to pre-production, production
and post-production; format and length of production; and the
medium you will be using (film, video or, now, multimedia
CD). Also very important, make sure you *date* the budget and
number it to indicate what version it is; note also the date of
the script it was based on. Make sure that your name and telephone number are provided, so that you can be consulted
regarding any assumptions that are not clearly explained. You
might also sign the top sheet to ensure that no one changes the
document that you have prepared or attributes its authorship
to anyone else. (The top sheet used in the Telefilm budget
template is shown at the end of this chapter.)

Defending Your Budget

Many of those who review your budget will approach it as
adversaries trying to find deficiencies or extravagances that
they will want you to correct. They will be only too happy to
point out these discrepancies to you. In part, it justifies their
existence when they discover weaknesses in your submission.

I once prepared a budget for a feature film that was considered by the central office of a well-known funding agency

to be too *under-budgeted*, for what we were planning to do. At the same time, the exact same budget was scrutinized and evaluated as being *over-budgeted* for our planned production by the regional office of the same agency!

However, budget reviewers, for the most part, are seasoned production managers who bring to their position experiences and learned assumptions about the cost of production. Although you may be tempted to argue your point of view, defending the way you estimated your costs, if you do not employ patience and discretion, you may end up undermining your ability to get financing. Even thoroughly and rigorously prepared budgets can have inadequacies from someone's point of view.

You have, nevertheless, a better chance of winning if you provide sufficient backup for the assumptions you have applied in calculating cost estimates in the budget. Some of your defence will come from clearly stating the parameters that your budget is based on, as discussed earlier. Backup may also consist of actual quotes from equipment suppliers, or contracts or deal memos from key crew personnel that indicate how much time they will be working for you and their rate of pay. It could also include location agreements, laboratory estimates, special set or prop "build" estimates, or a written quotation from a car and truck rental agency. Backup is especially important for categories where your budgeted amounts differ significantly from industry norms.

Most important, provide details! For example, if you need to rent a fleet of production vehicles, prepare an addendum for this budget subcategory that includes a breakdown of the rental period, rate of rental, and the anticipated operator of the vehicle. If you have several performers, complete a breakdown of each character's fee, including rehearsal time, wardrobe fitting, production time, and anticipated overtime and meal penalties.

Some of the templates for these breakdowns are provided in the standard budget forms. Others you will have to create. Whenever possible, use them to specify cost estimates. Do not present any assumptions or cost estimates that are not straightforward or might generate more questions than are answered. Remember, the more thorough and complete your budget is, the more likely it will be warmly received.

Sometimes, however, it may be imprudent to break down cost estimates in detail. There is a well-known accounting principle known as *materiality*. It suggests that separating and detailing specific expenses can sometimes be more time-consuming and "material" than the cost of the item itself. Therefore, it is more practical to group all the costs and round the total to a general estimate. For example, when you budget for courier expenses, you would not provide a detailed breakdown of how many couriers you would require each day for your production, with the exact cost of every run. It is simply not practical. More workable is to determine an overall estimate of your courier expenses based on the sum of averages of the cost of the different runs, how many deliveries you anticipate, and to where. This is generally referred to this as a *budgetary allowance*. When recorded in your budget, it is labelled as an *Allow*. However, be careful about summarizing in this fashion. The more you do it, the less confident others will be about the validity of your cost estimates.

IMPORTANCE OF ACCURACY

It is important to ensure that you are accurate in all your detailed calculations of expenses within the budget. It may seem self-evident, but you would be surprised at the number of simple arithmetical errors discovered by budget reviewers. Such mistakes undermine your reputation, and seriously jeopardize the possible funding of your project.

Always double-check and triple-check your calculations. Many computer programs can ensure the accuracy of your arithmetic, but be certain that you have provided the computer with the correct "rate" or "units" to complete the equation. Accuracy has its limitations, however; never submit a budget with cents included. It infuriates the reviewer. Always round to the nearest dollar.

Preparation of the Details of the Budget

Now let us turn our attention to the preparation of all categories and subcategories of the budget. If you have determined all your production parameters and gathered backup data as suggested above, you will find this process much easier.

As you progress through the *individual* cost estimates, ensure that none of the details contradict one another. For example, do not submit estimates for one labour category that indicates a different "production period" from the one used in another labour category. Similarly, do not provide for a transportation crew if no vehicle rentals are budgeted.

If you have properly broken down your script and prepared a detailed production schedule; if you have obtained quotes from suppliers and determined who are your key personnel, if you have accurately and thoroughly thought through and stated all the parameters specific to your production; then you are ready to proceed.

DIVISION OF SECTIONS, CATEGORIES, AND SUBCATEGORIES

The budget template we will be discussing here is the Telefilm version. It is divided into four sections: *Above-the-Line, Production, Post-production* and *Indirect Costs*.

Section "a," *Above-the-Line* expenses, generally refers to costs that are fixed and determined by the producer. Many producers will not reveal anything but the overall total of this section to people such as the production manager. (Of course, investors and completion guarantors would have full disclosure of *Above-the-Line* categories.)

Sections "b" "c" and "d" are known collectively as the *Below-the-Line* costs of production. Below-the-Line expenses "b" and "c" represent the heart of the budget. They are the actual costs necessary to produce the movie or television program and, for the most part, represent what you will see on screen. Production managers are generally responsible for determining these amounts and tracking the actual expenses of these categories via cost reports.

Section "d," or *Indirect Costs*, represents miscellaneous expenses that are either based on a formula related to the amounts budgeted in the preceding sections, or are overhead, infrastructure, or other indirect expenses for the production. They are generally determined by both the producer and production manager.

The 64 categories of costs, some with as many as 20 different subcategories, or budget "line items," are summarized at the front of the budget in a *Production Budget Summary* top sheet. This summary is distributed to more sources and used more often for submissions than are the budget details. Many who will review your budget do not want to spend their time sifting through all the details you have prepared. However, since these details provide the essential ingredients for the budget summary, they must be completed accurately. (A sample of the Telefilm Production Budget summary is at the end of this chapter on pages 99 to 102.)

Note that the Telefilm budget form provides columns where you display the following information: *Rate*, or the basic unit of cost (for example; daily fee); *Period*, or the amount of time required (may also be broken down into prep, shoot, strike periods); *Amount,* or the rate multiplied by the period; and *Total* of all the amounts in a specific subcategory. If we do not require this sort of detailed breakdown as we discussed above, print "allow" in the *Rate* columns with the estimated amount in the *Total* column. (Refer to the sample budget form at the end of this chapter.)

The Telefilm budget form also provides space for any notes or "refer to details" announcements beneath each of the sub-category names. All subcategories are coded numerically (for example, "04.05" refers to *producer fee*) to allow for easy cross-reference to the top sheet and for accounting procedures and cost reporting later. In the discussion to follow, we will make use of the Telefilm numeric codes. (Please note that the current Telefilm budget form does not include certain numeric categories, for example, 7, 8, and 9.)

LINE BY LINE THROUGH THE BUDGET

What follows is a brief review of the expense categories most commonly used when budgeting for a production. Keep in mind that there is no way to accurately review all the expenses you might require for your production in this chapter. One must first know the script, the schedule, and the amount of financing that the producer is able to raise.

Here are a few guidelines to help you:

- Complete only the expense subcategories that are required for your production.
- As much as possible, try to use similar units as "rate" and "period" throughout the budget: for example, hourly, daily, or weekly.
- Determine what will be the length of the average shooting day and use that as a base for all crew and cast calculations. (For example, a "12-hour" day might consist of the daily rate plus 4 hours multiplied by time-and-a-half; consult your rate books, determine the "base" unit, and use this calculation

throughout, even if weekly units are chosen as your base unit.)
- Use "Allow" cautiously, only when it is unreasonable to break down the expenses in detail.
- Complete "detail breakdown" forms when provided in the budget or when you deem their use to be appropriate.

ABOVE-THE-LINE ITEMS

These are budgeted items that for the most part are "fixed" and will not vary through the course of production. They have usually been decided and sometimes contracted before budget preparation. The producer has usually negotiated all these deals, and sometimes keeps this portion of the budget private, with the exception of investors, broadcasters, completion guarantors, and so forth.

1. *Property Rights.* The cost of acquiring the creative property, on which you will base the script for your production. Usually a negotiated contract; therefore, indicate as an "Allow."
2. *Scenario.* The writer's fee, as well as any story or script editor that the producer may desire. Most writers are members of the Writers Guild of Canada. Get a copy of the IPA (Independent Production Agreement): the collective agreement, that indicates terms and conditions of the writer's contract as well as minimum fees payable. Keep in mind that more established writers may demand more than minimum fees.

    The novice producer may have difficulty understanding how writers are paid. The *script fee* is what you pay the writer regardless of whether you produce the program. The *advance on use fee royalty* is the remaining amount you will pay the writer on first day of principal photography. The script fee is actually a portion of the total advance. In general, writer's fees are based on a royalty of approximately 4 per cent of the producer's take. Obviously how much the producer will earn from selling the production is unknown at the time of budget preparation. Therefore, the writer is provided with an initial advance based on approximately 4 per cent of the budget. As the producer earns enough from the sale of the production to cover the advance, the writer receives additional royalties. Read the agreement to fully understand how a writer is paid.

Other scenario subcategories include: *Clearances/Searches* — fees paid to an organization that checks your script to make sure there is no copyright or trademark infringement against existing protected entities; *Fringe Benefits* — all unions and associations require you to pay them for benefits to their members, as well as administration fees for the bodies that negotiate and monitor the collective agreement (Writers Guild of Canada and Canadian Film and Television Production Association). Currently the total fringe is about 13 per cent of the writer's gross fee.

3. *Development Costs.* These are expenses that presumably you have already incurred while developing the project up to this stage of pre-production. In essence, you record budgeted amounts in this "master" budget, even if you had already submitted and completed the development budget, completed the development phase, and have spent all of the funds that were allotted. However, if you are successful in obtaining production financing based on this budget, part of the "acceptable" expenses that will be financed will be the development costs. If other investors provided funding for the development of your project, they would now be paid back from the amounts budgeted herein.

Most projects will have some sort of development phase and funding, even if it is entirely provided by the producer. In Canada, keep in mind that only one in ten projects developed through traditional means (broadcasters, funding agencies, and so on), actually make it to the production stage.

There are many development expenses you may incur. Some examples are: *Budget Breakdown* — the cost of hiring a production manager to complete the master business plan; *Consultant Expenses* — cost of a director, art director, director of photography, graphic artist, post-production consultant, or anyone who helps to further develop and prepare the project; *Survey/Scouting* — an expense used while selecting locations; *Travel and Living Expenses* — used if the producer must travel to key cities and centres to find additional funding, select a distributor, or perhaps negotiate contracts; and *Other* — to cover other costs that could be incurred developing the project.

In the development phase, for example, you might pay the writer a script fee for a draft of the project or hire a story editor to put together a "bible" (a set of guidelines) for a series. Budget it here as opposed to under *Scenario* expenses. If the development phase is not funded from the producer's own resources, the producer is also entitled to budget 15 per cent of the overall development budget for his or her own fee, plus 15 per cent for overhead expenses.

4. *Producer.* Oh yes, producers do get paid for their work as well, if they don't defer their fee in order to help finance the production — a practice that happens often! If you are a novice producer, most agencies will insist that you obtain the services of an *executive producer* to help shepherd you through the stages of production. In this case, the executive producer's role is to provide the investors, completion guarantors, and so on with some comfort that the project will be completed on time and on budget.

Many of the subcategories here, as throughout this budget form, are superfluous. For example, rarely would you budget for a *Producer's Secretary* or *Fringe Benefits*. However, if you are shooting in a remote location, producer's *Travel and Living* expenses would be budgeted here. Overall, most funding agencies restrict the producer's fee, including the executive and associates, if any, to 10 per cent of the sum of sections "b" and "c" of your budget.

5. *Director.* Directors generally belong to an association known as the Directors Guild of Canada, and are covered by a collective agreement that indicates minimum pay rates for different types of production, such as movies, television specials, or episodes of a series. The agreement also indicates how much pre-production time directors are obliged to complete for every shooting day they engage in.

    Even if you do not hire a director who is a member of the DGC, the going rates for non-union directors will closely reflect what is in the agreement. Also, if you do use a DGC director, you will have the added expense of *buyouts*: a form of advance royalty payment, anywhere from 25 to 50 per cent of the gross fees, depending on the media and market in which your production will be exhibited. *Fringe Benefits* are also payable to the DGC on behalf of its members (currently approximately 17 per cent of the gross earnings of the director). Once again, avoid superfluous subcategories: for example, *Dialogue Director, Director's Secretary*, and so on, if they are not required.

6. *Stars.* Normally, *Stars* are performers who are distinguished from *Cast* on the basis of how much they are paid (usually well above the minimum required), and how much their name and likeness assists in the *packaging* (promoting and marketing) of your project. Since they will normally negotiate a flat fee contract, their fee is broken down within these subcategories. Note that you will still have to budget *Fringe Benefits* for them, since they will most likely belong

to ACTRA, the performer's association. Calculate fringes at 11 per cent of the star's gross fee.

Note that the stars will have to be from ACTRA or signed up as *permittees* if there are any other ACTRA performers used in your production. A *permitee* is a performer who is not a member of the union, who has to receive permission from the union to perform on your production, and pays a permit fee for working on your production with other union members.

BELOW-THE-LINE ITEMS

Now we get to the "guts" of the production. Sections "b" and "c," *Production* and *Post-production*, represent the actual day-to-day expenses of the project. It is essential that the producer not use up all his or her projected financing in above-the-line and indirect expenses; the more money spent on the actual production, the better the finished product will be.

PRODUCTION

10. *Cast.* All your performer's fees will be estimated in the many subcategories in this part of the budget. Almost every independent production shot in Canada uses performers from ACTRA. (A separate association, UBCP, has been established in British Columbia.) It is unlikely that you can assemble enough non-union performers for your production, although it has been done. For years, *"The Kids of Degrassi Street"* used many unknown child performers as well as adult actors with some stage experience.

However, once you chose one performer who is a member of ACTRA, it is almost impossible to continue without signing a *letter of adherence* with the association, agreeing to abide by the terms, conditions, and minimum pay scales outlined in their collective agreement (IPA). And, as are all collective agreements, this one is complicated. Make sure you consult with the producers' association (CFTPA) prior to signing, so that you understand what you are getting into.

On the topic of union versus non-union, you should be aware that the movie and television industry is like no other in terms of labour and management relations. When you sign a letter of adherence with ACTRA, this is no way obliges you to sign a collective agreement with another union (except the WGC, which has a "reciprocal" agreement with ACTRA). It could be that, on your production, you decide to sign letters of adherence with ACTRA, WGC, and the DGC (representing directors, production staff/production managers, assistant directors, production assistants, art directors and their assistants, editors and their assistants, to name only a few), but use a non-union technical and craftspeople crew.

You might also decide to use members of a crew union as your key personnel, paying them "non-signatory" rates, and use non-union members for the balance of your crew. This arrangement would not require you to sign a letter of adherence with the technical and crafts union. The terms and conditions of your contracts would be independently negotiated between you and each crew member. Keep in mind that each of your productions is treated as a separate entity and your signature does not bind you for future productions. However, certain unions and associations may ask you to sign a letter of adherence specifying a time frame as well, committing you to the terms and conditions of their collective agreement for a year, for example, rather than simply for one project.

As you can see, the scenarios are endless. Most often, your decision about which route to take is dictated by how much financing you can raise. Unions and guilds tend to be more expensive, due to fringes payable and other financial requirements defined in their collective agreements. But before you go out and hire a completely non-union crew, keep two things in mind: first, except for ACTRA, you can negotiate some of the financial terms and conditions of the collective agreement with the business managers of the unions (particularly during slow production periods); and second, the most experienced and talented individuals usually belong to a union, and they may, despite the additional cost of fringes, save you time and money through their knowledge and performance.

Returning to the *Cast* breakdown, ACTRA distinguishes three general types of performers, based on how many lines they deliver or their prominence on screen: *principals*, *actors*, and *extras*. (Extras are to be budgeted in the next category). Many other types of performers may also be required (*stunt performers*, *off-camera performers*, and so on.) Be sure to use the detailed breakdown sheets to determine the appropriate expenses.

In addition, all performers (except for extras) can negotiate a *buyout* representing an additional percentage of their fee, payable now in lieu of royalties later on. A chart in the ACTRA-IPA collective agreement will indicate the various percentages you must pay to buy out performers in your production, calculated according to the distribution of your program in particular markets and in specific media. In my experience, performers usually accept the guaranteed buyout above speculated royalty payments. All performers, including stars, generally receive the same buyout for their performance, which is determined by the producer before beginning production.

There are other subcategories here that should not be

overlooked: *Casting Director* and *Casting Expenses*, which will prove to be indispensable in assembling your cast; and *Fringe Benefits* totalling approximately 11 per cent of all performers' gross fees, payable to ACTRA on behalf of the performers.

11. *Extras.* The difference between extras and all other performers is that they do not speak in their performances and you do not pay them buyout royalties. There are several divisions of extras. Make sure you consult with the ACTRA-IPA collective agreement to understand terms, conditions, and fees payable for engagement. All extras are also paid *Fringe Benefits* of 11 per cent.

There is a category for *Administrative Fee* that represents 2 per cent of the 11 per cent fringe noted above, payable for *Stars, Cast,* and *Extras.* Normally, this administration fee is just included in the fringe subcategories within *Stars, Cast,* and *Extras.*

Tutor and *Children's Co-ordinator* are important line items if you are using children in your production. In our industry, there are many restrictions on the contracting of children, which regulate the amount of time they can spend in front of the cameras, the length of their working day, and educational tutoring that must be provided for them. Make sure you understand all the terms and conditions before you begin to budget.

12. *Production Staff.* This category includes the administrative staff both on and off the set: production manager, co-ordinators, assistant directors, accountant, and so on. Some may belong to a union; others may be non-affiliated. It is important to determine how much prep and wrap time each discipline requires, which is dependent on the type and length of your production. Generally, the production staff is onboard two to four weeks before commencement of princi-

pal photography. However, sometimes a production manager may be on payroll two to three months prior to production. "Weeks" are normally used as the unit for cost breakdown purposes.

13. *Design Labour.* The key personnel and their assistants, who are responsible for the look of the production, as well as the entire art department crew, are budgeted here. For small and moderate productions, an art director and an assistant and perhaps some "daily" graphic artists or draftspeople would normally be used. However, to qualify our discussion once again, how many would be needed in each department is dependent upon the unique nature of your production. As with the production staff, this department needs significant prep time.

14. *Construction Labour.* If you require the construction of a set or any special "builds," the labour is budgeted in these subcategories. Normally, this department has finished by the time production begins. However, it may be advisable to retain one or two stand-by carpenters or painters, etc., just in case material must be built or repaired during production. In some circumstances, sets are constantly being set up and struck, requiring the continuing services of certain tradespeople listed in this category. Note, however, that even if you have to build a set, you chose to sublet your construction needs. If so, budget in the form of an overall quote from a supplier in Category 35, *Construction Material.*

15. *Set Dressing Labour; 16. Property Labour.* These two categories represent the heart of your art department. The personnel budgeted here are the ones who do the physical work to realize the look of the set or location according to the art director's vision, and run around town gathering all the props and set dressing required for the production. They need to receive just as much prep time as the production

staff, and they generally work more hours than any other crew department during production. Wrap time will be required to strike the set and return rentals and supplies once production is completed. For most moderately budgeted productions, include at least a *key* and an *assistant* in each category. Usually, there is at least one more individual — a "buyer" or runner — whose duties are split between the two departments when money is tight. (These categories, as shown in the actual Telefilm budget template, are included at the end of this chapter.)

17. *Special Effects Labour; 18. Wrangling Labour.* These line items are reserved for highly specialized craftspeople. Unless your production contains special effects from beginning to end or is a program about animals, you will probably use these specialists only as the need arises. If there are many special effects and animals, you can rest assured that these specialists will insist on assistants in their crew. They are paid quite well relative to other disciplines, due to their uncommon skills. Be sure to budget for adequate prep time for each respective category, if they are to be used. Generally, quotes are provided before the production and included in this budget line item.

19. *Wardrobe Labour; 20. Make-up/Hair Labour.* If you are using union personnel, these individuals will be from the same union as set dressers, property personnel, and your technical categories. Therefore, minimum scale will be found in the collective agreement of one of the three main unions: Association of Canadian Film Craftspeople (ACFC), National Association of Broadcast Employees and Technicians (NABET), and International Alliance of Theatrical Employees-Technicians (IATSE). All three unions have similar technical and craft categories. However, if you chose to hire a union crew, you must select only one of

these unions for your production. You will need to decide which one will provide the least expensive labour and fringe costs, as well as determine which union posesses the most experienced and talented members for your needs. This information may be obtained from other producers or production managers who have engaged members of the particular unions.

If you chose to use non-affiliated personnel and resist signing a letter of adherence, basic pay rates are fairly similar. But you save on the fringes and can be more creative in how you pay overtime. Consult with an experienced production manager to determine what the non-affiliated rates may be at any given time. You will find that they vary a great deal but are usually proportional to level of experience.

Normally, the wardrobe department has at least a key and an assistant. They need as much prep and wrap time as you provided for the dressing and props departments. If your production has many characters or many wardrobe creations, you would probably budget for additional personnel on either a daily rate or flat fee per tailored costume.

Budget for at least one make-up artist and one hair stylist. If you have a large cast or have stars, you will probably require more people in this department. However, additional personnel could be costed on a daily basis based only on shooting days when many cast are being used. Normally, they do not require a great deal of prep time, unless special effects make-up will be used or you are producing a period piece in which many wigs and special period costumes are required.

21. *Videotape Technical Crew; 22. Camera Labour; 23. Electrical Labour; 24. Grip Labour; 25. Production Sound Labour.* All these categories (with their many subcategories) comprise the technical crew. You must decide which of these productions

requires and within which line items you will budget the cost. Most of these categories are used for film productions.

Although the *Videotape Technical Crew* category can be used to estimate your video production crew, you may feel, even if you are shooting on videotape, that it is more appropriate to cost out your technical crew in categories 22–25. This depends mostly on the method of production you intend to employ for your production. For example, even though you may shoot on videotape, you may use the same shot-by-shot method of production that is used when you shoot on film. In this case, you would probably use categories 21–25 to estimate your technical labour needs.

Normally, you should budget for at least a key and an assistant in each of these departments (unless you use the *Videotape Technical Crew* category, which will list all technical personnel — keys and assistants — required). Film camera departments generally require more personnel than the other departments, as there are several specific functions to perform that you cannot compromise. There is limited prep and strike time required by all departments, which will be less time than you budgeted for the art department.

26. *Transportation Labour.* In a non-union production, you can ask art department and technical crew personnel to drive vehicles you have rented. Main cast or stars should be driven to and from the set. You can assign one or two production assistants this responsibility, as well as giving the job of "running" deliveries and messages to numerous destinations. Therefore, you will not really need to allot costs to this category.

If you decide to use union personnel for your production, you may be required to provide a driver for every vehicle that is used. Certain unions insist on this! Other unions require you to pay the technicians or art department personnel an additional fee if they are responsible for driving their department's vehicle for production purposes. Having a staff of drivers is a godsend for any production; the question you must address is whether you can afford it.

27. Fringe Benefits. Now that most of your labour categories have been costed, it is time to add them up and determine the amount of fringe benefits you should budget for. Note that you have already budgeted fringes for writers, performers, and directors who have fringe subcategories in their respective sections of the budget. Since they are always considered "contractors," they won't require additional government benefits.

In the subcategories here, you cost out two separate elements. The first is union and association fringe benefits, if you chose to use union personnel in your production and if you sign a letter of adherence. This can range from 13 per cent to 17 per cent of the gross fee of the personnel, depending on the union(s) from which you select your members. As stated earlier, these expenses are sometimes negotiable with the business manager of the union.

Second, you will cost out government benefits for all crew members who are on payroll. However, if the crew member has set up a corporation to provide his or her services (commonly done in the industry for tax reasons), payment will include neither government fringes nor federal tax nor other deductions at source. On average, approximately one-third of crew members will work under their own corporations to provide labour.

For the balance of the crew, you must budget for the following fringes, regardless of whether the crew members are associated with a union: Worker's Compensation, Canada Pension Plan, Unemployment Insurance, Employer Health Tax, and Vacation Pay (if not provided for under union fringes).

Government fringe rates change annually. At the time of writing, they were approximately 13.5 per cent of gross earnings.

Faced with these expenses, you may be tempted not to pay government fringe benefits on behalf of your crew, and to treat all crew members as if they were personal service corporations. Be very careful! If any crew members do not pay taxes on their "unencumbered" earnings and are not actually incorporated, you as the producer could be responsible for paying the taxes that should have been deducted at source. If, after the production is completed, the crew member is deemed to be an "employee" by Revenue Canada, and that crew member does not pay the taxes owing on amounts paid while working on your production, Revenue Canada is entitled to make *you* pay. In such a case you have not only *not* saved any money, but paid even more than the contracted amount.

28. *Production Office Expenses; 29. Studio/Backlot Expenses; 30. Location Office Expenses.* In these categories, you provide cost estimates for the numerous administrative needs of your production, including facility rentals, equipment, and supplies. The production office is not necessarily your corporate office. A legitimate expense of producing is to set up a temporary office, fully equipped and supplied, to serve as headquarters. *Studio/Backlot Expenses* contains budgetary items for studio and facility rentals during pre-production and shoot for such items as set building and storage. *Location Office Expenses* are budgeted when you require a remote office facility as well as your primary production office. Use only those categories that are necessary. The budget reviewers frown on padded overhead!

31. *Site Expenses; 32. Unit Expenses.* These budget categories represent expenses for support and services for your production unit. For example, you will make estimates here for

location rentals, security, and pay duty police officers (whom you will have to hire on any location shoot in a metropolitan area). *Unit Expenses* include catering and other miscellaneous costs associated with looking after your cast and crew. This is one area of the budget that you don't want to compromise too much. A well-fed cast and crew (which will be your responsibility, for lunch at least) performs much better.

33. *Travel & Living Expenses; 34. Transportation.* This covers any travel and transportation requirements, including travel to and from a remote location, the fleet of production vehicles and motorhomes you will have to rent, gas, taxis, and parking. Remember to include vehicle insurance expenses and taxes in your estimates.

35. *Construction Material; 36. Art Supplies; 37. Set Dressing; 38. Props; 39. Special Effects; 40. Animals; 41. Wardrobe Supplies; 42. Make-up and Hair Supplies.* All imaginable art department supplies, rentals, construction material, and subcontracted "builds" are estimated here, in their respective categories. Many production managers simply indicate "Allowances" in these categories at the preliminary budgeting stage. As the budget is fine tuned, it is advisable to hire or consult with an art director to take the script and script breakdown and provide a fairly reasonable estimate of the costs in this area of the budget, with a detailed cost breakdown if requested.

This part of the budget is often controversial. Art directors always want more than a producer can afford. Their insistence is understandable, given that these categories truly determine what the production will look like. Often, however, production managers and producers leave estimating these areas of the budget till last, tossing in whatever is left of the financing after all other categories have been budgeted. It is easier to adjust and defend an "Allowance" here than it is a detailed cost breakdown. One must find the delicate balance between what can be afforded and what is required to make the production look good.

It is a smart idea to provide actual quotes from suppliers or builders for any budget items that appear to depart from industry norms.

43. Video Studio Facilities; 44. Video Remote Technical Facilities; 45. Camera Equipment; 46. Electrical Equipment; 47. Grip Equipment; 48. Sound Equipment. All technical equipment and supplies, whether rented or purchased, are budgeted in these categories. Department heads are usually consulted to help determine what should be in the equipment "package" for each area. However, a well seasoned production manager in consultation with equipment suppliers will be able to draft a fairly accurate list of equipment and determine any special equipment that will be needed on a daily rental basis.

Most equipment suppliers will offer to rent you equipment for a full week for a three-day rental charge. However, you can negotiate a much better deal than this, particularly when there is little other production activity and when the rental period is for several weeks. Very often, key department personnel will have their own equipment or facilities that they will gladly rent to you.

It is a good idea to consult with key personnel before completing this section of the budget. You would be surprised at how much can be overlooked. Above all, don't forget to budget a healthy amount for consumable supplies such as tape, sash cord, plywood, spare lighting bulbs; you will go through a lot of material while shooting.

49. Second Unit. If you intend to shoot a number of visuals in a remote location, it is much more cost-effective to hire a

small crew to shoot this footage than to schedule the main unit (of perhaps 50 crew members) to get the shots. The subcategories contained in this area provide line items that enable you to budget this expense in detail.
50. Videotape Stock; 51. Production Laboratory. Actual "stock," both film and videotape, and processing if necessary, is budgeted here. Make sure you have determined a shooting ratio before completing these categories. Take into consideration who the director is, how many "set-ups" and "takes" he or she usually requires, and how much time the schedule allows for shooting. Remember, videotape and film stock is relatively inexpensive compared to the expense of actually mounting the production. When estimating the amount of stock be sensitive to post-production and promotional needs (for example, additional videocassettes), as well as what format the investors and broadcasters will expect to have delivered to them.

POST-PRODUCTION

60. Editorial Labour; 61. Editorial Equipment; 62. Video Post-production (Picture); 63. Video Post-production (Sound); 64. Post-production Laboratory. This is an area that is often overlooked when budgeting. Many producers and production managers will do their best to ensure that sufficient money is set aside in the budget for production needs, but sometimes, on productions with limited financial resources, this means that there is not enough budgeted for post-production.

Be extremely careful not to shortchange the post-production needs of your project. You may have achieved the most beautiful footage containing the most stellar performances, only to have it ruined by allocating insufficient funds to put it all together properly in post. It is generally a good idea to consult with a post-production supervisor, editor, or service facility before finalizing your estimates in this section of the budget.

These five categories and their subcategories are where you will budget all your labour, material, and supply costs, and equipment/facility rentals for post-production activities. There are also categories for possible film or video effects, transfers, and graphics that your production may require. Decide how the project will be edited before calculating your estimates. Your options include: shot on film/edited on film; shot on film/edited on videotape; shot on film/edited on film/delivered on videotape. Remember that editing always takes longer than the production period, and usually longer than your initial estimate.

65. *Film Post-Production Sound; 66. Music.* You must make careful decisions about your post-production parameters before completing this section. For example: Will you be using an original score or previously prepared music tracks? Will you be using union musicians (AFM), or hire a "midi" (musical instrument digital interface) composer with his or her synthesizer to put together all of your music requirements? Will there be a lot of post-production looping of voices and ADR (automated dialogue replacement) needed? For these categories, it is a good idea to obtain quotations and estimates from the personnel you will hire and facilities you will use.

67. *Titles/Opticals/Stock Footage.* This category is used mostly for productions completed on film. (Video post-production titling and effects are budgeted in the *Video Post-production* categories mentioned before.) Film optical effects can become rather costly. If you intend to use many in your production, or are planning a sophisticated opening title sequence and credit roll, be sure to obtain an estimate from a reputable firm. Both film and video productions may

require stock footage. Be sure to budget the fee for the appropriate buyouts and royalties to ensure that the material you use can be exhibited unrestricted in the various markets and media when you sell your completed production.

68. Versioning; 69. Amortization (Series). These two expense categories are rarely costed in production budgets any more. Versioning refers to the cost of having your program dubbed or subtitled into other languages. Generally, this is an expense you incur after the production is completed, and is an "exploitation" cost that is dealt with once the completed production is being distributed. The *Amortization* section was at one time extensively used on series productions. Costs that could not be attributed to specific episodes of the series and costs that would be spread out over all the episodes produced would be summarized here. However, in my experience, these "common" expenses are now divided among the many production categories we have already discussed.

INDIRECT COSTS

70. Unit Publicity. This is a very important category to budget sufficiently; in fact, many funding agencies will actually *insist* that a percentage of your overall budget be spent here. If your production is not publicized enough to attract people to see it, what is the use of making it in the first place? The more attention you generate, the more likely it is that the public will watch your production, and the greater the potential for generating revenue, which will, of course, be returned to your investors.

Distinguish between a *marketing and promotion* campaign, which is generally estimated in a separate budget, and the *publicity* expenses necessary for the production. (More about this can be found in Chapter 9.) A unit publicist will

ensure that your production is given a "profile" and attention in the media while shooting. The publicist will require
a sufficient still photography (labour and material) budget
to work with, as well as substantial funds to put together a
press kit. Wrap parties and screening parties are often budgeted in this section, too.

71. *General Expenses.* All the important administrative necessities for the production are budgeted here. You will require
sufficient insurance coverage for a multitude of items: negative protection, cast insurance, props, sets, and wardrobe,
equipment, property damage, and comprehensive liability.
There are a number of highly specialized insurance brokers
in Canada who will put together the entire package for
you. Generally it will cost between 1 and 2 per cent of the
overall budget.

You will also require *Errors and Omissions* insurance,
which protects the producer, broadcaster, and investor
against copyright or trademark infringement litigation, as
well as slander, libel, or defamation charges. Most funding
agencies, broadcasters, and distributors will insist that you
have it. Cost for this insurance varies greatly, depending on
the nature of your production, the inherent risk involved in
the project, and the extent to which it will be distributed
and exhibited. Consult with an insurance broker to obtain
the most up-to-date cost estimate.

If you obtain cast insurance, which insures your production in the event that something happens to your performers, you will have to pay for their medicals, itemized in this
section.

You will require legal counsel to assist in drafting and
completing contracts and perhaps also to help you with negotiations, regardless of the acumen you possess as a paralegal.
Fees vary widely, depending on how much you use your

lawyer. This is a necessary expense. Use your lawyer judiciously, however; remember, they are usually paid by the hour.

Post-production accounting fees are a necessary expense
to ensure that someone keeps your books up to date once
production is complete. Most funding agencies and
investors will insist on a final audit of your expenditures by
a third party, which could cost anywhere from $1,500 to
$5,000, depending on the scope of production and the
investor requirements. Bank charges are the miscellaneous
service charges that will be assessed to your account, usually indicated as an "Allowance."

72. *Indirect Costs.* Although the previously mentioned *Unit
Publicity* and *General Expenses* categories are both part of
the *Indirect Costs* section of the budget, there is also a specific category in this budget template where you will find
other "indirect" expenses of your production, including the
following items. *Corporate Overhead*: even though you have
already budgeted for your production office needs, you as a
producer are entitled to budget a fee for your own office
and infrastructure needs as a company, known as the "cost
of doing business." Most agencies will limit the amount you
set aside here to 10 per cent of sections "b" and "c" of your
budget; the amount will vary according to how big your
actual corporate infrastructure is. The *Telefilm Administration
Fee* does not exist any more, so ignore it! Both *Interim
Financing* and *Other Financing* refer to the cost of loans to
bridge-finance your cash flow. When expenses for a given
period during the production phase outpace how quickly
you receive payments from your investors, you will need to
borrow money and budget for loan expenses.

80. *Contingency.* This amount covers overages caused by unforeseen circumstances or emergencies. As careful as you may

be at anticipating your production exigencies and costing them in a budget, in the movie and television industry, Murphy's Law always prevails. All funding agencies, guarantors, and investors will insist that you budget for a healthy contigency in case additional funds are required. Most of these parties hope that you will set aside 10 per cent of the overall budget as a buffer. Practically speaking, you will more often allocate between 4 and 8 per cent.

81. *Completion Guarantee.* The investors require some guarantee that you as a producer will complete the production as scheduled and as budgeted, so that they can recoup their investment and, hopefully, earn a profit. A Completion Guarantor is essentially an insurance agent who ensures that the production will be completed. They charge a fee of approximately 6 per cent of sections "b" and "c" of your budget (though this may vary among various completion guarantors and according to the nature of your production). It is my experience, however, that you may negotiate this fee to as low as 1.5 per cent of the budget, depending on the risk of the production and the skills of the producer and key production staff. If the production is completed on budget, the guarantor will normally rebate 50 per cent of this "bond" back to the producer as a reward for successfully completing the production on budget. Producers with "track records" and productions with limited risk factors may not require a completion bond at all.

The guarantor is given *take-over rights* to the production in the event that the cost of the production begins to exceed the budget. Producers with "track records" and productions with limited risk factors may not require a completion bond at all.

The guarantor can actually fire the producer or any key staff, in order to protect the right of the investor to be delivered a completed production for the budget that was approved. Since their staff comprises senior, experienced line producers and production managers, their "auditing" of your production can also be extremely helpful in organizing your production parameters and establishing your budget. However, completion guarantors do not provide budget preparation services. Usually, you would begin to consult with them when you need their services, once the financing is secure.

82. *Cost of Issue.* If you are intending to raise money from private investors you will have to prepare either an *offering memorandum* or *prospectus*. These are extensive legal documents that essentially indicate what you as a producer are offering to the investor in return for an investment in your production. The former is a document restricted to a limited number of potential investors, and is also limited in how many individuals you may approach. The latter is more sophisticated, actually having to be scrutinized and approved by the provincial securities commission, and is offered to the general public through brokerage houses. Both documents require you as a producer to declare a great deal about your production and your company: for example, the history of your company and other productions you have completed, and every possible risk involved for the investor.

Raising financing for your budget in this manner incurs many expenses that are itemized under this heading. They include legal fees to put together the proposal and commission fees for the broker for selling the "units" of investment to the public.

Cash Flow

After you have completed your budget, you will be required to prepare a *cash flow*. A cash flow, simply stated, represents the speed at which you are going to incur expenses on your production and spend the budget *versus* the speed at which you will be receiving revenue from all the financial sources that have agreed to support your production. All expenses in the budget are summarized in one column. Each expense is then spread out across several columns, representing discrete periods of production. Pre-production and post-production periods are generally summarized into bi-monthly columns, whereas production periods are divided into weekly columns.

Revenues are spread across the columns in the same manner, based on when you anticipate you will receive instalments from your financial participants. Be aware that most investors, broadcasters, and so on, rarely give you all of their contribution up front. They generally spread their contribution over several instalments. These instalments are known as *draw downs* and may correspond to any number of things, including the following: execution of your agreement with them; completion of a particular phase of production; or delivery of a certain aspect of the production, such as a rough cut or fine cut.

You will not prepare your cash flow in isolation. Generally, it requires the participation of the production manager and the accountant as well. It is a forbidding document but generally does not reflect anything about the contents of your budget other than how quickly you will spend it.

One of the main reasons the cash flow is required is to inform potential lenders and interim financiers. Rarely in the television and movie industry are revenues received quickly enough to offset our rate of spending. A cash flow will help the producer negotiate for faster payments by clearly demonstrating how quickly money is being spent and therefore, when cash inflows will be required. A cash flow must be prepared if a temporary loan or interim financing is required from a bank or other source to cover the shortfall of cash until the next revenue draw down is received.

Cost Reporting

The device you use to determine how well you budgeted and how smoothly, in financial terms, your production is proceeding, is the *cost report*. A cost report tracks actual expenditures and compares them to your original budget, to determine *variances*, which are referred to as "over" or "under." It is perhaps the most significant document prepared during production, since it represents a constant audit of expenses.

The cost report is prepared by the production accountant in consultation with the production manager, and is always approved by the producer before being sent to the financial participants and the guarantor. It is usually prepared weekly during production and monthly in the prep and post periods.All budgeted items are listed and broken down in the following column categories:

1. *Paid to Date* (or sometimes) *Cost This Week*;
2. *Payables* (or) *Commitments* (purchase orders, or monies actually committed);
3. *Cost to Date* (total of 1 + 2);
4. *Estimate to Complete* (how much the PM believes is yet to be spent in this category in the production);
5. *Total Cost* (total of 3 + 4);
6. *Budget* (the original cost estimates);
7. *Variance* (the difference between the original budget and the total cost 6 − 5).

The cost report is an extremely important document for the financial participants, since it always tells them how efficiently their money is being spent, and whether the production is still "on budget." If it should start to go over budget, the guarantor may have to step in to take over the production.

This situation may tempt a producer or production manager to hold back on declaring all expenses on the cost report at a particular point in time. They may feel that disclosing an overage might increase the likelihood of a takeover. They may believe that with more time, they will be able to bring costs under control.

However, it is extremely difficult to get away with this. To begin with, guarantors are generally staffed by very experienced production managers who know how to smell out this sort of lie. They can very quickly determine whether problems exist by reading the production reports submitted and comparing the declarations provided to cost report disclosures.

Furthermore, it would take extraordinary collusion to succeed in keeping the truth from investors and the guarantor. Don't forget that there are at least three parties who would have to co-operate in fudging the figures on the cost report: the producer, the production manager, and the accountant. Giving in to the temptation to make things appear better than they really are would ruin their reputations if it were discovered. And the odds suggest that it would be uncovered.

Summary

More than anything, what this chapter should convey is that preparing a budget is not simply a matter of making a few calculations here and there, reviewing a few collective agreements to determine crew or cast rates, or obtaining a brochure from a lab or equipment supplier indicating how much they charge for services or rentals. If thoroughly and accurately prepared, the budget represents a true "master business plan" for your production. Without it, no matter how wonderful your creative property may be, you don't have a hope of realizing your ambition of producing a movie or television program.

Film/Videotape Production Budget*

WORKING TITLE

SERIES TITLE

PRODUCTION NO.

PRODUCTION COMPANY

EXECUTIVE PRODUCER

PRODUCER

DIRECTOR

WRITER

PRODUCTION MANAGER

FORMAT	PREP PERIOD
LENGTH	SHOOTING PERIOD
	STUDIO
	LOCATION
	PICTURE CUT PERIOD
	POST PRODUCTION DURATION
FIRST DAY OF SHOOTING	ANSWER PRINT

SCENARIO DATE

DRAFT NO.

BUDGET PREPARED BY

NAME	TELEPHONE NUMBER

SIGNATURE

APPROVED BY	DATE
PRODUCTION COMPANY	TELEPHONE

ADDRESS

* *This and the following three pages comprise Telefilm's Standard Production Budget Summary "Top Sheet."*

Production Budget Summary

ACCT CATEGORY	PAGE				TOTAL
01 STORY RIGHTS/ACQUISITIONS					
02 SCENARIO					
03 DEVELOPMENT COSTS					
04 PRODUCER					
05 DIRECTOR					
06 STARS					
PRODUCTION TOTAL "A"					
10 CAST					
11 EXTRAS					
12 PRODUCTION STAFF					
13 DESIGN LABOUR					
14 CONSTRUCTION LABOUR					
15 SET DRESSING LABOUR					
16 PROPERTY LABOUR					
17 SPECIAL EFFECTS LABOUR					
18 WRANGLING LABOUR					
19 WARDROBE LABOUR					
20 MAKEUP/HAIR LABOUR					
21 **VIDEO TECHNICAL CREW**					
22 CAMERA LABOUR					
23 ELECTRICAL LABOUR					
24 GRIP LABOUR					
25 PRODUCTION SOUND LABOUR					
26 TRANSPORTATION LABOUR					

27 FRINGE BENEFITS					
28 PRODUCTION OFFICE EXPENSES					
29 STUDIO/BACKLOT EXPENSES					
30 LOCATION OFFICE EXPENSES					
31 SITE EXPENSES					
32 UNIT EXPENSES					
33 TRAVEL & LIVING EXPENSES					
34 TRANSPORTATION					
35 CONSTRUCTION MATERIALS					
36 ART SUPPLIES					
37 SET DRESSING					
38 PROPS					
39 SPECIAL EFFECTS					
40 ANIMALS					
41 WARDROBE SUPPLIES					
42 MAKEUP/HAIR SUPPLIES					
43 **VIDEO STUDIO FACILITIES**					
44 **VIDEO REMOTE TECHNICAL FACILITIES**					
45 CAMERA EQUIPMENT					
46 ELECTRICAL EQUIPMENT					
47 GRIP EQUIPMENT					
48 SOUND EQUIPMENT					
49 SECOND UNIT					
50 **VIDEO TAPE STOCK**					
51 PRODUCTION LABORATORY					
PRODUCTION TOTAL "B"					

60 EDITORIAL LABOUR					
61 EDITORIAL EQUIPMENT					
62 VIDEO POST PRODUCTION (PICTURE)					
63 VIDEO POST PRODUCTION (SOUND)					
64 POST PRODUCTION LABORATORY					
65 FILM POST PRODUCTION SOUND					
66 MUSIC					
67 TITLES/OPTICALS/STOCK FOOTAGE					
68 VERSIONING					
69 AMORTIZATIONS (SERIES)					
POST PRODUCTION TOTAL "C"					
TOTAL "B" + "C" (PRODUCTION AND POST-PRODUCTION)					
70 UNIT PUBLICITY					
71 GENERAL EXPENSES					
72 INDIRECT COSTS					
TOTAL OTHER "D"					
TOTAL "A" + "B" + "C" + "D"					
80 CONTINGENCY _____ % OF _____					
SUB TOTAL					
81 COMPLETION GUARANTEE _____ % OF _____					
82 COST OF ISSUE					
GRAND TOTAL					

Sample Page From the Telefilm Budget Template

04	PRODUCER				
SUB-ACC	DESCRIPTION	RATE	PERIOD	AMOUNT	TOTAL
04.01	EXECUTIVE PRODUCER				
04.05	PRODUCER				
04.10	CO-PRODUCER				
04.15	ASSOCIATE PRODUCER				
04.25	PRODUCER'S SECRETARY				
04.60	TRAVEL EXPENSES				
04.65	LIVING EXPENSES				
04.70	PUBLIC RELATIONS				
04.90	FRINGE BENEFITS				
04.95	OTHER				
04	TOTAL PRODUCER				

Sample Page From the Telefilm Budget Template

15	SET DRESSING LABOUR							
SUB-ACC	**DESCRIPTION**	**RATE**	**WEEK**				**AMOUNT**	**TOTAL**
			Prep	Shoot	Wrap	Total		
15.01	SET DECORATOR							
15.10	ASSISTANT SET DRESSER(S)							
15.20	SWING GANG							
15.30	LABOURER(S)							
15.95	OTHER							
15	TOTAL SET DRESSING LABOUR							

Sample Page From the Telefilm Budget Template

16	PROPERTY LABOUR							

SUB-ACC	DESCRIPTION	RATE	WEEK				AMOUNT	TOTAL
			Prep	Shoot	Wrap	Total		
16.01	PROPERTY MASTER							
16.10	ASSISTANT PROPERTY MASTER							
16.16	PROPERTY BUYER(S)							
16.30	OTHER PROPERTY LABOUR							
15.95	OTHER							

16	TOTAL PROPERTY LABOUR	

Cost Report

DISK COST60-61
CURRENCY: CN   LOCATION 01   SUMMARY
PROD: 900

PERIOD ENDING DATE

BASE CURRENCY/BUDGET RATE
INCLUDES PO COMMITMENTS
YR.   02

PAGE 1

RUN DATE 08/13/93
BASE CURRENCY: CN

ACCOUNT NUMBER	ACCOUNT DESCRIPTION	ACTUAL THIS PERIOD	ACTUAL TO DATE	PURCHASE ORDERS	TOTAL COST AMT.	EST. TO COMPLETE	ESTIMATED FINAL COST	TOTAL BUDGET	VARIANCE
ABOVE THE LINE									
02	SCENARIO								
03	DEVELOPMENT								
04	PRODUCER								
05	DIRECTOR								
ABOVE THE LINE TOTAL									
BELOW THE LINE									
10	CAST								
11	EXTRAS								
12	PRODUCTION STAFF								

13 DESIGN LABOUR	15 SET DRESSING LABOUR	16 PROPS LABOUR	18 STUNTS	19 WARDROBE LABOUR	20 MAKEUP/HAIR LABOUR	22 CAMERA LABOUR	23 ELECTRICAL LABOUR	24 GRIP LABOUR	25 SOUND LABOUR	26 TRANSPORTATION LABOUR	27 FRINGE BENEFITS	28 PRODUCTION OFFICE EXPENSES.	31 SITE EXPENSES	32 UNIT EXPENSES	33 TRAVEL AND LIVING

ACCOUNT NUMBER	ACCOUNT DESCRIPTION	ACTUAL THIS PERIOD	ACTUAL TO DATE	PURCHASE ORDERS	TOTAL COST AMT.	EST. TO COMPLETE	ESTIMATED FINAL COST	TOTAL BUDGET	VARIANCE
34	TRANSPORTATION								
35	CONSTRUCTION MATERIALS								
36	ART SUPPLIES								
37	SET DRESSING								
38	PROPS								
39	PICTURE VEHICLES/ANIMALS								
41	WARDROBE								
42	MAKEUP/HAIR SUPPLIES								
45	CAMERA EQUIPMENT								
46	ELECTRICAL EQUIPMENT								
47	GRIP EQUIPMENT								
48	SOUND EQUIPMENT								
51	PRODUCTION LABORATORY								
	PRODUCTION TOTAL								

BELOW THE LINE POST PRODUCTION

60   PICTURE EDITORIAL LABOUR

61   PICTURE EDITORIAL EQUIPMENT

62   VIDEO POST PRODUCTION

63   VIDEO POST PRODUCTION

64   POST PRODUCTION OFFICE

66   MUSIC

67   TITLES/OPTICALS

POST PRODUCTION TOTAL

BELOW THE LINE OTHER CHARGES

70   UNIT PUBLICITY

71   GENERAL EXPENSES

OTHER CHARGES TOTAL

BELOW THE LINE TOTAL

ABOVE & BELOW THE LINE TOTAL

TOTAL DIRECT COST

ACCOUNT NUMBER	ACCOUNT DESCRIPTION	ACTUAL THIS PERIOD	ACTUAL TO DATE	PURCHASE ORDERS	TOTAL COST AMT.	EST. TO COMPLETE	ESTIMATED FINAL COST	TOTAL BUDGET	VARIANCE
COMPLETION COSTS									
72	INDIRECT COSTS								
80	COMPLETION BOND								
COMPLETION COST TOTAL									
BELOW THE LINE CONTINGENCIES									
81	CONTINGENCIES								
CONTINGENCIES TOTAL									
PRODUCTION TOTAL									

4

Financing
Your
Production

by Steve Ord

S teve Ord is the vice-president and general manager of Atlantis
Films Limited, where he is responsible for overseeing and co-
ordinating all of Atlantis's television production activities, including
pilots, TV movies, miniseries, and series, with his main focus on the
financing of these productions. Atlantis Films Limited is one of
Canada's largest producers of television programming and is a public
company trading on the Toronto Stock Exchange. Prior to joining
Atlantis in 1993, he was the manager of Business Affairs at Telefilm
Canada in the Toronto Office, where he was involved primarily with
the Broadcast Fund and the Feature Film Fund. He is a graduate of
York University's MBA program (1985) and Concordia University's
Communication Studies program (1983).

Introduction

It has been said that financing film and television production
requires an equal mixture of business acumen and creative
ingenuity. No two Canadian productions have been financed
in exactly the same way. Raising production financing generally involves bringing together a number of different sources

of financing such as broadcasters, distributors, and investors (public and private), each with their own set of requirements and objectives. The producer must find a way to bring these sources together in a unique financing arrangement that allows a project to be produced — and ultimately released to the viewing public, whether in movie theatres or on TV screens.

As much as we should think about dramatic film and television production as a creative endeavour, involving the input of producers, writers, directors, actors, and other key creative individuals, we should also think of it as the making of "product" for a marketplace. The film and television industry in Canada and throughout the world is a business in which TV networks, pay channels, distributors, movie theatres, and other buyers need a regular supply of film and television programming suitable to the particular market of end consumers they serve. These buyers rely on producers or distributors for film and television programming. All successful producers must have a very good idea of which types of productions individual buyers want, and at what price.

This chapter will provide you with an overview of how to go about financing your project. The focus is on steering you through the complex process of raising production financing and guiding you to the main sources of funding available. The commentary provided deals primarily with dramatic productions, albeit many of the financing concepts apply equally to other types of programming, such as documentaries and children's productions. Although the lion's share of production activity in Canada is TV production, the chapter includes additional commentary on the particular challenges of financing theatrical feature films. Much of the information provided relates to the generalities of the business of production financing. Exceptions to the "general rules" occur all the time. In fact, some would argue that the film and television business is an industry where *every* project produced was a result of exceptions to the general rules.

SOME BASIC DEFINITIONS

To navigate successfully through the maze of film and television financing, it is useful to understand some basic definitions:

- The *project* is any production destined for release as a theatrical feature film, a two-hour television movie (also referred to as an "MOW" for Movie-of-the-Week), mini-series, television series, pilot, or a one-off special.
- *Development financing* is the cash required to turn an idea for a production into a complete creative package, including a final screenplay or teleplay, ready to go before the camera. This type of financing is usually in the form of an "advance."
- The *production budget* is the budget to produce and deliver a production. It is essentially a detailed cost estimate that covers development, pre-production, principal photography, post-production, and other associated costs.
- *Production financing* is the cash required to finance the production budget of a project. When a project is fully financed, the committed production financing equals the production budget dollar-for-dollar.
- The *financing structure* is a schedule that shows how an individual project is to be financed: that is, where all the money is to come from. It is usually in the form of a table that provides a breakdown of sources of production financing (such as investors and broadcasters), the nature of the participation — whether it be investment, pre-sales, or other forms — and the amount of money involved.
- *Interim financing* (also called *bank financing*), not to be confused with production financing, is the process of engaging a lender to convert production financing contracts into a

cash flow, which allows funds to be made available when the producer needs them, not when they are paid. Interim financing is a necessity, because many sources of production financing do not pay during production when most costs are incurred, but rather on some other basis such as holding back payments until delivery of the production.

Overview of Development Financing

Development is the first stage in every successful film or television project. It comprises all the activity associated with taking an idea that one believes would make an excellent basis for a feature film or television production, and developing it into a full creative package including a final screenplay or teleplay. This process is typically a lengthy one, requiring producers to have a great deal of tenacity to be successful at it. Feature films produced in Canada usually spend at least two to three years in development before being realized.

From a financial perspective, development is a high-risk area of the business, for the simple fact is that most projects developed are not produced. Consequently, all funds expended on abandoned projects must be written off. For this reason, it is prudent to spend only enough money on a project to find out whether or not it will proceed into production. The development process ends when either production financing commitments are arranged, allowing the project to be produced or it is decided to abandon the project for any number of reasons. The most common reasons are that the creative elements do not come together to the satisfaction of the producer or director, as the case may be, or that insufficient market interest exists for the project to proceed.

The traditional means of trying to beat the odds in development is to involve other participants in both financing the development process and participating in the creative process itself. The goals here are to lay off some of the development risk on other parties, and to involve a party that may ultimately be a source of production financing. The key is to attract financial and market interest in the project at the earliest possible stage. Canadian broadcasters, including the CBC, private networks, and individual broadcasters, take an interest, and get involved financially in developing projects that they may ultimately choose to license. Historically, Canadian theatrical film distributors have not demonstrated much of an interest in feature films at the development stage, but prefer to get involved later.

Involving a specific broadcaster allows projects to be developed with input from what could be the ultimate buyer of the production. Disregarding advice from the broadcaster about decisions such as choice of writers, story editors, and the creative direction of the project leads to an obvious conclusion when the broadcaster later makes programming decisions — they pass on the project.

In addition, development financing is available from Telefilm Canada, provincial film agencies, and some private film/TV funds such as COSEC Program Development Fund and the Foundation to Underwrite New Drama for Pay Television (FUND). These organizations have long realized the importance of development to the industry and provide valuable funds to assist in this risky enterprise.

THE PHASES OF DEVELOPMENT

How does a producer go about raising financing to pay for development costs? The first stage is to establish a phase-by-phase budget to take a project from an idea to a final creative package including a screenplay that is camera-ready, a director on board, and some key talent. The practice in Canada is for film funding agencies and broadcasters to fund on a phase-by-phase basis. Broadcasters will typically structure into their development agreements the right to opt out at the end of any stage of the process, should they elect not to proceed further. Film agencies such as Telefilm generally require the producer to reapply at the end of each phase of development, which allows them to opt out of continuing with a particular project.

What are the phases of development? In the case of feature films and MOWs (sometimes called MFTs — made for television), the development process usually commences with an outline, followed by a treatment, first draft, second draft, third draft, continuing to final draft and polish. Developing television series is more complicated, since usually only a handful of final scripts are commissioned and paid for in the development process. While it is difficult to generalize, the main development activity focuses on the production of a series "bible," which contains the premise for the series and character profiles, accompanied by story outlines for the first season of the series and up to five or six final complete scripts. Once production financing is arranged on a series, it becomes necessary to keep the writing team well ahead of the production team; shutting down production to wait for scripts to be written is a costly exercise.

BUDGETING DEVELOPMENT

Due to the high-risk nature of development, spend only as much money as you have to. For example, when acquiring the underlying rights to a story you are developing into a film or television project, the practice in the industry is to option rights for a reduced payment and to delay the actual purchase price to a production cost that is to be paid only if the project proceeds. Typically, the cost of the first option for the film/television rights to a book might be $5,000 for perhaps one year, with extensions costing lower amounts. The final purchase price for the rights could be $20,000, and usually the initial option fee and one or two extensions are applied towards reducing the purchase price. Writing fees make up the bulk of development costs. It is important to understand and adhere to the WGC (Writers Guild of Canada) collective agreement for independent producers. Negotiations with writers or their agents typically involve such issues as whether or not they will be paid scale for their services or scale plus a percentage, as may be the case for sought-after writers. In the case of television series, where more than one writer is usually involved, the services of an experienced story editor or head writer are helpful to ensure consistency among the scripts, and also to ensure that the stories work from one episode to another, particularly if there are story "arcs" involving several episodes.

During the final phases of development, other costs will need to be budgeted, which can include the services of the director, costs associated with preliminary location scouting, and travel costs that will be incurred to raise production financing. In all phases of development, it is important to ensure adequate legal fees have been budgeted, because mistakes made in development can prove to be very costly to fix in the production stage, particularly with respect to underlying rights. (See Chapter 10 for more on this subject.) People tend to get a little greedy when they find out, on the night before commencement of principal photography, that they hold some "right" that the producer has overlooked. It is also important to keep in mind that if the producer has failed to acquire necessary underlying rights, this lapse will be revealed at a later stage, when lawyers representing insurers, banks, or financing sources ask for evidence that clear title exists and that all rights have been cleared on the property that the producer or its distributors are intending to exploit.

Lastly, don't forget to budget producer fees and overhead to cover administrative support, faxes, couriers, and long-distance phone calls. These costs will add up over a period that can span a few years. If one is going the agency funding route for development, it is important to check their various guidelines, because these costs are typically capped as a percentage of direct development costs (such as writer's fee, option fees, and legal fees). Development budgets are typically broken down into phases: such as costs to treatment, costs to first draft, costs to second draft, and so on.

FINANCING DEVELOPMENT

The practice in the Canadian industry is to repay all parties who have contributed to development out of the production budget of the project if it is produced, on either the first day of principal photography or on some other repayment schedule as agreed to. Also, if the original producer sells or transfers the underlying rights (including the script) to a second producer, most financiers would require either consent to such a transfer or the right to demand full repayment. Consequently, development financing is typically in the form of an "advance" or some form of "loan." It is preferable from the producer's perspective that development funding neither be tied to a fixed repayment date nor bear interest, as is the case with funding from Telefilm and most Canadian broadcasters. In some situations, however, development funding may be in the form of a loan payable on a fixed repayment date, which serves to pass all the risk back to a producer if the project being developed does not proceed into production.

When developing a project, a producer should keep tight controls on funds expended, keeping in mind that development costs must ultimately be financed at the production stage. Projects that have a long history, with many different writers involved and perhaps many different producers, generally also have steep repayment obligations. These projects often become difficult to finance as their production budgets include ballooned above-the-line production costs caused by lots of baggage in the form of old development costs.

For television projects, involving a targeted broadcaster at the outline or treatment stage is a good place to start. An interested broadcaster would finance a portion of the agreed-upon development budget in exchange for the exclusive right to licence the production for telecast at a later date if it is produced. Such involvement typically binds the producer to that particular broadcaster under the terms of the development agreement. It is essential, therefore, to ensure there is a good fit between the producer, the broadcaster, and of course the project. When projects proceed into production, broadcasters typically apply their development advances against licence fees due as a kind of off-the-top deduction. While there are exceptions, Telefilm and most provincial agencies require the involvement of a broadcaster as a prerequisite for their support of a project in development.

In the feature film area, it is relatively rare for Canadian theatrical distributors to get involved in development during the early stages of a project. Unless the producer or director has a long-established relationship with the distributor, the practice is for Canadian feature film producers to develop projects on their own, often involving Telefilm and other private and public film funds, and to pitch the projects to the distributors at the near-final or final draft stage.

OTHER DEVELOPMENT CONSIDERATIONS

With the exception of television series renewals, every dramatic film and television program is essentially a new product that has to be designed from the ground up and produced on an individual basis. As our Canadian industry has grown and matured, the larger production companies such as Atlantis and Alliance have established development departments in recognition of its importance.

Development is typically the first exposure of a novice drama producer to buyers of programming and to the Canadian funding agencies. Early in the development process, broadcasters will be sizing up the producer to determine whether or not that producer has the makings of a reliable program supplier from both a creative and business perspective. Development is also the stage when novice producers gain exposure to the workings of funding agencies, and these organizations, in turn, gain insight into the experience and skillfulness of the producer.

Early in the development process, film agencies and/or broadcasters may advise a producer that they believe a project is beyond the scope and experience of that particular producer (or the director attached to the project), and that they will not support the project beyond a certain point in development or consider the project for production financing until an experienced executive producer or producer is brought on board. While these "judgement calls" are at times controversial, it is better to air these issues early in the process than later.

It is critical for the producer — and those funding him or her — to know ahead of time whether the intended budget is realistic for the production being developed. For example, at the time of writing, a typical low-budget Canadian theatrical film has a production budget of between $1.2 million and $1.8 million; it takes 20 to 22 days to shoot, in and around one central geographic area; and it will likely be a non-union shoot. The craft of writing for such films, therefore, becomes not only to tell engaging and original stories, but also to deal cleverly with the limitations imposed by production budgets. At this budget level, funds may only be available for a limited number of characters, locations, crowd scenes, and action/adventure or special effect sequences. As a reality check for all production assumptions, advice should be sought from a respected line producer, production manager, or first assistant director who has experience with the type of project being planned. Lastly, one must not forget that development is an unpredictable endeavour. It is not until the end of the process that the cumulative results of decisions such as story ideas, choice of writers, and structure will be known.

Production Financing

Assuming that development has been completed successfully, the next stage is raising sufficient production financing to allow the project to proceed. Keep in mind that, until sufficient financing commitments are arranged to cover the full cost of production, you are still in "development," albeit the final phase.

Raising production financing is usually done on a per-project basis, as opposed to on a per-company basis. Virtually all government-supported investment programs fund projects, not companies. For legal and accounting reasons, the practice in Canada is for production companies to set up single-purpose production companies, which are often referred to as "Prodcos," to produce and exploit one project. These companies hold all initial rights, apply for financing, contract with investors, and enter into licence and/or distribution agreements.

THE PRODUCTION AS A BIG "BUNDLE OF RIGHTS"

A starting point for this discussion on financing is to think of every production as an "asset," which is essentially a big bundle of rights to be exploited and protected. This is what is unique to the film and television industry and is at the root of every business arrangement involved with production financing.

A basic right is ownership of the asset. If a producer finds a production without any third-party owners (i.e., parties unrelated to a producer), he or she would own the asset outright. To raise production financing, it is often the practice in the industry to sell off portions of this asset to third-party investors, such as Telefilm or private tax-motivated investors, through limited partnerships. This asset can also be pledged to banks to help secure interim financing as collateral for a loan.

Other rights attached to the asset are the rights to "license" it for specific use. While a completed master negative of a film may cost millions of dollars to produce, it costs only a few hundred dollars to duplicate it. The industry is not about selling physical products but rather the right to use or to rent the physical product. (The home video business is an exception, of course, but even here consumers acquire only the right to home use.) Canadian copyright legislation and international copyright conventions provide legal protection for owners of film and television productions that allows them to sell and/or license specific rights they control. Raising production financing is, therefore, the process of strategically selling off or licensing specific rights to raise sufficient funds to allow the production to be made.

This concept is best explained using the example of a sale by a producer to a broadcaster. This sale is called a *broadcast licence* for a *licence fee*, which would be set out in a *licence agreement*. Specifically, the broadcast licence would allow the broadcaster to effective "rent" the production for a defined number of telecasts — typically three or four runs; for a term — typically no more than four years; and for a specific geographic area — typically the area covered by the broadcaster's signal. In most cases, broadcast licences are exclusive so that no other entity can encroach on the rights granted. Further, at the end of the term the broadcaster would have no further rights to the production. The producer would be free to relicense the production in that same geographic area to either the same broadcaster or another one, for additional licence fees.

Continuing with the preceding example, if the sale to the broadcaster is made before production commences (that is, if the broadcaster "orders" the production based on the script and other creative elements of the package, such as director and casting), the broadcast licence would be referred to as a *pre-sale*, which could be used to assist with the financing of the production.

A trade-off exists here between raising more funds at the pre-production stage by licensing the full value of the production, versus holding back various rights to be sold when the production is completed so that the production has long-term earning potential. While producers would rather hold back as many rights as possible, due to the realities of the marketplace and the high cost of production, in practice it is a luxury to hold back any great number of the available rights.

Finally, it is common for investors not to invest in the actual copyright of the production but rather to invest in the distribution rights to the production. This approach deviates from the very traditional investment approach used by some agencies such as Telefilm. It is in many ways a much more cautious approach, because it puts investors much closer to the revenue of the production, which is, of course, directly linked to the distribution rights.

THE CANADIAN PRODUCER AS A "PACKAGER"

Financing for Canadian film and television productions is almost always carried out on a piece-by-piece basis as opposed to raising the entire budget from a single sale to one buyer. That is to say, productions are financed by bringing together financing to cover the cost of production from a number of different sources, which are usually a combination of investors (public and private) and buyers who license various rights. The producing function in Canada is very much one of a "packager."

In my estimation, the average dramatic production produced in Canada has four to six different sources of financing. During my time at Telefilm Canada, it was not uncommon to use independent documentary films with 10 to 12 different sources of financing; the record would probably go to a project with 20 sources of financing! Ironically, as a general rule of thumb, the smaller the production budget, the more sources of financing are required. Big-budget feature films and drama series often have the fewest sources as they are often the most commercial projects with a higher level of interest from major buyers.

Raising financing piece-by-piece is one of the greatest frustrations experienced by many Canadian producers and filmmakers, but it is also one of the greatest strengths of the industry, which is now proving to be very beneficial as Canadian producers expand into the international marketplace. They are now using their skills to bring together Canadian buyers with American and other foreign buyers to finance productions. Our track record in co-production, as demonstrated by the number of international co-productions completed each year, is a testament to our industry's ingenuity.

It should be noted that, particularly in the case of television production, the Canadian experience differs significantly from that of our counterparts in the United States, Britain, France, and Germany, where traditionally a single domestic broadcaster has paid all or nearly all of a program's cost by a single licence fee. With the continued fragmentation of the world television market by cable and the licensing of more television services, however, a trend is developing whereby broadcasters around the world, including those in the United States, are pushing their producers to find partners, because they are no longer willing or able to pay the full cost of production.

Before turning to a detailed description of how to raise and structure production financing, it is useful to review the Canadian context in which it occurs: namely, the small domestic market, the impact of Canadian content regulations, and public financing, because these factors largely determine Canadian production financing models.

THE SMALL DOMESTIC MARKET

The Canadian domestic marketplace, by itself, is not large enough to support Canadian dramatic production. The ultimate Canadian marketplace for film and television productions is 22 million English Canadians and 7 million Francophone Canadians. The economics are quite simple. On the supply side of the equation, producing quality film and television production is very expensive, with production budgets for drama typically about $700,000 to $1,200,000 or more per hour. On the demand side of the equation, licence fees for television productions from English-language Canadian broadcasters typically fall somewhere between $60,000 and $300,000 an hour, with the higher fee being paid only in very exceptional circumstances. Most private broadcasters would argue that even these described licence fee levels are above what they are able to recover from advertising sales.

Only the CBC, and only for in-house productions, will fund the full cost of Canadian dramatic production. In the case of theatrical feature films, Canadian distributors will generally limit their distribution advances for Canadian rights to not much more than what a broadcaster will pay on a per-hour basis (and these advances are often indirectly supported by Telefilm's Feature Film Distribution fund). This economic reality explains why both public financing and the reliance on foreign markets are necessary to allow Canadian dramatic productions to be created.

THE IMPACT OF "CANADIAN CONTENT"

Experience has shown us that appealing, high-quality Canadian drama shows in good time slots attract audiences comparable to their U.S. programming counterparts. As well, Canadian broadcasters — from the networks through to individual stations, pay channels, and specialty channels — all operate in an environment where Canadian content levels must be adhered to as part of meeting their conditions of licence as regulated by the Canadian Radio-Television Telecommunications Commission (the CRTC). Conventional television broadcasters must telecast Canadian productions for 50 per cent of their programming schedule. In the last ten years, the CRTC has also encouraged broadcasters to rely on independent Canadian producers to meet their Canadian dramatic programming requirements. In addition, major Canadian broadcasters have specific programming requirements as measured in hours and dollars related to licensing and/or investing in Canadian productions. For example, the CRTC will require some broadcasters to spend predetermined levels of licence fees and investment for a predetermined volume of Canadian productions.

As a result, when broadcasters elect to license Canadian programs, they typically require evidence that the production qualifies as "Canadian content," which one obtains by applying to either the Canadian Audio-Visual Certification Office (CAVCO) at the Department of Canadian Heritage, or the CRTC itself. Both bodies have regulations that are based on a 10-point system (key creative positions, such as art director, count for a point, with the major roles of director and screenwriter being assessed two points each) and Canadian spending requirements, in addition to other criteria. It is vital for a producer to know these regulations inside and out, and to ensure that productions sold as Canadian content achieve certification by following the regulations.

One should also not overlook the importance of Canadian content to the film agencies and other incentives available in Canada such as the Ontario Film Investment Program and the newly launched Cable Production Fund. Telefilm Canada, through its main investment funds, the Broadcast Fund and the Feature Film Fund, will generally only invest in high Canadian content productions that qualify for at least 8 out of 10 points and that meet subjective Canadian content criteria: that is, the productions must be genuinely set in Canada and tell stories from a Canadian perspective. In addition, objective programs (involving no subjective assessments of the merits of the content of a particular production) such as the federal film Capital Cost Allowance (CCA) program, which is being phased out, require a production to satisfy CAVCO's Canadian content criteria. Official Treaty Co-productions can also achieve Canadian content status by applying to the Co-production Office at Telefilm in Montreal.

In the marketplace, Canadian content has more value to television production than to feature films, because what is shown in movie theatres is not regulated as it is in the case of broadcasters. In other words, while Canadian broadcasters must telecast Canadian productions, theatrical exhibitors screen any films they want, subject only to provincial censorship restrictions. Canadian content does, however, play a role with feature films, because it is a pre-condition to receiving any public financing. As well, Canadian broadcasters that are heavy buyers of Canadian theatrical films (particularly The Movie Network and Superchannel) have CRTC Canadian content requirements.

PUBLIC FINANCING

Since the publication of the first edition of *Making It*, one of the most positive industry developments has been the establishment of several public financing mechanisms to assist with the development and financing of Canadian productions. At the federal level, Telefilm Canada administers the Broadcast Fund (for TV productions) and the Feature Film Fund (for theatrical feature films), in addition to other funds such as the interim Loan Fund. The federal government also continues to support Canadian production indirectly, through accelerated Capital Cost Allowances for private investors who invest in Certified Canadian productions, although, at the time of writing, the federal government is in the process of phasing out this program in favour of a refundable investment tax credit program. In addition, most provinces have direct investment programs and, in some cases, private investment rebate programs. These funds are more fully described later in this chapter.

The Process of Raising Production Financing

Whether the project is a big-budget drama series or a low-budget feature film, the process of raising production financing is similar; it simply grows in complexity with the magnitude of the project. While there are always exceptions to the "general rules" of how things actually get done in this business, the vast majority of decision makers who control production financing at broadcasting and distribution companies and the public film agencies know the process of funding production very well. They expect the producer to have reviewed carefully all the steps required to ensure that all their requirements are met.

STEP ONE: THE PRODUCTION BUDGET

Since the production budget is essentially a detailed cost estimate for the completed project, it is important to determine at the outset how much money has to be raised, keeping in mind that the production is not financed until the committed and contracted financing equals the production budget dollar-for-dollar.

The production budget will also be the focus of considerable scrutiny from potential investors, broadcasters, and the completion guarantor. The budget, along with the production schedule, is a blueprint for how the production will be made. Most participants who contribute significant dollars to production financing require the right to approve the production budget, and they may object to certain costs and/or the absence of certain costs in the budget. The more money financial participants put up, the more they care how all the money will be spent. Film agencies need a detailed budget before they will assess an application for funds. Further, they will usually not proceed to a commitment stage until they have approved and accepted the budget, and most retain the right of approval over the final budget.

The place to start is to engage an experienced line producer and/or production manager to break down the most recent script into its component parts, prepare a shooting schedule, and then prepare a realistic production budget in the format used and accepted in the business — the Telefilm Canada format. The individual preparing the budget should know — before beginning — what budget range the project is intended to fall into. Inevitably, the first draft of the budget will exceed the level of financing that can realistically be raised. This brings us to an unavoidable point of conflict between those whose responsibility it is to raise money and those whose responsibility it is to spend money. It is a fact that it is easier to raise less money than more; it is also a fact that it is easier to spend more money on a production than less. It is the producer's job to find a balance between production and financing pressures.

It is important for the producer to review the budget carefully, to make sure that all necessary expenses are budgeted and that unnecessary costs are not budgeted. The budget is covered fully in Chapter 3, but I would like to note here a few points related to financing when budgeting that your production manager may not be aware of:

- Ensure that the *full* development costs are included, as these must be repaid from the production budget.
- If the targeted buyers require star casting, ensure that an adequate allowance for stars exists.
- In the area of talent residuals, ensure that the prepaid residuals budgeted are adequate to cover all pre-sales used in production financing. For example, if a pre-sale to a theatrical distributor for all Canadian rights is used in production financing, then one must budget the maximum buyouts for Canada. Budgeting world buyouts where not required is a luxury that only big-budget productions can afford. A "buyout" is a prepaid fee to actors and directors to cover all future and unlimited uses in the marketplace for predetermined medias and territories for a limited term (usually five years).
- Don't overlook *Producer Fees* and *Corporate Overhead*, with the former being a fee for producing the project and the latter being funds used to cover all non-project specific costs, including the cost of running an office during times when no fees are earned. If you are seeking funding from film agencies, most set a ceiling for these costs at 10 per cent of the "b" and "c" portions of their budget forms (essentially the below-the-line costs) for each of fees and overhead (that is, 20 per cent for combined "b" and "c"). Generally speaking, the agencies consider this cap to apply to the collective

costs of *all* producers — line producer, producer, and executive producer — on a particular project.

- Shooting on 35 mm film is more costly than on 16 mm film. While theatrical films are generally shot on 35 mm, the practice in Canada is to shoot on 16 mm for dramatic TV to keep costs in check. With the exception of TV shows for U.S. networks, most TV buyers will accept 16 mm, since the quality difference is negligible once transferred to videotape.

- Pay close attention to the post-production portion of the budget, so that funds are set aside for all of the delivery requirements of distributors and/or pre-sale licences. These might include: music and effects tracks to allow for foreign dubbing, and a French-language dub if a French-language sale is used in production financing. In the case of feature films with elements unsuitable for television use — for example, because of foul language — it is a good idea to do a "free-TV" version.

- Include a detailed allowance for interim financing to cash-flow the production, plus bank set-up and legal fees.

- If a third-party completion guarantor will be required, which is almost always the case, ensure that the fee budgeted is accurate.

Budgets are not unlike scripts. They generally change many times and are typically "locked" only days before commencement of principal photography, when final costs of certain suppliers are known. The producer, line producer, and director (for a movie) should sign off on the budget before it is submitted to investors and the completion bonders for their final approval. It is useful to involve a completion guarantor in the budget process because they hold a lot of control in this business.

STEP TWO: THE FINANCIAL STRUCTURE

Before approaching any potential financing sources, the second step is to determine a realistic financing structure to fund the production budget. That is to say, develop a financing plan or model to raise enough funding to cover the production budget. This involves a process of going through the many permutations and combinations of how the project can be financed, based on realistic assessments of how much broadcasters or distributors are likely to advance on a pre-sale basis, and the extent to which other financing sources such as film agencies and investment rebates can be accessed. This process may also involve revisiting cost assumptions used in formulating the production budget, if the financing keeps coming up short. In order to handle this stage properly, you need detailed knowledge of how the various financing sources function, and under what terms and conditions they are likely to commit production financing.

It is critical at this point to make an impartial assessment of the "fit" between your project and potential sources of financing. For example, to access the Ontario Film Investment Program (OFIP) for a feature film, an Ontario-based Canadian theatrical distributor must be involved. Hence, a theatrical commitment from a Quebec-based distributor will not be accepted by OFIP.

In most cases, the financing of a project is built around a primary pre-sale, which serves as an "anchor" for all other financing sources. For example, if the main buyer is intended to be a theatrical feature film distributor, that would be your first targeted financing source and the means by which you hope to access other financing. Telefilm Canada and most other provincial film agencies will not even review an application for feature film financing until you have obtained a financial commitment from an approved theatrical distributor. The jargon used in the business is whether or not a "trigger" is in place. These organizations require Canadian-owned and -controlled companies to be the triggers to the funds. If your project is intended primarily for the U.S. market and/or international marketplace, the reality is that the bulk of production financing will have to come from those sources. Hence, the anchor for the project is likely to be a pre-sale to a U.S. or international broadcaster, distributor, or pay channel for most of the production financing. In addition, if the story has American characters and settings it is extremely doubtful that Telefilm Canada would invest in the project, no matter how many Canadian content points the production achieves.

In the case of public financing, most film funding agencies set funding limits, expressed both as a percentage of the production budget and as a maximum amount. Many programs also vary their participation, depending on how many Canadian content points are involved. Taking Telefilm Canada as an example, it can invest up to 49 per cent of a production budget for a 10 of 10 (point) production; however, its normal maximum investment is $1.5 million for theatrical feature films and $1 million for TV movies.

An additional objective at this stage is to arrange for the orderly exploitation of the project to satisfy investors' requirements and to provide long-term earning potential. Investors will require the producer to demonstrate that real potential exists for them to recover their investments. Thus, when rights are being licensed, investors will often require that some rights remain unsold so that sources of revenue can be realized from the completed production to be applied towards recoupment of their investment. Telefilm typically requires that producers leave either the U.S. market or the foreign market (excluding the U.S.) as unsold territories as a pre-condition for their investment.

As budget levels rise, which of course heightens the need for production financing, negotiation with investors becomes more protracted, as the producer tries to find a financing structure that allows all financing sources with their seemingly incompatible goals to come together to allow the project to be made. For example, in order to attract a foreign sales company to put up a distribution advance against foreign distribution rights, the distributor will often demand rights to all unsold territories, to create the greatest possible opportunity for it to recover its distribution advance and, of course, to earn distribution fees. This often conflicts with the goals of investors, who may, as we said earlier, require that some rights remain unsold so that they have a more immediate return on their investment when they are licensed. This predicament illustrates the necessity for creative thinking to find ways to finance productions.

Financial structures are generally set out in chart form, indicating the intended financing sources, with the amount of financing and form of financing — for example, licence fees, investment, or distribution advance — clearly indicated. It is often necessary to develop various scenarios with fall-back strategies, so that if Plan A fails, the producer can work on Plan B, and so on, until all realistic financing structures are exhausted.

STEP THREE: OBTAINING PRODUCTION FINANCING COMMITMENTS

At this stage, you have a viable package, including the creative package, a budget, and a financing plan in which any combination of broadcasters, distributors, film agencies, and other sources of development financing have contributed to the project's development. It is relatively easy to get to this stage. It's the next stage that is often the most challenging and that decides the fate of projects — raising production financing.

MAKING THE MAIN PRE-SALE

The first commitment you must nail down is the anchor to the entire project: for example, a significant offer to license the production from a broadcaster or distributor. Carefully consider the order with which you approach potential buyers. It's considered bad form to approach your second choice before hearing back from your first choice. Every producer has her or his own style of pre-selling projects to buyers, and each buyer has her or his own way in which they typically buy into projects. If you are not a good "pitcher," team up with someone on the project who is. Some writers, directors, and actors are excellent at selling concepts. Printed material submitted should be organized and professional, and should be what the potential buyer asks to see: if the buyer wants to see a summary, for example, don't send the script. It's generally a good idea to reach a positive acceptance of the creative material before entering into business discussions and negotiations.

During negotiations, the following basic deal-points will be discussed:

- What will the production be like when it is finally delivered, and are the producers and creative/production team capable of delivering what is promised?
- How much licence, distribution advance, and/or investment money will the buyer advance?
- When will the commitment be paid, and what rights does the buyer get in return for a commitment of cash? For example, are the buyer's rights exclusive or non-exclusive? How many years will the term be? Other rights to be clarified include the territory, number of uses (for TV sales), the media involved, the options for renewal of rights, on-screen credits, credits on promotional materials, and the buyer's approval rights.
- What is the delivery date of the production?

- What are the conditions of the offer; for example, at what date does the commitment lapse if the producer is unable to secure the balance of production financing?

Unless you are very experienced at such negotiations, its a good idea to use the services of an entertainment lawyer or business affairs expert to guide you through the process.

An often overlooked deal-point is the delivery date. For TV shows, because broadcasters agree to buy a production based on a probable airdate, "value" to the broadcaster is not only determined by how good the show is, but also when it can be telecast: for example, during the fall line-up, as a replacement to an existing series, as a movie for sweep-weeks, and so on. Theatrical distributors often work backwards from what they believe is the likely launch date of a particular film to determine the delivery date. For highly commercial movies, for instance, they may work backwards from the release date, whether it be a summer release date, fall release date, or a Christmas release date. They may also work backwards from the cut-off date for submissions to the Cannes Film Festival or the Toronto International Film Festival. It is the producer's job to find a way to meet the delivery date while also juggling production factors such as weather considerations, crew and talent availability, and financial factors. It almost always takes longer to raise production financing than planned.

SECURING THE BALANCE OF PRODUCTION FINANCING

With a commitment from the primary pre-sale buyer in place, you now must put in place the balance of production financing as set out in the proposed financing structure. In Canada, the balance of financing may well involve a number of different sources, with the typical ones being public investments, provincial investment rebates, foreign pre-sales, advances from distributors, and deferrals. It is important that you understand the order in which you should approach the various funding sources. Most private broadcasters/distributors can be approached whenever they are receptive to new productions. As stated previously, government film agencies generally require that the "trigger" broadcaster/distributor be secured and that a viable financing plan is in place before they will even review an application. While you can usually apply at any time of the year, these funds typically work on a fiscal year basis, commencing in April. Most of the private investment funds, such as the Maclean Hunter Television Fund and the Shaw Children's Programming Initiative have quarterly decision schedules and corresponding cut-off dates.

Once the bulk of financing is arranged, you can then proceed to try to tap into other sources, such as private investment from tax-motivated investors. For Ontario producers, the Ontario Film Investment Program (OFIP), which provides rebates to producers for eligible investments, is typically the last commitment you can obtain. OFIP will not commit to a project until full financing and other requirements are met, as demonstrated by your entering into long-form contracts.

STEP FOUR: ARRANGING FOR A COMPLETION BOND

When your project begins to look like it actually might happen, add the completion bond to the top of your to-do list. Most investors and interim lenders will specify that a completion bond must be in place to guarantee completion of production. There are two types of bonding arrangements in use in the Canadian industry:

1. *A Completion Bond Company.* Several companies, such as Film Finances Canada (1984) Ltd. and Motion Picture Guarantors Ltd., are in the business of bonding productions

for a fee. The completion guarantor serves to guarantee that the production will be delivered on time and on budget for the benefit of the producer, the investors, the bank, and others providing production financing. These companies underwrite their policies with re-insurers, so that if a claim is made they will have the resources to complete production. Bond fees are negotiated on the basis of the track record of the producer and other key production personnel and on the production budget. Guarantors will focus on what they view as variable costs, such as below-the-line and star costs when setting a fee, which is in the area of 6 per cent of these costs.

It is important to understand that completion guarantors do not guarantee financing of productions (or even the cash flow), but rather that productions will be completed so that the producer meets all of the delivery requirements provided all production financing is made available. Guarantors pay close attention to production budgets, production schedules, delivery dates, and who is hired to ensure production risks are minimized. Early in the process, run all major decisions by your guarantor, including selection of a line producer and director, to reduce the risk of any "surprises" later.

In the event of a significant cost overrun, the guarantor will get involved. If the producer is unable to manage the production, the guarantor has the contractual right to take over the production and take control of production funds, including the production bank account. The guarantor would then ensure that the production is delivered and be responsible for all costs to get the production delivered. In the event of an outright production disaster (which is not covered by production insurance), the guarantor has the right to refund all production financing advanced to date and to abandon the production. This is referred to as the *strike price* in the completion bond agreement. In practice, modest production overages are usually paid by the producer and not the guarantor. (In this regard, the process is not unlike other forms of insurance: you are not going to claim on your car insurance policy if you cause a little fender-bender.)

Most newcomers to the business of financing production get a little too fixated on the completion bond. One should keep in mind that the Canadian industry has had very few completion bond horror shows. It is very rare for bonds to be called in Canada, although it does occasionally happen. In fact, some believe that current bonding fees have become inflated in Canada because of claims made in the United States, where guarantors have had a number of big claims in recent years, mostly over big-budget feature films.

The practice in Canada is for guarantors to refund half the bond fee to the producer in the event that there are no claims, as a reward for producing on time and on budget.

2. *Producer Self-Guarantees.* This is an alternative to third-party completion bonds and is only an option for low-budget productions, particularly in the television area. Under these guarantees, the producer takes responsibility for all overages by pledging producer fees against budget over-runs. In particular, many low-budget documentaries with film agency investment follow this approach. Self-guarantees involve a simple agreement between the producer and investors, whereby the producer agrees to withhold payment of fees to himself or herself until final costs are known and the production is delivered. In some cases, the producer is required to place these fees (often about 3 percent of the budget) in trust with a lawyer until the investors sign off on the final costs so the fees can be released.

STEP FIVE: ARRANGING INTERIM FINANCING

When production financing commitments begin to come together, you will need to determine the extent to which you will need interim financing, also referred to as "bank financing." To figure this out, you need to have your accountant and/or production manager prepare a detailed cash-flow projection from pre-production through to delivery of the final production, ending at audit of the production. Cash flows are very simple: they are a week-by-week spreadsheet that shows the net projected production account balance based on estimates outflows (that is, spending the budget) against estimated inflows (that is, the production financing). Each week ends with either a surplus of cash or a deficit of cash. If you are unable to either find a way to accelerate your inflows from financing sources or delay payment to suppliers to get the production in a positive cash position for every week, then you will need interim financing.

Interim financing is a form of financing that few producers have the luxury of avoiding. It's true that lower-budget features with considerable public investment are made each year with no interim lender. In these cases, film agencies try to structure payments schedules that will approximate the pace at which the production budget will be expended. Most productions, however, need interim financing. While commercial banks in the past tended to ignore the industry, its recent growth is bringing them slowly into the world of film and television production. The Royal Bank of Canada has led the charge with its long track record in this business. Other sources to consider are the very successful Rogers Telefund and Telefilm Canada, which administers its own interim loan fund. Some other film agencies provide production loans to varying degrees. To arrange interim financing of your production, you will have to:

- contractually prove to your bank that production financing is fully in place;
- prepare a detailed cash flow that lays out your borrowing requirements;
- assign future payments from your financing sources to the bank through a legal instrument called an *Assignment and Direction*;
- allow the bank to take a first-position security interest on the project (i.e., allow the bank to be the highest-ranked creditor), on all the assigned receivables, on the distribution rights, and on anything else the bank reasonably requires;
- arrange to have the bank named as an additional insured on the completion bond and the production insurance.

Bank financing is a costly endeavour, in both money and time. The producer is responsible for interest charges and all of the bank's legal fees in addition to the producer's own legal fees. It's a good idea to have someone in your office do as much legwork as possible on behalf of the bank and be as organized as possible, because if the bank's legal counsel does all the work the producer will be hit with an even larger legal bill.

In the case of commercial banks, the producer also must pay a loan set-up fee, which has to be negotiated. All of these costs should be included in the production budget. Don't underestimate the time and effort required to put in place interim financing, because it is not unusual for the process to consume more time and effort than lining up all other production financing commitments combined. A good relationship with your interim lender is key to making the process work on all fronts.

STEP SIX: CLOSING THE FINANCING

Unlike financial closing in other sectors where all financing participants get together to attend a late-night formal closing in a law firm's boardroom, film and television financing involves a series of closings. It starts with commitment letters and/or short-form deal letters from each financial participant and moves to long-form contracts. The most complicated aspect is determining the order in which various documents should be negotiated and signed. As the process proceeds, it is inevitable that points of conflict will arise, such as disputes over who gets screen credits and in what order. Once again, it is the producer's job to find the middle ground in these conflicts.

Most financial participants will not advance any production funds until the producer can demonstrate the "full circle of financing," and some will not advance any funds until all long-form contracts are in place, along with the completion bond and production insurance. The goal, therefore, is to close all financing commitments on or about commencement of pre-production. In this way, money is in hand to accommodate production cash-flow needs, before you have to enter into all of the cast and crew contractual commitments. Inevitably, however, closing the financing takes longer, which puts great pressures on the producer.

Complicating the closing process are each party's individual approval rights. Before many of the documents can be executed, they must be circulated for approval to other participants, particularly investors, to make sure that the various deals are consistent with each other. Further, if government film agencies are involved, they will want to see that the various licence and distribution agreements are consistent with their policies, which vary from one agency to another. Throughout this entire process, it is very important to communicate clearly with each participant, to ensure that all closing requirements are known with the longest possible lead time. As a general rule of thumb, the commitments usually closed first are licence and/or distribution agreements. The last commitment to close is usually the interim financing.

Closing film and television financing arrangements takes on an entirely new dimension when productions are made as co-productions, whether they be interprovincial co-productions or international co-productions under one of Canada's film treaties with other countries. In these arrangements a separate co-production agreement needs to be entered into between the two (or more) producers. These arrangements need to set out the various obligations of each producer, which will in turn, have an impact on the contracting entities of all licence and other financing agreements. (See Chapter 8 for more on the subject of co-productions.)

Most broadcasters and investors will require an advance ruling from CAVCO to confirm Canadian content status as a closing requirement. Producers of Official Treaty Co-productions generally must obtain an advance ruling from the Co-production Office (Telefilm, Montreal Office) to confirm the treaty status of the production.

Closing film transactions should be carried out with advice from legal counsel familiar with expertise in the legal and business aspects of this business. Lots of common sense is vital to getting productions financed, no matter what role one plays in this business, since the whole process revolves around a series of "chicken or egg" dilemmas.

A FEW WORDS ON RECOUPMENT OF INVESTORS' INVESTMENT

One of the most difficult aspects of closing investment deals is determining how future revenues from a production will be shared amongst all investors. This arrangement is usually set out in a document called the "recoupment schedule." The traditional approach to sharing revenue is as follows:

1. The first deductions from the after-sale revenue (i.e., rev-

enue not used to finance production) are the distributors' or sales agents' commissions, followed by distribution expenses and talent residuals. These deductions are usually referred to as "off-the-top" deductions and do not normally form part of the recoupment schedule. The net amount remaining, often contractually defined as "Net Receipts" or "Producer's Receipts," is then used to recoup any distribution advances.

2. The balance of net receipts is then paid to the producer on behalf of the investors. The investors are then usually repaid on a semi-annual basis of their recoupment schedule. Due to the difficulty of attracting private investment to the film and television industry, the usual practice in Canada is for government investors such as Telefilm to allow private-sector participants to recoup ahead of them or at a faster rate. This is usually done in a number of "tiers," which rank the order and amount each participant is entitled to receive. First-tier investors rank ahead of second-tier investors, and so forth. Several investors can share one tier, and in that case all funds flowing into that tier would be allocated on a pro rata basis, weighted on the basis of each party's entitlement.

   In recent years, because of budget cuts, Telefilm Canada and other government agencies have pursued a much more aggressive approach towards recoupment, making negotiations much more difficult and time-consuming to bring together a number of investment sources and distributors prepared to put up advances on one project.

3. At such time as all parties have recovered their investments, the balance of net receipts are deemed "net profits." The practice in Canada is for all investors to share 50 per cent of net profits, while the producer retains the other 50 per cent of net profits. However, on projects where there is very little investment in the financing, this formula is often not

used. For example, if investors put up only 5 per cent of the budget with the other 95 per cent coming from pre-sales arranged by the producer, it makes little sense to give up 50 per cent of the profits for 5 per cent of the financing. In these cases, net profits would simply be negotiated without the use of the "standard formula."

From the producer's perspective, the challenge behind recoupment negotiations is to find a plan that works for all investors and distributors, since the alternative is to lose production financing commitments. Recoupment arrangements can take on all kinds of forms and can, and often do, vary considerably from the approach described above.

The Canadian film industry has a tradition of setting out recoupment arrangements in numerical schedules in table form, which often include divisions of revenue by source, such as Canada, the United States, international, etc. In the film industries of other countries, particularly Britain and the United States, recoupment arrangements are almost always set out in lengthy prose with every other word being "whereas."

Be aware, finally, that involving a third-party investor in your project is a long-term relationship. The producer has an obligation to report to each investor for the term of copyright, which is 50 years. Because this creates a long-term administration cost, it is common practice in the industry to reduce reporting to an annual basis after the first few years when most revenue is earned. Telefilm, for example, has adopted this as their policy to alleviate administration costs on both sides.

SOURCES OF FINANCING FOR CANADIAN DRAMATIC PRODUCTIONS

Most public sources of financing for TV production and feature films have extensive policies and guidelines, which are available from the agencies themselves. The Canadian Film and Television Association (CFTPA) also puts out an excellent publication each year entitled *The Guide*, which summarizes the basic guidelines.

TELEVISION PRODUCTIONS

The combination of a growing demand by Canadian broadcasters for Canadian productions and the establishment of a number of public sources of financing, fuelled the growth of the independent TV production sector through the 1980s and into the 1990s. The major networks — CBC, CTV, and Global/Canwest (with near network status) — are active buyers of Canadian TV series, movies, and specials. Other key buyers and investors are the various broadcasting ownership groups such as Baton and WIC; the growing pay and cable networks such as The Movie Network (TMN), Family Channel, YTV, Showcase, the Life Network and other specialty networks; and in many cases individual TV stations. Each of these services has its own individual Canadian programming needs and price ranges for licence fees.

While Canadian broadcasters generally provide production financing in the form of licence fees, they will also occasionally provide additional investment funds and even interim loans. Broadcasters pick and choose among the many programming opportunities presented to them. They typically make programming and pricing decisions based on the perceived "value" of the programming to their audiences and their advertisers, as well as ensuring that their own Canadian content requirements are met. They generally don't set licence fees on the basis of what the producer needs for financing purposes but rather on the basis of what they are prepared to pay. Consequently, it is often the practice to increase licence fees by putting together more than one broadcaster on a single project. This can be done by selling off rights according to priority of use (windows); for example, a show could start on pay TV first and then it could move to free TV later. It can also be done geographically, by selling rights to a number of regional broadcasters on a market-by-market basis, not unlike what a television syndicator would do.

In television a very important concept to understand is the difference between pre-selling to a broadcaster and making a sale after the production is completed. When projects exist only on paper and can be tailored to a particular broadcaster's needs, they are referred to as *original programming*: broadcasters can get involved in the creative process from story scripts to final outlines through to casting considerations to ensure their programming needs are met. Original programming allows them to put their fingerprints on the project. For this reason, broadcasters will usually pay a premium for the show over what they would pay for a comparable production purchased *on an acquisition basis* (that is, after completion). In the United States, networks structure their programming departments along the lines of original and acquisition programming, since they are two distinct ways of buying a TV show.

FOREIGN PRE-SALES

As our industry has expanded its horizons to the international marketplace, pre-selling programming to foreign buyers — particularly U.S. cable and network buyers — is becoming a major source of production financing for Canadian productions. Many Canadian dramatic TV series and movies produced for private Canadian broadcasters are pre-sold to U.S. buyers. This provides levels of funding not available within Canada, even given our public sources of financing. Since Canadian audiences have grown up watching high-quality U.S. programming, Canadian productions have to compete head-to-head to

survive in the market; producing cheap programs to cut costs
is not a viable option.

CANADIAN TELEVISION EXPORTERS

Canadian distributors who sell into the international marketplace are also the source of production financing, in the form
of distribution advances and, of course, after-sale revenue used
to recoup investment in productions. The world television
market is centred on three major trade markets: NAPTE, held in
the United States each year for U.S. television syndicators/dis-
tributors; and MIP and MIPCOM, held each year in Cannes,
France, in April and October, respectively, which are geared to
international TV sales. Although held in Cannes, these markets
should not be confused with the Cannes Film Festival, which
is held separately and is unrelated to the TV markets. Canadian
exporters attend these markets and others. In addition, they
call on foreign broadcasters regularly to sell foreign rights on a
market-by-market basis. A successful Canadian television production may be licensed to more than 25 countries around the
world. In fact, Canada is now the second largest exporter of TV
programming after the United States.

If a Canadian distributor is interested in acquiring foreign
rights and is prepared to put money up against those rights, a
distribution advance is negotiated. These up-front funds (usually paid on delivery) are an advance against the producer's
share of net receipts — gross revenue less distribution fees, typically 25 to 35 per cent, and direct distribution expenses.
Distribution advances are a very valuable and sought-after
means of financing for Canadian producers.

A common point of negotiation is the distributor's fees. On
the one hand, producers and investors often try to reduce these
to as small a percentage as they can. On the other hand, distributors only survive and make profits by taking distribution

fees, so they negotiate for high fees. Sometimes producers believe they are improving their investors' position by reducing fees below market rates. This is usually a false economy, however, since distributors and their sales force are more motivated to sell when they can earn reasonable commissions. (For more about distribution for television programming, see Chapter 6.)

PUBLIC AND PRIVATE SOURCES OF PRODUCTION FINANCING

Complementing production financing from the marketplace are a number of other financing sources. These are the major ones:

1. *The Broadcast Fund*: This federal investment fund is administered by Telefilm Canada out of four offices (Halifax, Montreal, Toronto, and Vancouver). The fund usually has about $65 million to spend each year on production and development activities for English- and French-language production. This fund was established in 1983/1984 and has proven to have been a catalyst for kick-starting the Canadian dramatic TV production industry. Accessing the Broadcast Fund requires Canadian broadcasters to pre-buy the project at minimum licence fee levels, calculated as a per cent of the budget. Depending on whether the production is regionally produced or not, the licence fee requirements are in the 15 to 30 per cent range. Telefilm will invest up to 49 per cent of the budget, with their typical investment levels being more in the 25 to 33 per cent range.

   The Broadcast Fund is very much driven by the priorities of Canadian broadcasters. Each individual application is subject to an extensive creative, business, and distribution assessment. Decisions are based on objective and subjective criteria, and also on Telefilm's own priorities and those of the broadcasters.

2. *Provincial Investment Funds:* A number of provinces have put in place provincial film agencies with mandates to develop and invest in film and television production. These funds can only be accessed by producers operating full-time in the respective provinces involved. Each fund has its own policies and guidelines and generally requires minimum levels of provincial expenditures and the contracting of local creative and production personnel. The provincial agencies in place are British Columbia Film, the Alberta Motion Picture Development Corporation (AMPDC), SASK-FILM, the Manitoba Cultural Industries Development Office (CIDO), the Ontario Film Development Corporation (OFDC), Société de développement des entreprises culturelles de Québec (SODEC) in Quebec, and the Nova Scotia Film Development Corporation (NSFDC).

3. *Provincial Investment Rebate Programs:* At the time of writing, there are three provincial investment rebate programs in place: the Quebec Refundable Production Tax Credit, the Ontario Film Investment Program, which is administered by the OFDC, and the Nova Scotia Production Rebate Program. These programs all have fairly complex objective eligibility requirements. Rebates are calculated as a percentage of eligible investment amounts, which comprises all private investment including investment made by the producer through pre-sales. These programs also have provincial expenditure tests and fairly tight local residency requirements for key creative and production personnel.

4. *Private Investment Funds:* The Maclean Hunter Television Fund (MHTV) and the Shaw Children's Programming Initiative were established to invest in Canadian productions pre-sold to Canadian private-sector broadcasters.

MHTV supports series production and Shaw supports children's programming. Other private funds include the Foundation to Underwrite New Drama for Pay Television (FUND) and the Global Canadian Program Investment Fund, administered by CanWestGlobal.

5. *Private CCA Tax-motivated Investment*: Since the early 1970s, the Canadian industry has raised private investment through limited partnerships by which individual investors can take advantage of accelerated Capital Cost Allowance (CCA) write-offs for investments in Canadian CAVCO-certified productions. Although this mechanism has proven to be costly and a complex source of production financing, the industry has grown to rely on it with roughly $430 million of certified Canadian production being tax sheltered in 1994.

Tax shelter financing is typically arranged by brokers who specialize in the business. They arrange for limited partnerships to buy the underlying ownership of a production and a revenue stream from the producer and through a series of complex financial transactions the investors are able to take advantage of accelerated write-offs and the producer receives an additional cash infusion used for production financing. The producer's share of new money generated by the deals typically represents 8 to 10 per cent of the underlying copyright conveyed to the limited partnership. While this percentage may seem low, in this business the last piece of financing is often the hardest to get, and proceeds from tax shelter proceeds are often that source.

In recent years, the vast majority of Canadian dramatic series, TV movies, and big-budget feature films have accessed tax shelter financing. Unlike funding from film agencies, this source is completely objective as there is no subjective assessment; it is strictly a business arrangement.

In the 1995 federal government budget, the government

notified the industry of its desire to phase out tax shelter financing by December 31, 1995, to be replaced by a federal tax credit program.

6. *The Federal Refundable Tax Credit*: The federal government announced it will put in place a tax credit rebate program to replace the existing CCA program. The net tax credit program is intended to provide rebates to "qualified taxable Canadian corporations" for investment in eligible Canadian productions that meet CAVCO certification requirements. The credit will be an amount of funding equal to the lesser of 25 per cent of qualified salaries as part of the production budget or 12 per cent of the total production budget.

At the time of writing, the federal government will be putting into place policy guidelines and an administrative process for the refundable tax credit. The program is intended to become effective for productions produced in 1995.

7. *The Cable Production Fund*: A further development is the recent introduction of the Cable Production Fund, which is funded by cable operators in Canada (and indirectly by Canadian cable subscribers). It is intended to increase Canadian dramatic, documentary, and children's programming by providing financial incentives to both Canadian producers and broadcasters of programming with high levels of Canadian content (8 CAVCO points or more). The fund is tied to licence fees of Canadian broadcasters on a percentage basis, and is intended to contribute up to about $50 to $60 million per year into Canadian programming, both English and French production. The first year's budget (1995) is set at $39 million. To qualify for this fund, licence fees (including the contribution by the Cable Production Fund) must be at least 35 per cent in the case of drama productions and 25 per cent in the case of children's and documentary productions. Depending on the type of produc-

tion, the Cable Production Fund will, in effect, subsidize 35 to 40 per cent of the licence fees. This program is likely to be of significant benefit for Canadian dramatic productions.

SOURCES OF FINANCING FOR CANADIAN THEATRICAL FEATURE FILMS

For the most part, experience has shown that Canadian feature films are much more reliant on public financing and dramatic TV programming. The big exception is movies made primarily for the video market for which the U.S. market has a very high demand. As compared to TV, it is also less common for Canadian feature films to be pre-sold to foreign buyers. The world theatrical market is dominated to a very high degree by the U.S. studios, leaving Canadian films to compete, for the most part, with independent films from other countries (including the United States) for a small portion of the theatrical market.

Since the mid-1980s with the establishment of Telefilm Canada's Feature Film Fund and the Feature Film Distribution Fund for Canadian theatrical distributors, government policy has focused on linking Canadian feature producers and Canadian theatrical distributors. This is where you start to finance your feature film.

Canadian Theatrical Distributors: There are a handful of Canadian companies active in distributing Canadian feature films into Canadian movie theatres and the other major markets for movies, namely: home video, pay TV, pay-per-view, free TV and ancillary markets (such as airlines). The major Canadian theatrical distribution companies are Allegro Films, Alliance Releasing, Astral Distribution, C/FP, Cineplex Odeon Films, Norstar Releasing, Max Films, and Malo Films Distribution.

For financing purposes, Canadian theatrical distributors

will put up distribution advances for Canadian rights, with the usual level being from $50,000 to $500,000 per movie. The advance is dependent on the expected revenue potential in the Canadian market. Because of the high-risk nature of this business and the enormous costs associated with launching a film theatrically, Telefilm Canada, through the Feature Film Distribution Fund, assists theatrical distributors by providing those that qualify with an "envelope" from which to draw to finance their advances. As films generate revenue, they repay this capital to Telefilm.

A producer's decision to accept a commitment from a theatrical distributor is based both on the financing the distributor is prepared to bring to the table and on the distributor's commitment to launching the film effectively (keeping in mind that a theatrical release is often a "loss leader" that allows the distributor to make sales and profits in other media). It is generally difficult for producers to hold back any non-theatrical media rights from the distributor since these are usually the up-side revenue sources. However, a runaway box office release is clearly a profitable enterprise all on its own and is what the producer and distributor ultimately strive for. Under their distribution agreements, distributors are able to cross-collaterialize losses in one media with revenues from another. (For more about theatrical distribution, see Chapter 7.)

Foreign Exporters of Canadian Feature Films: A second source of financing is distribution advances put up by foreign exporters against foreign rights. Canadian domestic distributors who are also active in selling into the foreign market, of which there are very few, may also be interested in representing the film abroad. In fact, some companies will only commit to a film if they can acquire both Canadian and foreign rights.

For Telefilm Canada and other agencies to participate in financing feature films, Canadian rights must be distinct from foreign rights. That is to say, distributors can put up separate advances for their markets but cannot put up one advance for all rights. Further, so as to allow for real potential for recoupment of investment, it is also the practice in Canada to exclude one major territory from the foreign advance to be reserved for investors. In practice, this is usually the U.S. market. The foreign distributor can sell this "open territory" but the net receipts will not be applied against its distribution advance.

Foreign theatrical exporters represent Canadian films at the major annual feature film markets around the world, including the AFM in Los Angeles, at the market that is part of the Cannes Film Festival, and MIFED in Italy. Films are sold market-by-market, with the buyers typically being subdistributors in a particular market (such as France) for which they would usually seek to acquire rights to all media. Sales are also made directly to home video distributors and broadcasters, particularly to pay services. Besides maximizing revenue, the ultimate goal is to arrange for Canadian films to be theatrically released outside of Canada.

Telefilm Canada, as an investor in Canadian feature films, requires Canadian films to be offered first to all Canadian exporters before a non–Canadian exporter can be signed up. The few Canadian feature films produced at the big-budget level (budgets of $10 million or more) are usually made only when foreign distributors put up large advances against foreign rights, such as U.K.-based foreign sales agents and/or U.S.-based independent distributors. Fortunately, times are changing as our own Canadian theatrical exporters are developing more clout in the market place.

PUBLIC AND PRIVATE SOURCES OF FINANCING FOR CANADIAN FEATURE FILMS

1. *Telefilm Canada*: Telefilm is a key source of investment

financing. It provides investment and development funds of approximately $24 million per year for Canadian feature films. For 10-out-of-10 point productions, it will invest up to 49 per cent of the production budget to a maximum of $1.5 million per film. Telefilm will typically fund about 15 to 18 English-language films per year and 8 to 10 French-language films per year. In recent years, Telefilm has loosened many of its policies to allow for U.S. star casting in secondary roles, and to exceed its dollar cap of $1.5 million per production on films requiring additional funds for star casting and other elements that will increase the chances of commercial success.

Telefilm has considerable expertise in exploiting Canadian feature films and can offer valued advice in structuring deals and distribution arrangements. In recent years, Telefilm has focused on the marketing of Canadian films. As a result, the agency has put considerable pressure on producers and distributors to think through their marketing approach well before a film is made.

2. *Provincial Agencies:* Additional investment is available from all of the provincial agencies, namely: BC Film, Alberta Motion Picture Development Corporation (AMPDC), SASKFILM, Manitoba Cultural Industries Development Office (CIDO), The Ontario Film Development Corporation (investment funds and investment rebates through the Ontario Film Investment Program), Société de développement des entreprises culturelles de Québec (SODEC), and Nova Scotia Film Development Corporation (NSFDC).

As noted previously, access to a provincial fund is limited to producers resident in that province. There are usually additional requirements, such as shooting in the home province and/or spending a minimum level of the budget in the province.

3. *Other Sources*: Other organizations involved in production financing of feature films include The Foundation to Underwrite New Drama for Pay Television (FUND) and The Movie Network, which make investments (as well as development contributions), the National Film Board of Canada, which occasionally gets involved on a co-production basis, and the various arts councils, such as the Canada Council, which provides grants for very-low-budget films. Also, sources of funding such as CCA-related investment and the new refundable investment tax credit are also available for feature films.

4. *Deferrals*: For both TV and feature productions, one final form of financing you can consider is deferrals and/or investments by suppliers in either cash or goods and services. While it is usually preferable and simpler to negotiate lower costs, thus reducing the production budget you have to finance, you can also arrange for parties to agree to defer payment until revenues are received, not unlike the manner in which cash investors get back their funds.

   Deferrals and investments in goods and services are probably the most misunderstood and mismanaged forms of financing in the business. A deferral is not simply an arrangement to defer payment from a cash-flow perspective, such as extending payment terms until, for example, the producer receives delivery payments from the distributor; rather, it is an arrangement whereby suppliers are only paid if and when the production earns sufficient after-sale revenue to pay out the deferrals, in accordance with a recoupment schedule that would include all investors. Deferrals impose future reporting obligations on the producer and can be very difficult to factor into the recoupment deals of other cash investors.

   A word of caution here: check all the guild and union

agreements on union/guild productions before pursuing deferrals, because some agreements forbid it. Make sure, too, that your production accountant accounts for deferrals and any other non-cash contributions such as goods and services separately from the cash costs of production. Most standard accounting software packages don't seem to be able to separate the two out. Many Canadian films have ended up with accounting bird's nests by mixing together underages and overages in cash and non-cash accounts such as deferrals and goods and services. Long after everyone else involved in the production has gone on to other endeavours (often including the original production accountant) the producer, the guarantor, the auditors, and the investors are left to sort out these messes.

Conclusion

My hope is that this description of production financing will be a road map for how to go about finding development and production financing for your project. While sources of funding for Canadian productions will come and go or evolve with the times, the underlying premise behind production financing as the selling off of rights in the production to pre-sale buyers and/or investors will be around for some time. This is the model used by every market-driven film and television industry around the world. The goal, at the end of the day, is to get projects funded so that they can be seen by the largest possible audience and for each individual project to realize its full potential in the marketplace. With a lot of hard work, some clever thinking, and a little luck, it is possible to get your project financed so that you end up with more drama on the screen than behind the scenes!

5

Pre-production, Production and Post-production

by Tom Dent-Cox

Tom Dent-Cox is currently one of the producers of the dramatic series "North of '60". Prior producer credits include 12 episodes of the "The Ray Bradbury Theater" science fiction series, and numerous short dramas and documentaries. Line producer and production manager credits include the feature film Blood Clan, *the Japanese Samurai epic* Heaven and Earth, Bye Bye Blues, Cowboys Don't Cry, *and the Swedish/Japanese co-production* Friends. *Tom is a principal in two active production companies — WDC Entertainment and Alberta Filmworks — and is the chair of the board of directors of the National Screen Institute. He lives with his family in Calgary.*

Introduction

Motion picture production is one of the most creatively collaborative processes currently undertaken in the name of industry or art. It is therefore one of the most highly organized ventures you will ever embark upon.

In order for you to triumph in this endeavor, three principles must be adhered to: careful planning, calm flexibility and clear communication. Your production must be planned and executed with military precision, yet with the knowledge that the most thorough plan will be altered many times or even abandoned over the course of the production. The only way to survive the process with any hope of success is by maintaining concise and constant communication. The only way to survive with any hope of sanity is by maintaining a well-oiled sense of humour.

This chapter will cover the nitty gritty "front line" of the filmmaking process: pre-production, principal photography and post-production. These three phases are usually the most intense and expensive stages of production. Combined, they are often the shortest part of the filmmaking process, sandwiched between interminable development and distribution phases.

For the purpose of the chapter, we will assume that you have a completed script in hand, have incorporated a company through which you will produce your film, and most important, have your financing in place. In other works, development has been completed. This may mean that you have already contracted a director, a star, or other "promotable elements". Or it may simply mean that you've emptied your bank account and are setting out armed only with vision and determination. If the later is true, may God bless you and keep you from harm. If the former is true, God may no longer be willing to get involved. In either case, get friendly with a good lawyer.

Seriously, if you are new to the task of producing, the best way to avoid, or at least minimize the effects of, the pitfalls that will confront you is to find a mentor; a seasoned and sympathetic producer who will be willing to look over your investment agreements, budget, schedule, key creative contracts, etc.. If you know, or know of, such a person, involve them at the outset. Used judiciously, mentorship can save you untold heart- and headache without unduly taxing a long-standing or budding relationship.

Pre-Production

This is a heightened state of activity lasting anywhere from 3 to 12 weeks, during which you finalize your script, budget, cash flow, production design and schedule; secure insurance and a completion bond; negotiate and sign with applicable unions and guilds; negotiate and sign all cast, crew, and locations; build and dress sets; rent studio space, production offices, grip, electric and camera equipment; buy film stock; contract a lab and post-production houses; dress and rehearse your actors; communicate all plans to all investors on a timely basis; and, if you're really organized, eat a sandwich and do your laundry.

RE-ALLOCATING THE BUDGET

First things first. The *budget* — which, since you are financed, should exist in some form — will need a certain amount of re-allocation to match the changes that occur in prep. Your budget may have originally been done using a computer spreadsheet. If it wasn't, rectifying that shortcoming will be the first order of business. There are many software spreadsheet packages available that can serve your purposes. The best packages contain both budget and schedule forms, and link one to the other so that when you make changes to the schedule, as you undoubtably will, the changes can be automatically reflected in the budget. There are numerous budget formats available within most software packages. The Telefilm budget format is probably the most widely accepted in Canada, and is included in most budget software packages available here. There may be categories or cost centers within the Telefilm format that you won't need. If you are new to budgeting, however, a line-by-line exploration of the spreadsheet will invariably unearth cost centres that you have overlooked in your initial figuring, so it's well worth the effort.

HIRING A PRODUCTION MANAGER

One of the first crew members you will want to hire is the *production manager* (PM). Your production manager will be responsible, under your supervision, for preparing the budget, supervising preparation of the schedule, supervising location scouts and surveys, negotiating union and crew contracts, renting equipment and vehicles, purchasing film stock, and securing production insurance. She or he will approve all production expenses, call sheets, production reports, and cost reports. The production manager will also be your eyes and ears on set, providing services as confessor, psychologist, or drill sergeant, depending on the circumstances. PMs should be hired on the basis of their experience in the type of production you are undertaking, not because they love you, helped fix your car, or play in the same band, And don't do it yourself. Hire a professional who will allow you to focus on all aspects of production without becoming mired in minutiae.

The first task your PM should undertake is tuning the budget to match whatever new information is available as you start prep. The PM can do an initial breakdown of the script for budgeting purposes and, within the existing budget parameters, begin to move the money around, allocating more specific or appropriate amounts to each category.

THE CONTINGENCY

Ideally, you have included a *contingency* in your preliminary budget. If not, your PM will have to carve a contingency out of the existing total. The contingency is a segregated amount of money, to be set aside for use only in the event of unforeseen expenses. An accepted percentage is no more that 10 per cent of the total below-the-line budget (that is, the portions of the budget that are not fixed and may vary depending on changes in schedule, and so on). The amount of contingency needed will depend on the complexity of your production. If you are shooting all exteriors and need numerous special effects, stunts, and crowds, you will need a much larger contingency than you will if you are shooting a film with a small cast in a studio. Whatever amount you set aside for contingency, treat it as you would your children's inheritance. Better yet, treat it as you would like your parents to treat your inheritance. You may will need to address unforeseen elements in post-production, so spend your contingency very, very carefully in production, if you have to spend it at all. You will not be frowned upon for *not* spending it, unless there are deficiencies in the delivered film that might have been corrected by freeing up contingency funds.

INSURANCE

You or your PM will need to get quotes early in prep for production and errors and omissions insurance. You should get quotes from several companies specializing in entertainment insurance packages, since prices can vary significantly. The more information you provide about the specific demands of your production to the companies offering quotes, the more accurate the quotes will be, and the more thorough your coverage will be. Purchasing an inexpensive policy that fails to cover certain aspects of your production is equivalent to playing financial Russian roulette. By being clear about your specific needs, however, you can limit your coverage and your costs to the real necessities.

Two of those necessities will be insuring your cast and your director. Cast coverage can be restricted to those actors without whom you could not continue production within your schedule and budget. You will probably need to arrange medicals for your insured cast, and to provide a letter from your director stating that she or he is in good health.

Coverage for sets, props and wardrobe, camera, grip and electric equipment, and third-party liability should be included in your basic policy. You may find, however, that certain locations require additional property damage and liability insurance, with, preferably, coverage limited to the time during which that location is in your care and control, or is occupied by any of your crew for work purposes. Because the need for specific location insurance will likely become evident after your initial policy is written up, you should have a separate insurance allotment within your locations budget.

Train, plane, boat, and automobile insurance can be quite complicated, and hideously expensive. It should therefore be looked into very early and very carefully. Your basic rental agreement with your production auto supplier may cover some or all of your rental auto insurance requirements. However, you may be able to get a better rate on collision insurance from your production insurance company, so you may want to limit the insurance provided by the auto supplier to liability coverage. Certain picture vehicles (vehicles appearing onscreen for story purposes), or any vehicles in use by the production whose worth exceeds a preset limit, will require additional coverage. Non-owned aircraft and boat insurance is particularly complex. You may want to acquaint yourself with a low-budget trick aptly called "poor man's process", whereby your picture vehicle never leaves the parking lot, airstrip, or dock. It's not pretty, but it is cheap and occasionally effective, and it can limit the amount of picture vehicle insurance coverage you need, as well as limiting the time required to film the scenes in which the vehicle appears.

The same company that provides you with production insurance can supply you with errors and omissions coverage, which insures the production against copyright infringement, libel, or defamation suits. You will need to have the script title and contents "searched" to ensure that your title is original and that your fictional material does not defame a living person. If you are documenting or dramatizing a living or historic person, you may need to get a release from that person or his or her heirs. Any well-known or distinctive property seen in your film may need a release, even if you are not using it as a shooting location. Any music used as part of your score or as background source will need to be licensed. Your insurer will give you an application that outlines all the requirements for enacting an E & O policy.

THE COMPLETION GUARANTOR

Depending on your production, and the investors involved in it, you may also need to contract a *completion guarantor*. In return for a fee equalling up to 6 per cent of your budget, a completion guarantor will ensure that your production will be completed with a product delivered to the appropriate bodies. This guarantee provides tremendous comfort to investors, and will probably be a contractual requirement of one or all of them. The guarantor will require a copy of your script, crew and cast lists, the final budget, a faxed copy of each shooting day's call sheet and/or production report, and each week's cost report. If, at any time during the course of production, the guarantor determines that your are in jeopardy of going seriously over budget, or are in danger of not being able to deliver a finished product, the guarantor has the right — indeed the obligation — to step in and provide whatever resources are necessary to complete the film in accordance with all applicable contracts. Those resources may be limited to additional financing, or may include augmenting or replacing whatever element is deemed to be an impediment to completion. Unfortunately, that element may, in certain circumstances, be you.

PREPARING THE CASH FLOW

One of the next tasks to be undertaken by the PM, in concert with the production accountant, will be preparing a *cash flow*. The cash flow sets out the amount of money you will require in each week of pre-production, production, and post-production. With any luck it will match the draw down schedules presented by your various investors. If it doesn't, it will disclose the discrepancies between draw downs and cash flow, allowing you to negotiate revised draw downs with your investors, or at least find interim financing to fill any gaps. To prepare the cash flow, your PM and production accountant will list each budget item, and the cost of that item divided in columns under the appropriate week of prep, shoot and post. Once the cash flow is drafted, go through it carefully with the PM and accountant until you are all satisfied that the needs of the production can be met without delays or undue anxiety. The cash flow, along with the budget, will certainly evolve as you finalize cast, crew, locations, equipment, and so on. An experienced PM or accountant can make knowledgeable estimates at the outset that will be close to the mark, however, allowing you to project with some authority what your needs will be.

THE 1ST AD

Not long after you start your PM, and in consultation with your director, you will want to engage your *first assistant director* (1st AD). The 1st AD will be responsible for preparing a script breakdown, board, shooting schedule, and cast "day out of days"; will organize and attend all location surveys; will work closely with the director as a shot list is developed; will organize and run production meetings, read-throughs, and rehearsals; will supervise the preparation of each day's call sheet; and will run the set, ensuring that the director's needs, and the production's needs, are met within the confines of the schedule.

As with the PM, engaging an experienced AD is not simply an asset to the production, it is critical to your director's ability to deliver the best film possible. If your director is inexperienced, all the more reason to give her or him the best available help. (A rule of thumb worth following says that you should train only one key individual on any single project. If you want to work with a director with little experience, try to ensure that all other key creative personnel are veterans. In that way you give the director every chance at developing her or his craft in a secure and nurturing environment. This approach certainly increases *your* chances for producing a cohesive and successful film.)

THE SCHEDULE

The 1st AD's initial task is to break down the script and prepare the schedule, a document that sets out each day's work, including listing the scenes to be shot and the location of each scene, noting whether the scene is day, night, interior or exterior, listing the actors required in each scene, and noting the *script day*. (The day within the story on which a scene occurs.) The *"day out of days"* forms an important addendum to the schedule, and deals specifically with cast scheduling. It is usually laid out in graph form, listing each day of the production schedule as a column head and each cast member as a row heading. Beside each cast name, and under the appropriate production day, are marked showing whether that actor is travelling, working, or on hold. You are thus able to see at a glance whether your schedule makes efficient use of each actor, or whether actors are travelling or on hold more than they need to be, or more than you can afford, in order to accommodate another aspect of the schedule that might easily be changed.

The schedule should be done using a software package (one that interfaces with your budget). If software is not available, the schedule can be done on the traditional "board", with each scene represented by a cardboard strip, colour coded to show whether that scene is day, night exterior or interior, and with all cast, special crew, equipment, special effects, and location information marked on the strip. Many decisions you will make during pre-production will affect the schedule, and minor revisions can continue through the last day of shooting. Your AD's two most pressing concerns related to schedule are the final choices of cast and locations. Once cast and locations are "locked", your AD will be able to create a schedule that weaves all the variables for maximum use in the production, with the least impact on the budget. As long as cast and locations are under discussion, the board and schedule must remain somewhat theoretical.

LOCATIONS OR STUDIO?

Your decision on the use of *locations and/or studio* will have a critical impact on the budget and on the amount of time your director has with the cast in front of the camera. The time your cast and crew spend in vehicles, moving from location to location, is time that could be spent filming. You might find that cheap warehouse space, well-placed insulation, and burlap or theatrical drapes can create cost-effective studio space in which to place interior sets that would otherwise necessitate unreasonable travel. Flats for interior sets can often be rented or borrowed from theatrical companies or universities, further cutting the cost of set construction. The advantage of studio shooting, apart from removing travel from the equation, lies in your ability to fully control light and sound on your set, and human access to it. Having full control of these elements should mean than it takes your crew less time to light and shoot each scene.

The advantage of locations is that they ar often "dressed", requiring little or no construction or decorating to render them camera-ready. In addition, locations offer the possibility of directly connecting interior and exterior action (being able to have the camera follow an actor from inside to outside in one shot), a feature that most directors find desirable, and that, depending on your script, may be necessary. The best way to decide whether to use locations or a studio is simply to determine which route contributes to the best possible film. Scrutinize that ideal from the perspective of the budget and the schedule, and then revisit the ideal to see how close you can come to it. Some combination of elements will work for your production, and a good AD will discover that combination and lay it out succinctly for you.

OTHER MEMBERS OF THE TEAM

At the same time that the budget and schedule are being "built", your *production designer* will need to be hard at work, creating a look for the picture that translates the written material into evocative imagery while respecting the limitations of the budget and schedule. Once you, the designer, and the director are happy with the design in principle, the designer will need to work closely with the PM, AD, director of photography, and location manager to ensure that desire and reality are in sync. This may seem relatively simple on low-budget projects where sets, if there are any, are minimal. The truth is that design is far more crucial when financial resources are scarce, and bringing that design to fruition within extreme time constraints is an art of the highest calibre. The designer will not only set the overall look of the picture, collaborating with the director and director of photography to ensure a cohesive design, but also co-ordinate and supervise every aspect of production that affects the visual image, including art direction, set decoration, props, hair, make-up, and wardrobe.

You and your director will have to decide early on who the best person is to engage as *director of photography* (DOP). Your director may have a long-term collaborator who will be at the top of your list, or you may decide with your director that this film needs a new and particular "eye" to fulfill your collective creative vision. If you are hoping to engage someone with whom you have not worked before, it will be important that, before you make your decision, she or he read the script and meet with your director to discuss the desired style of imagery and of working. The relationship between director and DOP is arguably the most important creative partnership on the set. Their ability to communicate, and to share a common vision, will be deciding factors in the relative achievement of your film, and in the success of the production process.

Another artist who can truly enhance the process and product of your production is the *location manager*. This unsung hero will not only assist in creating the right look for your film, but will function as your ambassador to the community; preparing the way for your unruly army; getting special permissions and permits from various bureaucracies; negotiating great rates for the use of public and private locations; keeping owners and property managers happy during shooting; and mending fences after the unit has moved on. Given the dependence we all have on great locations, and on our ability to return to them time and time again, your choice of location manager/world ambassador is pivotal.

Another unsung hero working quietly in pre-production is

your *production co-ordinator*, whose impeccable organizational skills must be matched by an ability to keep cast, crew, and you smiling as your unit careers around the town or country invading airports, hotels, and restaurants like commandos in search of a bomb. The co-ordinator will be responsible for setting up and maintaining the production office, and for the preparation and distribution of scripts, scrip revisions, crew and cast lists, call sheets, and production reports. She or he will also co-ordinate all travel and accommodation, and shipping of equipment, film stock, and rushes, and any required medical examinations or visas for cast and crew.

Along with the co-ordinator, your *production accountant* is one of the most important members of the prep team. No simple bean-counter, a good production accountant will be an invaluable ally, ensuring that you and the PM have allotted the requisite amounts in all categories. Your production accountant will also be largely responsible for creating and maintaining a safe cash flow; will set up and maintain your banking relationships; will identify and secure the best payroll and accounting computer service; and will set up relationships and payment terms with your innumerable suppliers. During production, this life-saving individual will also provide accurate weekly cost reports indicating the money spent that week in each budget category, money spent in each category to date, estimated costs to complete in each category, and any variance between estimated final costs and the budgeted amounts. In extremely low-budget situations, on-the-ball production accountants have been known to provide daily "hot sheets" showing the previous day's crew and cast overtime costs.

It is unadvisable to combine any of these principal crew positions. If, for financial reasons, you do have one personal doing more than one of these jobs, know that they can not possible be as effective as two people would have been.

CASTING

While all of these dedicated professionals are preparing for production, you are continuing to work with the writer or with the script itself, massaging it until it reflects the realities of production without having lost any of its mood or message. You are also continuing to *cast*, either through a casting director or on your own. This means negotiating with actors or their agents to get the best talent available within the confines of your budget. If you are "going union", it also means negotiating with your local council of the Association of Canadian Television and Radio Artists (ACTRA) to create a contract that fairly reflects the nature and resources of the production. In this event, you must become familiar with the ACTRA Independent Production Agreement (IPA). This is a confusing, dense little document that, once you decipher it, sets out the perimeters under which ACTRA members or permittees (non-union actors permitted by the union for a single engagement) may work. Most experienced film actors in Canada are members of ACTRA, and the IPA is a negotiated and binding agreement for union productions, so if you are contemplating a union production, study it carefully. It is also more open to interpretation than the Bible, so don't presume to always understand the intent of a clause. If you are unsure of intent, get advice from your local ACTRA office and from the Canadian Film and Television Producers Association (CFTPA).

If you have a government agency, broadcaster, distributor, or private investor involved in your project, chances are that one or all of them will have *contractual vetoes* over your casting choices, and restrictions with regard to Canadian content. Create a short list of the actors you are interested in, and can afford, and get necessary approvals before approaching the actors in question. Your short list should include several choices for each key role, any of whom you would happily cast. You don't want an investor pulling out just because you can't get Ms. X. Get all applicable investors to sign off on Ms. X, Ms. Y, and Ms. Z so that you have the leeway to look elsewhere if Ms. X is unavailable or undesirable to a veto-holding investor. If an investor wants someone in particular, and that person is out of your price range, the investor should be encouraged to cover the "breakage" — the difference between what you have budgeted for the role and the amount necessary to secure that person.

Once you have an approved short list, either you or your casting director can begin calling agents or unrepresented actors to begin negotiations. A good *casting director* will know the going rates for U.S. and Canadian leads. She or he will also have worked with most agents and, based on previous relationships, may be able to get an actor to read a script that you couldn't even get an agent to read. Engaging a casting director, even if that engagement is restricted to "star" casting, should allow you access to a broader talent pool, and should allow you to create a more favorable agreement than you would have been able to create on your own. On the other hand, if your budget simply does not allow you to engage an experienced casting director, don't be afraid to jump in and ask for who or what you want. Audacity is not without its benefits in extremely low-budget situations.

When you negotiate your cast deals, make sure you know what *buyout* is needed in order for you to fulfill all your contractual obligations and sell your film in all applicable markets. The buyout (defined in the IPA as a Prepayment Option) is a fee for the use of an actor's performance in a particular market or territory beyond the *Declared Use* (the single use paid for within a performer's contracted minimum fees.) The buyout is based on a percentage, stipulated by the IPA, of the actor's contracted fee, and is paid in addition to the contracted minimum fee. Read your investment, broadcast, and distribution agreements, as well as the ACTRA IPA very carefully to determine what markets and territories you need to buy out. Rustle up a boilerplate "star" contract, from your venerable mentor or from a lawyer, study it until you understand the reasoning behind each clause, and get a legal opinion before offering your version to an agent or actor. Having a clear and thorough contract protects you *and* the performer from misunderstanding and acrimony down the road.

Principle casting should be completed quite early in the pre-production process. Your ability to negotiate will be severely compromised if the actor or agent knows that you really need that actor, and you start shooting in 48 hours. In addition, your schedule will be impossible to finalize until you sign your cast.

If your cast includes children, become especially familiar with the relevant Articles in the ACTRA IPA, and read through your provincial labour laws with respect to employer responsibilities when engaging children. You will find that your potential liability as an employer of minors is substantial. Child labour laws have been enacted to prevent abuse or accidents. Should an accident occur involving a minor who is engaged by a production found to be in violation of child labour codes, the resulting lawsuits and negative publicity will be disastrous to the production, and to the producer.

CREWS

While you are casting, your PM should be engaging all department heads, always in concert with you and the director. In turn, each department head will have input into the choice of personnel within their respective departments, in concert with the PM. Depending on where you are mounting your production, there will be four to six guilds and unions with which you have the potential of working. They all offer highly trained, experienced craftspeople who will be of great benefit to your production. Depending on where you are working, there will also be very good dedicated and experienced non-union crafts-people with whom you can work. The decision to go union or non-union should be made solely on the basis of what is best for the film, creatively and financially. Most unions and guilds are willing to negotiate coid to ask the local business represen-tative or council for help. You may find a creative way of work-ing together that satisfies everyone's needs.

The best production teams are just that: teams, composed of friends who have collaborated on many projects, have a common approach to the production process, and work together without wasting time or energy. Your ability to hire, or create, the right team will determine how smoothly the shoot will go. In my experience, positive relationships and a positive work environment will translate into a better film than can be achieved though fear, intimidation, or even monetary reward. The art of producing will, in part, be found in your ability to assemble and empower your team, allowing as much input as cast and crew wish to give, short of robbing the process of momentum and without ever diluting or relin-quishing the relative vision.

Your PM will be knowledgeable about industry-standard crew rates. Acquaint yourself with them. Even if you aren't offering industry-standard rates, it will be useful to know what your crew would ordinarily be making.

Each department head — designer, location manager, wardrobe designer, set decorator, props master, gaffer, key grip, and so on — should submit a budget for their own depart-ment. It is critical that they feel confident in their ability to deliver the required elements within the allowances made for their department. The director of photography, while not expected to do a budget for grip, electric, and camera rentals,

and purchases, should provide the PM with a list of all requirements for those departments. As with all department heads, the
DOP should be given every resource available to create the best
picture, within the confines of the budget and schedule. Every
department will want to bring more to the production than
the production can afford. Every department will compromise,
and will still bring more to the production than the budget
allowed — for no more, and sometimes for less, than the budgeted amounts.

CHOOSING A FORMAT

One of the critical choices to be made affecting the look and
cost of your picture is the recording medium itself. Should you
shoot on one of the many video formats, or on 16mm, super
16, or 35 mm film? You may have broadcast or distribution
requirements that dictate what format you will use. If you do
not, you will have to weigh the standards of your intended
markets against the limits of your resources. If you are anticipating a theatrical release, your choices are limited to 35 mm,
super 16, or, for limited art house release, 16 mm. If you use
16 mm or Super 16, you will have to blow the final print up
to 35 mm for theatrical distribution. Depending on your story,
and the style in which you intend to tell it, the blowup process
does not necessarily detract from your ability to sell your film
in many markets. Super 16 will certainly allow you to create a
better 35 mm blowup than you will be able to coax from 16
mm. super 16 (and certainly 35 mm) also allows your product
to be transferred to high-definition video, an option not available if you use 16 mm. High-definition video is without a
doubt a growing "market," with the potential to develop a
voracious appetite for good products.

Given the proliferation of broadcast and narrowcast entities, and the subsequent variety of programming being

licensed, producing for television markets allows for a much wider range of recording choices. These choices are being made more viable by the ever-growing array of technologies available in post-production to enhance your images.

In making your choice, you will want to research your intended markets carefully, making sure that you don't limit your distribution potential more than you have to.

Production

This is a ridiculously heightened state of activity, lasting anywhere from 3 to 5 days for a half-hour drama, 6 to 10 days for an hour drama, 18 to 30 days for a television movie, and 18 to 80 days for a feature film. During this time you monitor the progress of the unit; watch rushes; discuss shot lists and rushes with the director; encourage or "tune" the cast and crew; begin the editing process; communicate with all investors, broadcasters, distributors, and guarantors as they respond to production reports, cost reports, and possibly rushes; anticipate problems and avert them; react calmly and swiftly to any problems that do arise; promote your film; exert strict quality control over catering; and send your laundry out.

THE PRODUCER'S ROLE — STAY CALM

The producer's role in production is as individual as the producer and the project. I have known producers who were complete strangers to the cast and crew, well-dressed visitors seen only in the lunch line. Other producers are on the set before crew call and don't leave until the last cable is rolled at the end of the day. Every day. I have never seen a production that didn't benefit from the producer's presence and influence, as long as both are manifested in a calm and constructive way. In fact, regardless of what happens, stay calm. By doing so, you are bound to have a positive effect on the outcomes of the project. One of the inevitable side effects of this ridiculously heightened state of activity is panic — caused by bad weather, a missing cast member, a misplaced costume, a misdirected special effect. These are all perfectly reasonable things to panic about if they're not where they need to be when they need to be, or aren't working as well as they should. Your job in this situation, preferably in concert with the PM, is to calm the panicked director, AD or department head, offer solutions to the problem causing the panic, and ensure that action is taken immediately to bring about that solution. You can usually assess the situation, and deal with it most effectively, if you have been consistently monitoring the progress of the shoot from close at hand.

You will need to stay actively involved in any changes being made to the schedule during the shoot, and ensure that you are apprised of wardrobe, hair, and make-up decisions or special equipment requests (a call for a camera crane to use in a scene that was originally scheduled to be shot on tripod will be a clue that your budget and schedule are about to be compromised). It will also be prudent to keep an ear to the ground for on-set rumour that might be based on, or might create, real problems that need attention before they affect the production.

Having said this, it must be remembered that *your primary relationship during production must be with the material being shot.* This is a difficult truth to keep in focus when there are anywhere from 60 to 160 people vying for your time and attention, and these good people are all passionate interpreters of that material. However, they are also all professionals, hopefully capable of solving most problems on their own or with the assistance of the PM or director. In the heat of production, you will be the person most capable of maintaining a clear and objective overview, and only by continuing to focus steadfastly on the material — the script and rushes — along with everything else, will you maintain that overview.

THE SCRIPT DURING PRODUCTION

In a perfect world, the script is locked long before the camera rolls, and nothing that occurs in shooting alters that. In the world most of *us* inhabit, shit happens. You may find that the script is playing too long and cuts are required in order to achieve the desired length. Conversely, the script may be playing short and additional material would be helpful. These problems are more prevalent in television, where strict delivery requirements must be met. However, distributors of feature films have delivery requirements as well. Even if Kurasawa or Oliver Stone is directing, a film that runs four hours is very hard to sell, and impossible to complete on a limited budget. You will be extremely unhappy if necessary cuts are not made until you are in editing, *after* the money has been spent, or if additional material is required after the director, cast, and crew have gone on to other work.

Your *script supervisor* will issue a *script timing* before you start filming, and will issue revised timings after each day's filming. This information is critical to your ability to track the progress of the shoot, and will inform your decisions about trimming or adding to the script during production. Revised script timings will be include on the daily *production report*, which will also include information on the length of the shooting day, the number of hours each cast and crew member worked, and number of scenes and pages shot, the amount of film and sound stock used, and any occurrences that affected the progress of the day. This report will allow you to track the progress of the overall production with respect to the budget and schedule. It is a critical document to have on file, in that it makes note of any problem that might require action — such as an insurance claim — in the future. The daily production report may also be one of the delivery requirements of an investor, agency or completion guarantor monitoring your progress from afar.

Your knowledge of the script, your vision of the finished film, and your ability to impart that vision to your director, cast and crew, will be revealed and tested in *rushes*. It is here that you will see, for the first time, whether you, the director, and the rest of your creative team are truly on the same wave length. At this time, communication with your director is critical. If you feel that more or different coverage is needed, or that an actor is misinterpreting a character, say it. If you are delighted with what you're seeing, by all means say it. Whether your director is inexperienced or a veteran, your thoughts on the work in progress will be very important for her or him to hear. Be sensitive, be supportive, but be honest and candid. If you have assembled the right team, and have set out clear parameters for communication in prep, you should be able to get your point across without creating a division or rancour.

PUBLICITY

During production, and even in prep, you will need to pay close attention to a critical and oft-neglected element of the overall production process: *unit publicity*. Good publicity can be vital to the success of your film and to your continued success as a producer in the motion picture industry.

One or more of your investors may have required that you submit a *marketing strategy* prior to production. This document will include a description of your target audience, a strategy for reaching that audience, a list of your film's attributes that will allow your strategy to succeed, and a breakdown of your publicity budget. If your investors don't require you to prepare this, do it anyway. It will clarify where your film will fit in the world marketplace and will begin your preparation for the distribution process.

One of the most crucial elements of publicity is *stills photography*. Unless you want your distributor to sketch a poster and restrict promotion of your film to radio ads, make sure you have great photographs of all your lead actors, taken during the filming of scenes and in "gallery" poses (posed photographs taken on the set when scenes are not being shot.) Get great production shots of your charismatic director at work and even submit to a few good shots of you.

Another valuable marketing tool is an *electronic press kit* (EPK), a promotion video showing behind-the-scenes footage of your production in progress, intercut with sage and witty interviews with you, your director, and your lead performers describing the unique and wondrous nature of your story and your production.

The process of getting press coverage during production is greatly assisted by the presence of an experienced and reputable *unit publicist*. This person should come armed with long and close relationships with editors, critics, columnists, and reporters from all major media, and she or he should be able to create an irresistible angle on elements within your film that will have the media flocking to your set for a story. If that fails, invite the media to lunch, and make sure your fabulous caterers are apprised of the invitation.

Post-production

This is a relatively calm state of activity, lasting anywhere from three weeks to six months, during which you lead a deceptively normal life, are lulled into a sense of security, and then are slapped upside the head by news of video anomalies that jeopardize foreign broadcast, requests for different sounding footsteps after you've mixed, demands for different titles or credits, legal complications, audits, and so on.

PROCESSING THE FILM

Post-production actually begins on the first day of principal photography. As soon as film has rolled through the camera, it has be be sent somewhere to be processed, printed, and/or transferred. If you live in a city where post-production houses exist, this is a relatively straightforward process. A driver or production assistant drives your footage to the lab at the end of the shooting day, dropping it into a night box for overnight processing. If you are shooting in a region not currently blessed with post-production facilities, a bit more thought, time, and money is required. You may have to "break" film before the end of the workday in order to get film onto a plane destined for a center where lab and transfer work can be done overnight, in order to get a print or transfer tape back on a plane in time for your viewing by the end of the next working day. One of the rustic charms of film as a recording medium is that you don't really know what, if any, image has been captured until long after the filming has taken place. Depending on your depth of experience and/or cynicism, this aspect of the process will seem either humorous or nauseating. For even the most experienced and cynical producer, this quaint attribute can bring on the dry heaves within seconds of hearing that "the driver had a little accident on the way to the airport," "the air cargo carrier has no record of your shipment," or "the lab just called to say you've got a stock or camera problem."

But let's be optimistic. Your co-ordinator has successfully orchestrated the shipment of your precious cargo to the lab, and that cargo has been transformed into images on celluloid and/or plastic and has made its way safely back to you. Once your have screened rushes and have discussed them with all appropriate members of your team, you should get right down to the task of editing. Your *editor* should start no later that the day your first set of rushes, also known as "dailies," comes in.

Admittedly, it would seem cost-effective to amass all the footage and have the editor attack it all at once when shooting is over, as opposed to having the editor pick away at it each day as it arrives. The advantage to having your editor on board from the start is twofold. You will have rough and fine cuts, which are usually triggers for financial draw downs, much sooner and, more important, you will be able to determine whether scenes work as well as they should while production is underway and you still have some chance at a pickup or two that will really make a scene sing.

With the advent of *non-linear editing* systems, the process of editing has been revolutionized. The latest technology in non-linear editing, utilizing computer hard drive and disk technology and known as "third-generation" editing, dramatically increases your ability to reconstruct and shift scenes, as the time it takes to make changes decreases just as dramatically. This flexibility means that you can get the most out of your material, assembling it in an infinite number of creative configurations. If your resources do not allow you to utilize a third- or second-generation non-linear suite, a linear (first-generation) video system will still allow a modicum of flexibility at a slightly greater speed than film editing does. If your film is destined for broadcast and video release only, there is no reason, other than dire financial straits, to edit on film. Even if you plan a theatrical release, the flexibility offered by tape editing is so advantageous that film editing must be viewed as the avenue of last resort. If any editing purists still wants to "run the film through her or his fingers," assuage her or him with a trim bin full of waste for Christmas.

DIRECTOR'S CUTS, ROUGH CUTS, AND FINE CUTS

Once production is completed, and your final shipment of rushes has been incorporated into the rough assembly, your director will have the first pass at a cut. The Directors Guild of Canada makes specific provision for this stage in its basic agreement, with minimum time allowances for a *director's cut*. I suspect that the allowances currently set out in the guild agreement were established in the era of film editing, and may be ready for review in light of these computerized times. However, it will behoove you to establish a comfortable time frame with your director that ensures that she or he has the time needed to complete a director's cut, being mindful of draw down and delivery requirements.

You may decide that the director's cut is your official *rough cut*, or you may want to make adjustments before you deliver a rough cut to all relevant parties. This is always a vulnerable stage, given that for those who have not seen rushes, the rough cut will provide their first look at, and impression of, the film. The temptation will be to continue honing the material until you have a fine cut, in order to create a great first impression. You will have to balance your desire for perfection with the need to adhere to your post and draw down schedules.

Between the official rough and *fine cut*, you may go through up to a dozen intermediate cuts, as you continue to massage the footage into its ultimate order. At some point, however, time and money will dictate that you invoke closure on this process. I have to say that I have never delivered a film that I haven't seen later and wished for just one more day in the editing room. Somehow, I don't think that I'm alone.

Eventually, the proud or fateful day does come when you *"lock picture."* If you have been editing on tape, your editor will ship an *edit decision list,* or EDL, (the time codes of each picture edit) to the picture post-production house handling your film. If your are delivering on tape, they will *"on-line"* edit, using EDL to select footage from the 1-inch daily transfer masters, thus giving you your edited master. For a film finish, this EDL will go to a white-gloved negative cutter who will conform your film negative, creating your edited negative master. The edited 1-inch master, or edited work print, will then go to the sound post facility, where an *audio EDL* will be done, leading to an *audio conform* from the 1/4-inch production sound tapes to a multi-track.

SOUND EDITING

Sound editing begins at this time, with a dialogue editor, effects editor, and Foley artist working to create a rich and realistic sound bed for your film. The *dialogue editor* may identify lines that need to be re-recorded ("looped") in a sound booth, a process also known as *automatic dialogue replacement (ADR)*, to replace lines obscured by background noise or mumbled by Brando wannabes. You may also have lines that you want looped for performance reasons. Hopefully that list is short, as the chance of getting the appropriate emotional level from a actor lip syncing to her or his own image while standing in a foam -lined booth the size of an outhouse is slim. The cost of this procedure can also be quite prohibitive, so it is best to pick up many of these lines on set during production, either by reshooting the offensive dialogue or, for off-camera lines, by having your location sound mixer record "*wild lines*" (lines recorded without picture) in the same environment as the scene from which they originated.

The *effects editor* will add background sounds that were not evident on the production of the 1/4-inch tapes, but which the editor feels are needed to flesh out the soundscape. The *Foley artist*, armed with a strange bag of very effective tools — including Styrofoam cups and kitty litter — will enhance existing sounds such as footsteps, so that they are not lost beneath dialogue, effects, and music.

THE MIX

Once the sound edit is completed, you are ready to pre-mix the music, dialogue, and effects separately to their own appropriate levels, and then *mix* all sound elements together to picture. Depending on the complexity of your sound bed, and the amount of money you have allotted to this important process, you will have anywhere from 4 to 100 production, dialogue, effects, Foley, and music tracks to blend, creating the final aural feast to accompany your presumably stunning pictures. At the *playback* of the mix you will hear the mixed tracks, and you can give notes on any elements that you feel still need work. The pre-mix, mix, playback, and subsequent "*fixes*" can take anywhere from a day for an uncomplicated short film, two days for a television series episode, three days to a week for a television movie, or much much longer for an effects and action packed, big-budget feature.

The final mix of all your tracks is transferred (by a process known as a *layback*) to a single sound tape for video delivery and/or magnetic stock for film delivery. If you are delivering a film print, the mag master will go to an optical house, where your picture effects and titles have been created and are waiting to be married to the sound track. The combined sound and picture elements go back to your lab, where a colour timing is done and your answer print is born. From your answer print you will clone the required number of release prints.

For tape delivery, the mixed sound elements are married to the picture master tape, which, while the sound editing team was at work, was being *colour corrected* — a process that allows you to match shots and scenes for colour and brightness and, with the current technology, change a grey sky to blue. You may be changing your Confederate rebels into Union infantry in the process, but they're working on that.

Regardless of whether you are finishing on tape or film,

you will have to construct and approve your titles and credits. Along with deciding on the style, colour, and placement of your titles, you must now tiptoe throughout the minefield of credit size and placement. In order to successfully navigate through this process, you will need to review all of your contracts — with investors, broadcasters, distributors, cast, crew, locations, unions, and suppliers — to see what credit, credit size, and placement you promised to whom. A good rule of thumb says that your credit list should not exceed your film in length. However, if you are producing a low-budget film, you have probably pulled favours from everyone involved in the process, in return for which a credit often goes a long way toward replacing financial remuneration. For those who have been good enough to assist you for a credit of thanks in lieu of payment, just make sure you spell their names right.

Before we leave the lab and other post-production facilities; a bit of advice. For beginning producers, money for post is usually tight, and inexperience occasionally leads to, well...mistakes. Your lab and post-production houses can deliver you from the darkest hell of your own creation back into the light (sometimes quite literally!). If you are sincerely humble and appreciative of their efforts, they will sometimes orchestrate that deliverance for much less than you should have had to pay. Even though they are not on set, and often not even in the same city, they are creative collaborators, and a critical part of your team.

MUSIC

Many a film has been elevated from mediocrity to a more satisfactory standing throughout the magic of *music*. Many more have been lifted from being simply excellent to being utterly sublime by the same means. We still tend to think of motion pictures as just that — photographs in motion — but I have been struck numerous times, while watching films and television programs, by how may emotions were being aroused and manipulated, not by an visual element, not by dialogue, but by music and effects. I have been moved to tears by scores composed for a single instrument, and I have been moved to the exit by the most lavish and expensive orchestrations. Obviously, the reverse can be true as well. Whether the mood is being evoked is sad, mysterious, buoyant, or horrific, music can literally create the mood, or sink any chance of producing the desired atmosphere regardless of other aural or visual cues.

In choosing your *composer*, it helps to find a musical reference that you can have the composer listen to: existing film scores, existing music unrelated to film, or even sounds that evoke the kind of mood or emotion that would be appropriate for your picture. If you are contemplating engaging an experienced composer, listen to everything she or he has done. If the composer seems appropriate, have this person read the script, see some footage, and express some thoughts on musical direction. If you don't hear anything that sounds or feels close to what you are "hearing" for your film in the composer's existing scores, and her or his instincts based on your script and footage seen foreign, you should listen elsewhere.

Good film composers are versatile, with scores spanning a wide variety of styles and genres, yet most do have a signature that will be identifiable throughout their body of work. The simplest approach, though not always the most creative, is to find someone whose basic signature seems close to the style of music you imaging for your film, and discuss with this composer the specifics relevant to your story, style, and period. If you are hiring a composer with limited experience, get her or him to compose a theme, either for the film or for a character, that might give you a sense of where her or his instincts lie. You then have a basis for discussing the score as a whole.

Any existing music that you hope to include in your music score or as background *source music* should be licensed well in advance of mixing. Negotiations for source music can be protracted, and the song you are interested in may prove too costly, requiring you to look for another appropriate piece of music. All cue sheets, listing the authors and publishers of licensed compositions, must be registered with the Society of Composers, Authors and Music Publishers of Canada (SOCAN).

And on to the Next Production

Once you have delivered the appropriate materials — film prints, videotapes, stills, press clippings, final financial reports, etc. — to your broadcasters, distributors, investors, and sponsors, one might legitimately presume that a glass of champagne, a hearty congratulation extended to yourself in the mirror, and a nice little holiday might be in order. In my experience, a sense of completion on any one project is denied the producer, as you continue to monitor, encourage, and/or orchestrate the promotion and sales of your film for years after its completion. In addition, if you are planning to produce more than one film in your life, you really can't afford to rest for even an instant after completing a film. While you were giving 100 per cent of your time and energy to your current film during production, you were, by necessity, giving at least another 50 per cent of your time and energy to the projects in development and distribution. When you "finish" one film, there will be much catching up to do on the projects that have only had the benefit of 50 per cent of your attention during the months of production.

Even if math isn't your strong suit, it must be obvious by now that, as a producer, you are going to be in a heightened state of activity most of the time. It will be important for you to learn to set limits in order that you might, in addition to being a successful producer, have a fighting chance at being a sane, happy person, enjoying relationships with the world, and with family and friends.

In my experience, and again I suspect that I'm not alone, setting those limits consistently is far easier said than done. So, to quote a little ditty penned by Stephen Stills, "If you can't be with the one you love, love the one you're with." In your role of producer, the one you are with is your production, for better or for worse. Given the amount of time and passion required to produce a film, the single most important criterion for your job is not a love of money (there are far easier ways to make a living), not a love of film as an art form (you can audit a university course or buy a video membership and find much more satisfaction), but a love of the *process*. It is the process by which, like it or not, you will be utterly consumed.

Sample Script Break-Down

BREAKDOWN FOR AUGUST 18, 199- DRAFT

SCENE NUMBER		LOCATION	
THIRTY-NINE		INT. POLICE STATION	
DESCRIPTION	**CAST**	**PAGES**	**DAY/NIGHT**
Dave is introduced to the staff	1. Dave 2. Jerome 12. Erica 13. Orest 14. Wes 19. Joe 28. Jim 29. George 31. 32.	2 1/8	**DAY** **(Afternoon)**

SET	**WARDROBE/MAKEUP**
Interior police station	All cops in formal uniform including gun holsters, Dave's suit, inc. white shirt and tie

PROPS	**VEHICLES/ANIMALS**
Jerome's report, Orest's file, car keys,	**Exterior — squad cars parked out front

SPECIAL EFFECTS	**SPECIAL EQUIPMENT**

EXTRAS	**SOUND**
Note: exterior pass-bys	Radio in background (ADR)

NOTES	

Sample Call Sheet

EXECUTIVE PRODUCER	DAY/DATE	SHOOTING DAY #20
PRODUCER:		FRIDAY, SEPTEMBER 3RD, 199—
DIRECTOR:	SPECIAL CALLS	10:15 CRAFT SERVICE ON SET
PRODUCTION MANAGER:		
PRODUCTION COORD.:	UNIT CALL	10:00 ON SET
COORDINATOR:		
HOSPITAL: LEDUC HOSPITAL, 4210—48 ST.,	SUNRISE/SUNSET	SUNRISE: 06:47 SUNSET 20:19
POLICE: RCMP:		
CATERER: COOKING FOR CROWDS (MEAL @ 4727—50TH AVE.)	WEATHER	MAINLY SUNNY, 21 HIGH, 6 LOW

Sc.	SET	D/N	PGS	CAST	LOCATION NOTES
Sc. 141	**IF NOT COMPLETE** **INT. HAMELIN POLICE STN.** Where's Marylin's File?	DAY 9	7/8	1, 2, 12	Leduc
Sc. 143	**INT. HAMELIN POLICE STN.** Eileen is the key	DAY 9	2	1, 2, 12	Leduc
Sc. 147	**INT. HAMELIN POLICE STN.** Walter confesses	EVE 9	3/8	1, 2, 9, 12	Leduc
Sc. 149	**INT. HAMELIN POLICE STN.** Walter is sorry	DUSK 9	5/8	1, 2, 9, 12	Leduc
Sc. 153	**INT. HAMELIN POLICE STN.** So tell her	N9	1 3/8	1, 2	Leduc
Sc. 115	**INT. HAMELIN POLICE STN.** Erica radios Jerome, Re.: Prints	N8	3/8	12	Leduc
Sc. 120	**INT. HAMELIN POLICE STN.** Erica on radio — keep looking	N8	3/8	12	Leduc
Sc. 130	**INT. HAMELIN POLICE STN.** No word from Jerome	N8	3/8	12	Leduc
Sc. 24/25	**INT. SUBURBAN AT POLICE STN.** Mike Friesen escaped	DAY 3	6/8	2, 4	Leduc
Sc. 118pt	**INT. POLICE SUBURBAN (P.M.P.)** They're bounced around	DUSK 8	1/8	1, 2	Leduc
Sc. 34	**INT. SUBURBAN — TRAVELLING** A twelve-year man	N3	4/8	1, 2	Leduc
		TOTAL	7 6/8		

CHARACTER	ARTIST	P/U	MAKEUP/UP/HR/WDRB	SET	REMARKS
1. DAVE		09.40	10.30	11.10	AB. PLACE, 10049–103 ST.
2. JEROME		10:00	10:30	11:10	14608–82 AVE.,
4. KAREN		O/T	13:00	13:45	
9. WALTER		O/T	11:30	12:00	
12. ERICA		09:15	10:30	11:10	10719–123 ST,

EXTRAS/STANDINS	P/U	MAKEUP/UP/HR/WDRB	SET	REMARKS

NOTES NOTES NOTES NOTES NOTES NOTES NOTES NOTES NOTES NOTES NOTES NOTES NOTES NOTES

PROPS: Sc. 141: Marylin's Case File
Sc. 143: Dave's/Jerome's Guns, Coffee, Cups, Marylin's Case File
Sc. 147: Notebook, Pen
Sc. 149: Dave's/Jerome's Guns, Fax from Forensics, Marylin's Case File, Practical Fax Machine
Sc. 118pt: Dave's/Jerome's Guns

VEHICLES: Sc. 24/25: Hamelin Police Suburban
Sc. 153: Dave's Car, 1 x Hamelin Black & White
Sc. 34: Police Suburban, rigged, Tow Vehicle

MAKEUP: Sc. 149: Tears to Work

SETS: Sc. 120: Clock reads 4:30

SPECIAL EQUIPMENT: Sc. 34: 3/4 Front Driver's Side Mount

•••VISITORS ON SET: STEPHANIE CRAIG AND TASHA MICH (K-97)

1ST AD: JIM LONG	2ND AD: T. LONG	3RD AD: B. TURNING	LOCATIONS: P. RAYMAN
PH:	PH:	PH:	PH

DAY: TWENTY   **DATE: SEPTEMBER 3, 199–**

1st AD: J. Long	10:30	Art Director: Louise Middleton		O/C
2nd AD: Tracy Long	10:30	Set Dec. Doug Blackie		Per. L.M.
3rd AD: Brenda Turning	10:00	Ass't. Dc: J. Murray		Per L.M.
A.D.'s P.A.: Susan Long	10:30	Props: Peter Kalven		10:30
Location Mgr. Paul Rayman	O/C	Props Buyer: Shelly Godsack		10:30
Ass't Location: Bill Sorochan	Per Paul	Swing: Carol Lavellee		Per L.M.
DOP/Camera Op: Peter Wunstorf	10:30	Cos. Designer: Kerry Hackett		O/C
1st Asst. Cam.: Rob DeCoste	10:30	Wardrobe: Joanna Johnston		10:30
2nd Asst. Cam. Kathy Deugau	10:30	Wardrobe P.A.: Sam Musgrage		10:30
Cam. Asst. Trainee: T.Mutcher	10:30	Make-Up: Prudence Olenik		10:30
Stills: Myrl Coulter	O/C	Ass't. Make-Up: Bev Wright		10.30
Sound: Clancy Livingston	10:30	Hair: Rosemarie Karpinsky		10:30
Boom: Janie Kidd	10:30	Head Carpenter: D. Cooksey		Per L.M.
Gaffer: Vete Dorchak	10:30	SPFX: Lee Routly		N/A
Best Boy Electric: Chris Tate	10:30	Stunt Coord: Tom Eirikson		N/A
Key Grip: Jeff Connors	10:30	Wrangler: L. Bourassa		N/A
Grip: C. Hodson	10:30	Transportation Coord.:A Holmes		O/C
Dolly Grip: Bill Mills	10:30	Driver: Garry Saunder		O/C
Gen. Op: Tracey Chapman	10:30	Driver: Dennis Fitzgerald		O/C
Grip P.A.: s. Whiting-Hewlett	10:30	Honeywagon: Bob Townsend		O/C
P.A.: Blair Freeman-Marsh	10:00	Craft Service First Aid: Ava Karvonen		10:15
Dailies:		Catering: Lunch x 50		16:00
Script: Nancy McDonald	10:30	Publicity: Myrl Coulter		O/C
Script Trainee: Adriana Salvia	10:30	Ass't Public: Maureen Prentice		Per Myrl
Prod. Mgr: Linda Chapman	O/C	Accountant: Susan Lewis		O/C
Prod. Coord.: Kim Goddard	Per Linda	Bookkeeper: Franco Dottor		O/C
Coordinator: Brenda McDonald	Per Linda			
Trainee: Sandy Nichol	Per Linda			

ADVANCED SCHEDULE
Day: 21   Date: Tuesday, September 07, 199–

		Location:		Call time:	

Sc.	SET	D/N	PGS	CAST	LOCATION NOTES
Sc. 95	**INT. AMY'S SHOP** Amy comes clean	D7	2 3/8	1, 2, 22 1 Cust. leaving	Studio
SC. 8	**EXT. PRISON – SOLEDAD** ECU's Mike into Van Insert foil in door	D2	2/8	5 2 x Soledad Guards	Studio
Sc. 5A	**INT. TORONTO SQUAD ROOM** Dave decides	D2	2/8	1 1 x Uniformed T.O. Cops 5 x Plain Clothes Cops	Studio
Sc. 10pt	**INT. CORRECTIONS VAN** Mike frees himself	D2	2/8	5	Studio
Sc. 10pt	**INT. CORRECTIONS VAN** Mike looks out the window	D2	1/8	5 2 x Soledad Guards	Studio
Sc. 11	**INT. CORRECTIONS VAN** Mike bursts out	D2	1/8	5 2 x Soledad Guards	Studio
Sc. 32pt	**EXT. LAKE** Marylin dead in the water	N3	1/8	10	Studio
Sc. 138pt	**EXT. SALVAGE FIELD** Aftermath of killing Mike	DAWN9	4/8	1	Studio
Sc. 121pt	**EXT. SALVAGE FIELD** CU's Mike checking back trail	M8	1/8	5	Studio
Sc. 134pt	**EXT. SALVAGE FIELD** CU cartridge in Jeromes hand	M8	1/8	2	Studio
Sc. 12	**EXT. HIGHWAY INTERSECTION** Mike takes over	D2	3/8	5 2 x Soledad Guards	Leduc

ADVANCED SCHEDULE
Day: 21   Date: Tuesday, September 07, 199–

		Location:		Call time:	

Sc.	SET	D/N	PGS	CAST	LOCATION NOTES
Sc. 95	**INT. AMY'S SHOP** Amy comes clean	D7	2 3/8	1, 2, 22 1 Cust. leaving	Studio
SC. 8	**EXT. PRISON – SOLEDAD** ECU's Mike into Van Insert foil in door	D2	2/8	5 2 x Soledad Guards	Studio
Sc. 5A	**INT. TORONTO SQUAD ROOM** Dave decides	D2	2/8	1 1 x Uniformed T.O. Cops 5 x Plain Clothes Cops	Studio
Sc. 10pt	**INT. CORRECTIONS VAN** Mike frees himself	D2	2/8	5	Studio
Sc. 10pt	**INT. CORRECTIONS VAN** Mike looks out the window	D2	1/8	5 2 x Soledad Guards	Studio
Sc. 11	**INT. CORRECTIONS VAN** Mike bursts out	D2	1/8	5 2 x Soledad Guards	Studio
Sc. 32pt	**EXT. LAKE** Marylin dead in the water	N3	1/8	10	Studio
Sc. 138pt	**EXT. SALVAGE FIELD** Aftermath of killing Mike	DAWN9	4/8	1	Studio
Sc. 121pt	**EXT. SALVAGE FIELD** CU's Mike checking back trail	M8	1/8	5	Studio
Sc. 134pt	**EXT. SALVAGE FIELD** CUcartridges in Jerome's hand	M8	1/8	2	Studio
Sc. 12	**EXT. HIGHWAY INTERSECTION** Mike takes over	D2	3/8	5 2 x Soledad	Leduc

**Second Unit Shoots the following,
Tuesday, September 07, 199–**

Sc.	SET	D/N	PGS	CAST	LOCATION NOTES
Sc. 9	**EXT. CALIFORNIA HIGHWAY** Van through countryside	D3	1/8	2 x Soledad Guards	TBA
Sc. 152	**EXT. HIGHWAY** Dave's car, fast passby	DUSK 9	1/8	1	TBA
Sc. 13	**EXT. BAL-HEADED PRAIRIE** Dave's Car passby	D3	1/8	1A, #A, 15A	TBA
Sc. 40	**EXT. HAMELIN STREETS** Suburban travels alley	D4	1/8	1A, 2A	Ponoka
Sc. 22pt	**EXT. HAMELIN STREETS** Dave's Car cruises the town	D3	2/8	1A, 3A, 15A	Leduc
Sc. 41pt	**EXT. HAMELIN STREET** They take off	D4	1/8	1A, 2A	Leduc near RR
Sc.22pt	**EXT. HAMELIN STREET** They leave town for farm	D3	1/8	1A, 3A, 15A	Leduc
Sc. 102	**EXT. POLICE STATION** Insert rotating lights	N7	1/8	—	TBA
Sc. 118pt	**EXT. SALVAGE FIELD** Headlights swerving	DUSK 8	1/8	1A, 2A	TBA
Sc. 114pt	**EXT. COUNTRY ROAD** Off road, into field	DUSK 8	2/8	1A, 2A	TBA
Sc. 131pt	**EXT. SALVAGE FIELD** Footprints	N8	1/8	—	TBA

6

Television
Distribution

by Ismé Bennie

Ismé Bennie became head of acquisitions for TVOntario in 1972 and rapidly established a presence in the international marketplace. Moving to the private sector in 1981, she was vice-president of sales for Televentures Program Management before setting up her own distribution company, Ismé Bennie International in 1983. It is now Paragon International, a successful division of Paragon Entertainment Corporation. Its catalogue includes "The Raccoons," seen on major networks worldwide; the award-winning "Degrassi Junior High;" the ABC movie of the week, Held Hostage; "Ready or Not," seen on Global TV; and the prestigious HandMade Film Library; as well as animated specials and series. Paragon International also represents selected foreign product in Canada.

Ismé has played an active role in industry organizations such as the Canadian Film and Television Production Association (CFTPA), the Academy of Canadian Cinema and Television, and Toronto Women in Film and Television. In 1990, she received the CFTPA Personal Achievement Award, and in 1995, its Jack Chisholm Award for Lifetime Contribution to the Motion Picture/Television Industry.

The Role of the Distributor

With the development of new technologies, television distribution has become a highly sophisticated business. Programming or "product" has to be guided as effectively as possible through a series of "windows" of opportunity including any or all of: non-theatrical or institutional; pay-per-view; pay TV; satellite-delivered; cable TV; free TV (network, regional, public or educational, and station); various forms of home video; closed-circuit, including airlines, hotels, and ships-at-sea; interactive TV and formats such as CDI or CD-ROM; video-dialtone (telephone-delivered); publishing and merchandising, and other ancillary uses. The marketplace is further complicated by constantly changing language and territory permutations and groupings, created by satellite "footprints" or new strategic alliances.

The "product" includes theatrical films that have had their theatrical release and are available for further exploitation via television, and various kinds of programming produced specifically for the television medium.

Distributors have their specialties and their strengths, and crucial to the marketplace success of any production is matching it to the right distributor. Government organizations such as Telefilm Canada and the provincial funding agencies can provide lists of names, and other producers can make recommendations. Chemistry is very important; it does not bode well for the producer-distributor relationship if it starts off in an adversarial way during contract negotiations. It is also important that there be a frank discussion of the producer's financial expectations, and whether the distributor's revenue projections meet them. The distributor has experience in the marketplace and will give a realistic assessment of the production's potential return over a period of time. This often comes as bad news to the producer who may, along with others, have invested heavily in the project.

Working with a distributor early on in the production process therefore makes good sense. At the concept stage, a distributor can provide valuable information on the viability of the project and help enhance its saleability. The producer can also assess the distributor's ability to "package": that is, to look for pre-sales, co-production parents, or sponsors. The producer may also want to find out if the distributor is willing to make a direct financial commitment to the project financing by way of an advance or bankable guarantee against distribution rights. The guarantee is an irrevocable commitment by the distributor to return to the producer a minimum amount of future sales revenues. The producer can use this as security against which to raise money from a bank or other funding source. However, unless a project is outstanding, most distributors will be reluctant to invest money in first-time projects or neophyte producers. A producer's relationship with a distributor should be evaluated for the long term, in that success builds on success, and a distributor can be a valuable resource for the future.

THE DISTRIBUTION AGREEMENT

Agreements between producers and distributors, whether for domestic or international rights, all have basic standard deal points.

- *Territory*, the geographical area for which sales rights are granted to the distributor. This could be, for example, France, or possibly French-speaking Europe. In the latter case, the French-language rights for Switzerland would be included. Another distributor could then have rights to German-speaking Europe, to include German-language rights for Switzerland. Usually territories granted are broad; for example, world, excluding North America.
- *Term*, or the number of years for which the distributor may represent the product.

- *Media*, the various forms of television and related media for which the distributor will have representation. These could include a range of ancillary rights such as home video, CD-ROM, books, soundtracks, and character licensing.
- *Exclusivity*, granting the distributor the sole right to represent the product in the media and territories designed in the agreement.
- *Delivery requirements*, the material or technical elements the producer has to supply to the distributor.
- *Sales Commission*, the percentage of sales revenues the distributor may charge the producer.
- *Distribution Expenses*, the costs incurred in the sales process, and how and when they will be accounted for.
- *Warranties*, or agreements by both parties that they have the right to enter into the agreement on the terms included, and that they will observe them, and legal remedies should either of them fail to do so.

All terms are couched in the appropriate language, and all are negotiable. The more financially committed the distribution company, the more favourable the terms it can negotiate for itself! As the marketplace grows more complex, so have distribution agreements. Most distributors have standard agreements. But each deal is unique and has to be considered on its own merits and according to its special circumstances.

A distributor — as opposed to a sales agent — will usually have the right to enter into licence agreements with broadcasters directly, without consultation with the producer, providing the licence terms are within the terms of the distribution agreement. (A licence agreement is in effect a "lease" of a program for specific telecasts over a period of time. The actual ownership remains vested in the producer.)

The producer may give world rights for a production to one distributor, or divide them among several distributors by hemisphere, language, media, or "domestic" versus "foreign." The arrangement is determined by various factors. For instance, the nature of the product may make it suitable only for certain markets. If an English program is too difficult to version into other languages, it may be saleable only in English-speaking countries. If it has pigs in it — this is an unlikely sounding but actual example — it will not sell in the Middle East where pigs are considered unclean. If the programming has been co-produced, the territories available will have been divided out under terms of the co-production, and a producer can only grant distribution for those territories he or she controls. If the producer has pre-sold some territories as part of the production financing, similar restrictions will apply. Funding agencies such as Telefilm Canada, as investors in new product, may impose certain conditions, including perhaps the way a new project is distributed. And of course the producer may prefer to have eggs in several baskets. The media that the distributor will handle will also be part of the negotiating process, and can range from television to merchandising, often including "any systems of video transmission to members of the public now known or hereafter developed!"

CLEARING RIGHTS

The producer, when clearing rights during production, should be aware of the various exploitation possibilities and ensure that those rights are available. The producer has to warrant that he or she owns and controls the rights being granted to the distributor, and that these are free and clear. Archival footage and the music and performing rights within the production must be cleared, and the producer has to accept responsibility for any payments due for these and other residual rights during the term of the agreement. Clearing rights involves getting written permission from all third parties involved in the project to exploit their material under certain defined conditions. This applies to all talent, whose contributions are usually covered under union agreements, as well as to any piece of film or sound use in the production.

If a production containing stock footage bought from a third party is sold, for example, to German television, not only must the right to use the footage in the production be bought or "cleared," but also the right to licence the production with the footage included in it. Rights can be cleared on a selected basis — the right to one broadcast on Canadian television for example, or on a worldwide basis, for a few years or in perpetuity. A distributor's preference is for a world buyout of all rights, and the distributor must be made aware of any restrictions or limitations on this.

FINANCIAL TERMS

The financial terms and conditions will be determined by the extent of the rights given, and the extent to which the distributor is willing to guarantee returns. The sales commission can be a given percentage across the board, or different percentages for different media or territories. Generally, the more work entailed, the higher the distributor's commission. Basically, there are two kinds of deals: a *gross deal*, in which the distributor's commission comes off the top, before deductions of any kind; and a *net deal*, in which the commission comes off after allowable costs are deducted. If the distributor has given an advance, this is paid to the producer "up front." If a minimum guarantee has been promised, then the distributor commits to pay the amount of money over a specific period of time. In either case, the money is really just an advance against the producer's share of sales revenues, and is fully recoupable by the distributor from the distribution income. There is no set formula for the size of the advance or guarantee. It is based on the distributor's realistic revenue projection.

A distributor normally pays for the costs of promoting and servicing sales, and then recoups these costs from the distribution income. Allowable costs will be defined in the negotiating process, and can include: audition cassettes; duplication, conversion or formatting of film and videotape for servicing sales; delivery, shipping, and customs brokerage; storage and maintenance of materials; duplication of scripts; various taxes; foreign-language dubbing; bank charges; trade fair participation; and the distributors' catch-all, "all other necessary and usual distribution costs for which television distributors are customarily reimbursed." A cap may be put on costs: either a percentage of sales, or an agreed-upon figure.

Periodic statements will be issued by the distributor — monthly, quarterly, or annually — showing financial details relating to the relevant period, and they may, at the producer's request, include backup documentation such as invoices and receipts. The producer may also require that there be no "allocation." This means the distributor must sell and account for each production separately and on its individual merits, rather than selling a package of productions from various sources and allocating the revenues to the distributor's benefit; for example, to those productions that earn a higher sales commission.

SERVICING MATERIALS

The right servicing materials are a key requirement in distribution. These materials have to satisfy a wide range of broadcasters, some of whom will telecast in English and others who will dub or subtitle in other languages; who will take any of a variety of television formats; and who will have the occasional unusual or special request.

The physical elements available to the distributor are affected by decisions that were made throughout the creative process;

for example, shooting on film or tape; finishing on film or tape; how sound was recorded; choice of titles, subtitles, or graphics; placement of commercial breaks or bumpers; music and lyrics; and program duration. The ultimate effect of these decisions on future sales is usually not on the producer's mind during production, so that the distributor may have some difficulty assembling the necessary broadcast-quality materials.

Videotape is the normal format for servicing television sales, and the distributor will require either a top quality submaster or laboratory access to the producer's master. Other delivery items include a good music and effects track, textless title back-grounds, an as-broadcast script (which means a word-for-word transcription of dialogue matched to visuals); music cue sheets; credit lists; a Canadian content certification number; chain of title documentation; copyright registration; and errors and omissions insurance, usually in the amount of $1 million to $4 million, to protect both the distributor and ultimately the licensee from trademark, copyright, or slander violations. A full list of items required by the distributor can be found at the end of this chapter.

The distributor's marketing plan will likely include the preparation of sales tools such as trailers, ads, one-sheets, and press kits. To produce these, the distributor will require from the producer a good selection of colour transparencies and black-and-white stills, synopses, bios of cast and production team, and title and logo stats. These materials will later to be used to assemble packages of publicity materials for the use of the broadcasts in promoting the telecast of the production or in creating videocassette boxes.

Once the selling process starts, the producer-distributor rela-tionship need not be confined to the quarterly report. If the distributor is encountering problems in selling the producer, the producer should be aware of them, so that producer and distributor can work co-operatively to overcome them. By the same token, a producer should trust the distributor. The selling process takes time and patience: the decision-making process at a network can be a long one; time slots and budgets have to open up; windows need to be maximized in logical sequence; market forces change; and program fads come and go.

International Television Distribution

New services are proliferating all over the world. In many countries, where one government broadcaster once had autonomy, there may now be a wide range of services. The distribution opportunities in the international marketplace are proportionately greater, but so too are the risks, as new services come along, struggle to survive, change ownership, or fold. The new services and the new means of delivery, such as satellite, have also complicated the licensing process. The distributor has to keep abreast of changes and developments worldwide, whether financial, technical, cultural or political, and to be cognizant of the ripple effects created by every sale made.

TRADE SHOWS

Each distribution company selling internationally has its own modus operandi. Some work through local subagents; some have their own offices in key territories; some work directly from home base. All, though, participate in international television trade sales where buyers and sellers from all over gather, which are essential to establishing the sales company and the product. These shows have been well supported by Canadian government agencies, and a great deal of Canadian programming is seen on broadcast outlets around the world.

The major television shows are NATPE (National Association of Television Program Executives) held each January in a U.S. city and aimed primarily at selling to the U.S. market, though it is becoming an increasingly important international event; MIP (Marché International des Programmes) and its offshoot

MIPCOM, each held annually in Cannes and probably the best-attended and most valuable trade events; and Monte Carlo, held each February in that city. There are also many "niche" events specializing in genres such as animation, documentary, and children's programming.

WILL YOUR PROGRAM TRAVEL?

Not all Canadian-produced programming is suitable for the international market place. The subject matter or references may be too local, or the programming may be date-specific or may date quickly. The programming may be too costly or difficult to version (dub or subtitle) by virtue of being continuous on-camera discussion or by depending heavily on lyrics to tell the story. Some countries don't broadcast contact sports, while some don't take motor racing; many countries have cultural mandates to produce their own preschool programming, and some have quota requirements; a pop star who sells a huge number of records may mean nothing to television; cultural or religious factors may prevent sales, particularly in the Middle East or Asia. Too few episodes can also be a factor, since buyers want to build audience loyalty.

World events can affect a program's acceptance in unpredictable ways. A country in political turmoil, for instance, may not want a movie dealing with a hostage-taking incident. In a world of increasing political correctness, buyers will assess the program's attitudes to women, to "challenged" groups, to violence, and to racial and ethnic stereotypes. The most universally sought-after genres remain action-adventure drama series, high-profile TV movies, and high-quality animation, though the new niche services have provided more outlets for other genres. But even as some markets are burgeoning and have more channels and more hours to fill, they are also — as in Southeast

Asia — turning to increased local programing, which is what succeeds best with their audiences. However, there are many Canadian success stories. The *"Degrassi"* series, produced by Playing With Time, are seen in over 60 countries.

COMPLICATIONS

In long-term planning, it's important to be aware of how borders, or their breakdown, influence sales patterns. A broadcast on free TV in France spills over into Belgium and Switzerland, precluding a later sale of the program to those French-speaking markets. A sale to a British satellite-delivered service with a "footprint" over Europe can affect price or sales in those European countries. A TV sale may preclude a later video sale, and vice versa. Merchandising deals usually work best when planned ahead in tandem with the television release, and are usually effective only with long-running series or major films.

The distributor steers the program through this complicated world of rights. The television client is usually the telecaster: a TV network, station, or cable service. However, the buyer can also be a middleman who licenses rights for an area or group of countries: say Latin America, or French-Europe, and subdistributes them. It is often better to get one good cheque out of one reliable bank and to service with only one set of materials, than to have to cope with country-by-country idiosyncrasies, such as censorship, or taxes or blocked funds, in difficult parts of the world.

License agreements between distributor and licensee specify certain basic elements: medium, number of transmissions, period, territory, language, exclusivity, payment of shipping and material costs, the license fee and its pay-out terms, and renewal options, if any.

PRICING

Pricing, for TV at least, is based on a country's population size and number of television sets. Within each country the prices are based on the reach of the individual broadcaster. Japan, for instance, is a market that, depending on the product, can pay large license fees. But a sale to English-language cable in Japan, with its limited audience, is worth only a few hundred dollars per half-hour. Price is also affected by the terms of the license agreement. The more telecasts and the longer the license period, the higher the price. Genre and fad play their part. Obviously, a huge international hit such as *"Baywatch"* will fetch competitive prices. Children's programming tends to fetch lower prices than, say, adult drama, because it is played in non-prime-time slots, and often in slots in which advertising is not permitted.

Variety and some other trade publications issue price guides periodically. These tend to reflect prices for U.S.-produced mainstream product. Nevertheless they provide a guide to going price ranges. A recent *Variety* price quote for the United Kingdom for a one-hour series episode was $15,000 to $100,000. U.S. Regardless, a one-hour episode might only fetch $1,000 U.S. if the sale is to a small cable outlet, or it may not sell at all. Prices quoted are for finished productions, not for pre-sales. Prices for home video and other ancillary media are less standard, and are continually evolving. In making these non-TV sales, the distributor is, in effect, placing the product with the appropriate subdistributor; monitoring the agreement, and collecting royalties on behalf of the producer.

SERVICING MATERIALS FOR INTERNATIONAL SALES

The servicing of these international sales is complex, demanding up-to-date knowledge of technical requirements country by country, and involving tape conversion to broadcast standards such as PAL or SECAM, and formats ranging from ¾-inch to D2.

It is very important to deliver a package of elements that facilitates dubbing or subtitling into foreign languages: most importantly, a good music and effects track, an accurate dialogue script, textless title backgrounds so that the titles can be replaced with titles in the foreign language, and opening and closing credit lists.

In almost all cases, except for French and Latin American Spanish, the licensee is responsible for versioning, either by subtitling or dubbing. The distributor, on behalf of the producer, usually arranges and pays up-front for dubbing into French and Latin American Spanish, because these particular tracks can be used to service sales in a number of countries. In negotiating distribution rights, it may be more cost-effective to have one distributor handle all French-language territories, including French Canada. Telefilm Canada provides dubbing assistance if the French-language or English-language dubbing goes through a recognized Canadian distributor. Though problems arise and quotas exist, Canadian programming versioned in Canada is usually accepted in France, provided the French is international.

SELLING TO THE UNITED STATES

While Canada is often considered to be part of U.S. domestic distribution, the United States is considered "foreign" by Canadians. Selling to the United States is affected by sales made in Canada, and border situations created by these sales. A Canadian network, for instance, may demand an exclusive North American window, or a Canadian broadcast signal spilling over the border can affect the exclusivity requirement of a U.S. sale.

The U.S. marketplace is made up of the traditional networks — ABC, CBS, NBC, and the new quasi-networks of Fox, Paramount, and Warners, which are made up of affiliations of stations; pay-per-view and pay-TV services, such as HBO and Showtime; the proliferating cable services; public broadcasting — PBS and station buying-groups such as APS or CEN; and individual stations both public and commercial. Station-by-station "syndication" in the United States is highly specialized, and most Canadian programming suitable for syndication is probably best handled or subdistributed through a U.S.-based syndication company. Barter is an important part of U.S. syndication. Simply put, it involves the exchange of airtime for ads. In other words, the distributor pre-sells some or all of the commercial time slots in the program to an advertiser, and then places the program with telecast outlets on some basis, either for free or for a combination of cash and the station's retention of some ad time to sell off itself.

In the past, it was very difficult to sell Canadian programming in the United States, but as cable services have increased, Canada has become a major supplier to this market. In addition, the larger Canadian production companies have begun to be recognized as suppliers to the networks. However, for the average distributor of off-the-shelf product, the networks are still difficult to access and a U.S. sale, cable or otherwise, can never be assured. Should it happen, though, it means that , recoupment of the production budget may become a reality!

Domestic Television Distribution

Canadian domestic television distribution is defined by U.S. domestic distribution. The border between the two countries can be a great help or a huge hindrance. For instance, a Canadian show, telecast on a U.S. network and "simulcast" in Canada on a Canadian network at the same time, increases the show's Canadian value by virtue of a government regulation that makes the Canadian cable carrier replace the U.S. signal with the Canadian, thus doubling the exposure of the program and its Canadian advertising. Disadvantages are great, on the other hand, if the conditions of either a U.S. sale or a Canadian sale limit the sales potential in the other market. A broadcast sig-

nal spilling over the border can affect the exclusivity requirement of a sale in either market, or each market may demand to
pre-release the other.

Canadian television is made up of both English-language
and French-language outlets. Like the rest of the world, this
marketplace has become exceedingly complex, with the introduction of many new U.S.-originating services such as A & E,
The Learning Channel, and CNN; as well as pay-per-view, and
pay-TV services such as The Movie Channel and The Family
Channel; specialty cable services such as YTV, TSN and
Muchmusic; and a host of new pay and specialty services featuring women's concerns wildlife and adventure, the arts,
Canadian drama, classic movies, and country music. Many more
of these services will come onstream as we move into a more
deregulated television environment in Canada. The free-TV
market includes the national networks, regional or other groupings, provincial public or "education" services, and individual
stations to which a distributor "syndicates": that is, sells station
by station. The last involves distributing over vast distances and
into differing local conditions from East to West, to sell to as
many local stations as possible. barter, very much part of U.S.
distribution, is relatively limited in Canada.

Government Canadian content regulations require the
inclusion of certain minimum percentages of Canadian programming in the broadcast schedule. This is further encouraged by incentives such as the 150 per cent Canadian content
time credit for prime-time telecast of 100 per cent Canadian
drama produced after 1985, and for Canadian children's drama
broadcast in appropriate viewing times.

Selling Canadian — and indeed any programming — in
Canada is not much different from selling it internationally. It
requires the same careful release pattern to maximize revenues
from each potential window. While pay TV usually comes first,

the number and variety of production financing relationships, and the need for Canadian content programming, has made for a more flexible marketplace. Even if all windows are properly exploited, recoupment of the production budget from Canadian sales is highly unlikely. (For more on Windows, see Chapter 7, Theatrical Distribution.) While English-language programming, dubbed into French, is widely accepted in French Canada, English Canada seems to resist dubbed or subtitled programming, whatever the source.

In addition to licensing the product in Canada or worldwide, the distributor can provide other services, such as taking care of entries into local or international festivals, registering copyright, collecting retransmission or performance royalties, as well as organizing promotional activities that ultimately enhance the product as well as the relationship with the licensee and the audience, and create a climate favourable to receiving the next production.

BASIC LIST OF TECHNICAL DELIVERY ITEMS AND PROMOTIONAL REQUIREMENTS FOR TELEVISION PROGRAMS

A) **Technical Delivery Items**
   ¼" cassette(s)
   ½" cassette(s)
   Compositive positive 18 mm colour print(s) with properly synchronized optical sound track
   Internegative to above, as required
   *International M & E track on second channel of master videotape and/or as required (i.e., ¼" or ½")
   *One set each of NTSC and PAL 1" videotape of picture and sound (stereo where applicable)
   Dubbed versions, if available

B) **Promotional Requirements**
   Unit publicist

Stills photographer
*Contact sheets
Negatives
*Set of 8" x 10" photographs
Colour transparencies
TV clips
The cost of the following items can be absorbed by either the producer or the distributor:
Flyer (one sheet)
Press kit
Press reviews and clipping
Graphic elements (logo, title, etc. . . .)
Prospectus (pre-production)

C) **Documentation**
   Synopsis
   Complete list of credits (i.e., actors, staff, opening and closing credits)
   *Spotted dialogue list (including narration, songs and voices)
   *Music cue sheets
   Biofilmography of actors, director, and artistic staff
   Production notes
   Final script

D) **Rights**
   *Certificate of copyright registration
   Certificate of Canadian origin
   Contracts for the acquisition or use of literary, dramatic, or musical material
   Contracts with producer, director, actors, and musicians
   Contractual obligations regarding credits, promotion, advertising
   Statement of restriction to the dubbing of the voice of any actor
   Information related to payments to professional guilds (UDA, ACTRA, etc.)
   Errors and omissions insurance policy

Items often "missing"
Reprinted by permission of Telefilm Canada

7

Theatrical Distribution

by Marie-Claude Poulin

M arie-Claude Poulin is vice-president of Sales and Acquisitions at
Malofilm International, a division of Malofilm Distribution, where
she is also in charge of acquisitions of European and Canadian films
and sales to domestic television. She has been with Malofilm for six
years, handling foreign sales of English and French Canadian productions such as The Lotus Eaters, Eclipse, The Glace Bay Miner's
Museum and Le Vent du Wyoming. She regularly attends all major
festivals and markets around the world. On the domestic side, she has
been in charge of acquiring Canadian films, working with producers
from the beginning and planning the marketing strategy.

Prior to 1989, Marie-Claude Poulin worked with Norstar/Simcom
International, handling sales for films such as Prom Night II and
Jack's Back. She was also assistant editor of the first and second edi-
tions of Who's Who in Canadian Film and Television.

Introduction

In the filmmaking process, each artist and crew member has his
or her area of expertise. From the director to the actors or the
gaffer, each person has a certain responsibility and talent and

performs a specific task. Why is it, then, when it comes to distribution, that certain producers and directors tend to think they can do it themselves? Perhaps it is the fear of losing control of their "picture" or not wanting to share the revenues with an outsider? Since it is the producer's responsibility to the investors to ensure that the picture returns the greatest possible revenue from the marketplace in all media both here and abroad, it is wise to work with an experienced distributor.

As on the production side, the distributor has his or her area of expertise and employs talented people to perform each specific task involved in the distribution process: marketing, selling, promotion, publicity, and so on. In today's marketplace, the distributor is also usually part of the financing structure of the film and therefore indispensable. In Canada there are two categories of distributors: the shrinking independent sector and the U.S. studios such as Paramount, Twentieth Century Fox or Columbia, usually referred to simply as "the majors."

As a Canadian producer and particularly if you are accessing Telefilm Canada or the production funds of another agency, you will have to make a deal with an independent Canadian distributor in the financing stages. You may, however, make a separate distribution deal for the United States (either with a major or an independent). It is also likely that you will need a foreign sales agent for your film at that stage.

Whether or not you are compelled to do it, it is in your best interest to use a Canadian distributor, other than for nationalistic reasons. Independent distributors in most parts of the world — including Canada — are more knowledgeable about releasing pictures in their own market and may be more committed to producing a profitable result in the territory where they work and live. In addition, most Canadian distributors are eligible for financial assistance from Telefilm Canada and other government agencies to offset distribution costs, which encourages them to develop a more ambitious publicity campaign for your film.

In this chapter we will look at a number of areas related to the distribution of your picture in the domestic and foreign markets. We will consider first what your distributor can and should do for you, and how to choose the right one. We'll take a detailed look at the items included in a distribution contract, and the theatrical and non-theatrical distribution process. The chapter concludes with an examination of how foreign sales are made.

The Domestic Market

WHAT YOUR DISTRIBUTOR CAN DO FOR YOU

As mentioned earlier, getting a commitment from a Canadian distributor in the earliest planning stages is quite important, since the distributor's work should begin prior to the production of the picture. Obviously, the distributor's responsibility is to maximize revenues in all media. More specifically, before and while the film is in production, the distributor can help by:

- making comments and suggestions for the final draft of the script;
- making casting suggestions that can enhance the marketability of the film;
- ensuring that all the necessary materials for the campaign (stills, slides, proper shots of the actors and director and crew, and shots of the sets and locations) will be available;
- obtaining press coverage in the local press and properly targeted publications;
- obtaining television coverage;
- supervising and organizing the production of an electronic press kit (EPK); and
- preparing the campaign or a preliminary campaign (poster and trailer concept) before completion of the production.

Once the picture is completed, the distributor should be undertaking the following tasks:
- creating the final campaign (posters, ads, trailers, etc.);
- securing the right theatre(s) and date(s) for the release;
- implementing publicity, promotion, and advertising strategy;
- exploiting the picture in all other media (video-television-non-theatrical); and
- reporting properly, to you, the producer.

CHOOSING THE RIGHT DISTRIBUTOR

Ten years ago, there was a proliferation of independent distributors, due in part to the burgeoning new technology that created after-markets for the theatrical film: in particular, home video and pay television. Theatrical revenues have gone up and down since then and the number of independent distributors has diminished considerably. There is now only a handful of distributors in Canada.

The first step in finding a distributor should be sending a script to a few distribution companies, along with the pertinent information on your project. You should always provide a budget, production schedule, casting suggestions, biographies of principals involved, and a director's reel if the director is unknown. It is also important to send your script to the right person — that is, the person in charge of acquisitions.

When choosing your distributor, there are a number of factors for you to consider. First, is the picture appropriate to the distributor under consideration? If your picture requires a slow, careful, and selective release in the most upscale cinemas in the country, then you should choose a distributor who has a reputation for distributing art or specialty pictures; an understanding of the need for getting your film screened at film festivals and critic's screenings; and knowledge of the best time of year to open your picture. If, however, your film is a wide-release action comedy or exploitation film, needing saturation bookings in each market and appropriate electronic media advertising support, then you must make sure that the distributor has the financial strength and exhibitor relationships to achieve these ends. In Canada, most independent distributors will handle both kinds of pictures. However, there are still small "boutique distributors" who will only take on specialty films that require careful handling.

Second, will you get along with these people? The film industry is very much a people business, and it is extremely important that the producer and distributor trust and respect each other. This will ensure that the distributor feels confident that you're not going to take the money and run if the film becomes a huge success, and, on the other hand, that you will not automatically blame him or her if the film fails at the box office.

Third, how crowded is the distributor's schedule? Is it possible that the distributor has committed to too many pictures and will not be able to give your film the attention or financial commitment it deserves ?

Fourth, what kind of reputation does your chosen distributor have? Have you spoken with other producers who have dealt with him or her in the past ? Have you read about them in the trades or elsewhere?

Fifth, what resources can your distributor command? Does this distributor have offices across Canada? Does he or she distribute directly in Quebec (or English Canada) or go through another distributor? Does your distributor distribute directly for video and television? Do they have an in-house publicity department? Do they have a foreign sales department?

The most important thing for you to do is to establish your priorities and decide what is important to you. Then look for a distributor who has the attributes you are looking for.

THE DISTRIBUTION AGREEMENT

If a distributor likes your project, he or she will make you an offer: probably a short deal memo or letter of interest to begin with. When you accept that offer, a long-form agreement will be drawn up and you will begin negotiations.

There can be as many deals as there are pictures, and the permutations and terms and conditions in a distribution agreement are virtually unlimited. Described below are the items that should be included in the agreement, and the main types of distribution deal you will be offered. The distribution agreement is usually provided by the distributor.

GRANT OF RIGHTS

In this clause the licensor sets out and grants to the licensee (distributor) the exclusive rights to rent, lease, license, exhibit, and distribute the picture in all media and for any purposes. Subject to negotiations between the producer and distributor, the rights include all formats and gauges (including those that might be devised in the future!) including any combination of the following: theatrical, non-theatrical (airlines, ships, schools, associations, armed forces, buses, and so on), home video rights (including video discs, CD-ROM), and television, broken down into the following categories: free, pay, pay-per-view, and cable. This clause may also cover foreign language versions, authorizing the licensee to exploit the picture in any language.

The distributor also usually reserves the right of *first negotiation* and *last refusal* for the distribution rights of theatrical sequels and remakes of the picture. "First negotiation" means that distributor will have a certain number of days in which to be the first to look at the sequel script and make an offer. "Last refusal" means that distributor will again have a certain number of days to match or better a bona fide offer from a third party.

THE TERRITORY

The territory will be defined specifically. In the case of Canada, it is usually defined by the language: English-speaking Canada, French-speaking Canada. In this way, for example, a distributor will be allowed to release a French-language version in the Maritimes or in Alberta.

THE TERM

The term of the agreement will generally be for a period of 15 to 25 years and may be negotiated for a term that extends to perpetuity. When the term expires, the rights revert back to the rights holder, usually the producer.

THE PICTURE

In this clause, the licensor (the producer) will warrant that the picture is (or will be) of first-class technical quality, and that the running time will not exceed a specified number of minutes (usually 120 minutes) and will not be less than a specified number of minutes (usually 90 minutes). Additionally, the distributor's offer is usually conditional on his or her approval of the following: Canadian content certification, budget, principal cast and crew, director, producer, production schedule, terms of a completion bond and completion guarantee naming distributor as a beneficiary, proof of errors and omission insurance coverage, proof of underlying rights and chain of title documentation, and proof of financing agreements. When some or all of these elements are already in place, the distributor's approval will be noted on the agreement.

DELIVERY

The producer will be required to deliver any and all necessary printing materials for the picture to the distributor, on or before a specific delivery date. The elements should be sent to a laboratory designated by the distributor, together with a laboratory access letter that gives the distributor legal access to these materials for the purpose of ordering prints, masters, or any other materials the distributor might require to properly distribute the picture. Standard delivery items (which should therefore be budgeted into a picture), usually include the following:

Film Delivery Items

1. interpositive (access)*;
2. internegative (access);
3. check print (access);
4. negative sound (optical sound track) (access);
5. magnetic master conformed in all respect to the answer print;
6. music and effects tracks;
7. main and end textless titles;
8. NTSC video submaster.

* Access means that the original element will be placed in a laboratory designated by the distributor for the term of the agreement, and that the distributor will have access to it at all times.

Other Items

1. music cue sheets;
2. dialogue list;
3. all necessary agreements for the music rights;
4. screen credit obligations;
5. pre-production portrait photos (colour and black-and-white);
6. production stills (colour and black-and-white);
7. all written publicity material and notes;
8. necessary information for the calculation of all royalties and residuals payable in connection with the picture;
9. copyright registration;
10. title report and copyright search by companies acceptable to the distributor;
11. chain of title documents.

DISTRIBUTION FEES

There are almost as many deals as there are pictures and distributors, and producers must work out a deal that is acceptable to both parties. However, there are two main types of financial arrangements: the net and the gross deal. A *net deal* represents a sharing of the gross receipts (that is, all monies received from all sources for the rental of the picture) *after deduction of fees, expenses, and advances.* For the theatrical rights there are two frequently used types of net deal:

1. *50 per cent/50 per cent costs-off-the-top.* In this deal, the following items will be deducted from gross monies received from the theatrical exploitation of the picture:
   • distribution expenses;
   • distributors' share of the receipts (50 per cent);
   • any advance already paid to the producer.
     The percentages may be negotiated to 40 per cent/60 per cent or even 30 per cent/70 per cent, once the advance is recouped by the distributor.
2. *30 per cent to 35 per cent fee to distributor.* In this deal, the following items will be deducted from gross monies received from the theatrical exploitation of the picture:
   • distributor's fee;
   • distribution expenses;
   • any advance already paid to the producer.

THE GROSS DEAL

The gross deal is much simpler, but in most cases it is more difficult for the producer to obtain from a distributor. In such a deal, the producer would receive his or her percentage of the gross receipts derived from the distribution of the picture *from first dollar, without deductions of expenses of any kind* (other than the distributor's advance to the producer if there has been one).

Here, the producer will get a smaller piece (usually 20 per cent to 30 per cent) of the pie, but will be guaranteed to receive some monies. This puts the distributor at risk, since he or she must absorb 100 per cent of the distribution costs. If the film performs well, this will be an advantageous deal to the distributor, but if it fails at the box office and the expenses exceed the revenue, the distributor will lose money. A distributor will very seldom enter into such a deal for a Canadian film. However, if he or she were offered the rights to, let's say, *Jurassic Park*, there would be no hesitation!

There is another type of gross deal, which will more commonly be offered to a producer, the *straight distribution* deal. In this case, there will be no monies advanced to the producer by the distributor and the distributor will take a commission from gross receipts, recoup the expenses, and, if there are additional revenues, split them with the producer. The distributor's fee in this case is usually between 20 per cent to 30 per cent of revenues. Since the producer will receive 70 per cent to 80 per cent of the revenues if the picture is successful, it is definitely an option that should not be ignored if offered.

With both deals, all rights are usually *cross-collateralized*, which means that the losses incurred in the exploitation of one right (for example, theatrical) may be recoupable from the revenues of another right (for example, video or television). If the advance and the distribution expenses are unrecouped after the theatrical release, then the distributor may retain the producer's share of revenues from other rights until the distributor's share is fully recouped.

HOME VIDEO RIGHTS
In the video market, the distributor sells to a wholesaler (for rental), who in turn must sell to the retailers. In this case, the producer's interests are best served by taking a *royalty* — a

percentage of the wholesale or sell-through price. A producer usually receives a royalty of 20 per cent to 30 per cent of the distributor's wholesale price for the rental market and between 10 per cent and 15 per cent for the sell-through market. For the other media, the income split is usually as follows:

Type of Media	Distributor's Fee	Producer's Share
Non-theatrical	50%	50%
Pay TV	20% – 30%	70% – 80%
Cable TV	20% – 30%	70% – 80%
Pay-Per-View	25% – 35%	65% – 75%
Network TV	20% – 30%	70% – 80%
Syndication	25% – 35%	65% – 75%

PAYMENT

The payment schedule is entirely negotiable and may vary between starting payments on signature of agreement or beginning of principal photography to payments being made on completion and delivery of the picture. The distributor will most likely insist on reserving part of the payment until acceptance of all delivery elements.

RELEASE REQUIREMENTS

When the agreement is negotiated prior to production, it is a good idea to include certain release requirements in the contract. Usually they include a minimum number of cities in which the film must be released and minimum and/or maximum print and advertising expenditures (P&A).

REPORTING

This part of the contract deals with the distributor's accounting obligations and practices. It lists the distributor's obligations related to keeping good financial records, as well as specifying how often statements (producer's reports) will be sent to the producer. For example, the distributor might undertake to remit reports quarterly for the next two or three years and bi-annually or annually thereafter. This clause will also define the right of the producer to audit the appropriate records for his or her film.

DEFAULT

This clause is used to protect the distributor and/or producer by including certain default provisions: actions that would render the agreement null, such as:

- if the producer does not deliver picture according to the schedule;
- if the producer or distributor becomes insolvent or files for bankruptcy; or
- if any of the provisions in the agreement are breached.

In addition, the distributor will include the standard terms and conditions in the agreement, which will usually include the following: list of allowable distribution expenses, ownership clause, editing and credit requirements, offset rights, merchandising rights, producer's and distributor's warranties, definitions of standard industry terms, financial conditions, litigations provisions, and music and publicity rights.

THE THEATRICAL DISTRIBUTION PROCESS

Independent Canadian distributors usually do not operate with branches in each market, unlike the U.S. majors, which will have satellite offices in several markets. They handle all bookings from one or two offices. However, some will hire an independent publicist or send their own publicist to specific markets to handle local press and co-ordinate any local promotions. Distributors will work with one or both of the two major theatre chains in Canada — Cineplex Odeon and Famous Players — as well as the independents.

Ten years ago, distributors worked exclusively with one chain. Now, however, even though independent distributors will usually have an allegiance to one chain, they will sometimes work with both simultaneously, since theatres are not always available at the right time and place for a certain picture. The American majors will essentially work only with one chain (for example, Paramount with Famous Players; Columbia with Cineplex). Since the majors book screen time for packages of films, distributors sometimes have very limited access to screens. It is therefore very important to choose your release date carefully. It is essential to find out what other films will be released at the same time and shortly afterward, to determine how long your picture will be able to remain in the right theatre (even if its box office is not outstanding). At certain times of the year — summer, Thanksgiving, Christmas — if a picture is performing not very well, it may be bumped from the screen when a big studio picture is scheduled for release. At other times, the same weekly box office would allow the film to remain on a given screen for a longer period of time. This only serves to illustrate the domination of American studio films in Canada. It is the same in many parts of the world.

Here are some examples of comparative box office results in Canada. In 1994, U.S. films garnered 85 per cent of the box office with 56 per cent of the titles; Canadian films (both English and French) had 4 per cent of the box office with 11 per cent of releases; French films took in 5 per cent of the total, but had 19 per cent of all releases; and all other foreign films took in 6 per cent of the box office with 14 per cent of releases.

Canadian Films

Louis 19th (Golden Reel Award*)	$1,800,000
Exotica**	875,000
Octobre	390,000
Love and Human Remains	359,097
Camilla	275,000
Le Vent du Wyoming	200,000
For the Moment	160,000
The Return of Tommy Tricker	97,124
Whale Music	70,000
Max	20,000
Road to Saddle River	15,000
Ordinary Magic	11,571
Harmony Cats	11,000
Ski School 2	3,324
Red Hot	2,400
Cadillac Girls	1,220

Non-Canadian Films in Wide Release

Jurassic Park	$20,873,072
The Mask	15,304,754
Pulp Fiction**	8,500,000
Schindler's List	8,231,000
The Crying Game	6,200,000
The Piano	5,500,000
Four Weddings and a Funeral**	4,132,226
The River Wild	2,121,181
Bitter Moon	700,000

Non-Canadian Films in Platform or Limited Releases

La Reine Margot	$800,000
Little Buddha	673,391
Barcelona	553,942
Eat Drink Man Woman	400,000
La Fille de d'Artagnan**	400,000
Go Fish	180,000

The Trial	100,000
In the Soup	75,000
Bank Robber	50,000
What Happened Was ...	50,000

Canadian film with the biggest box office results of the year.
**Still in release at time of publication.*

The above figures reflect box office from the major circuit only. An additional 10 per cent to 25 per cent should be added for the independent bookings.

Your marketing plan should be done two to four months in advance of its release date, and for this you need to know who is your target audience and therefore the appropriate marketing approach to reach that audience. In fact, you ought to have known who your target audience was while you were still at the script stage. You should always ask yourself: who will be interested in seeing my film, besides my family and friends?

The decision about the type of release will be made at the same time as decisions about release date and appropriate theatres (for example, downtown theatres for more sophisticated audiences). Most Canadian films will receive a *platform* or *limited release*, which means that the film will be released with three to twelve prints, not necessarily opening at the same time. By starting in one to three larger cities and then booking play-dates in secondary and tertiary markets, you can reduce expenses and allow word of mouth to build. In these cases, to give the film a high profile, promotional efforts and print and advertising expenditures will be concentrated on local activities and targeted innovative approaches to select audiences. For example, when releasing a film dealing with mental illness, support groups and associations should be contacted directly to promote the film.

For a film that is more commercial (for example, *Highlander*

III), a wide release would be appropriate . A wide release will range from 40 to 150 prints (the high end is mostly for American studio pictures) and will entail a much larger investment. This type of release should be supported by television and radio advertising, which are much more expensive than print advertising. The film will then open in all locations at the same time to maximize the impact of the electronic media purchases.

When booking the film, the distributor will negotiate the following items with the exhibitor:

- the opening playdate in each city;
- the most appropriate theatres for the film;
- the minimum and maximum terms for each particular week on a descending scale;
- guaranteed length of playing time; and
- minimum guarantee to distributor (for some independents).

The terms given by an exhibitor can vary from 90/10 to 30/70. In the former case, this means that the exhibitor, after deducting and retaining house expenses (rent, heat, salaries, light, everything involved in running a theatre) will remit 90 per cent of remaining monies to distributor. The 90/10 term is, however, usually reserved for powerful studios or very commercial films. Most conventional terms start at 60 per cent and scale down in subsequent weeks to 40 per cent or even 30 per cent. In most cases, if the box office receipts do not cover the house expenses in the first week, the distributor will be guaranteed 50 per cent of gross monies; however, the picture will usually not remain in the theatre!

PRINTS, TRAILERS, AND CLIPS

The logistics of theatrical distribution can be very expensive and time-consuming — which is why you need a distributor. To begin with, distributor will need 35 mm prints of your film. The distributor will order a certain number of prints from his or her lab. The release prints will be struck from the internegative supplied by the producer.

The distributor will also need 35 mm trailers, as well as TV ads and clips. It is the distributor's responsibility to create a trailer that will adequately promote the picture. A trailer is an assemblage of scenes from the film and should be as enticing as possible. It is arguably the most important tool to promote your film, since it reaches people who already go to the cinemas. The earlier the trailer gets on as many screens as possible, the better chance you have of building audience awareness. It is also important that the trailers be placed in front of the appropriate films. For example, a trailer for a subtitled film will not reach its audience if it is played before an action film aimed at teenagers. Since trailers have to be censored, it is important that the trailer receive a *general* rating to get onto as many screens as possible: an R-rated trailer cannot play before a PG-13 film. A general rating means the trailer can be screened by audiences of all ages.

There should be between three to five trailers ordered per release print. The trailers can start playing as early as six months before the opening and should remain on the screens in the same locale as the cinema that will be playing your film once the film has been released. In Canada and the United States, there are centralized services that handle the distribution of trailers to the theatres on behalf of distributors.

If your production uses electronic media for promotional purposes, you will need a short version of the trailer for TV advertising. Again the ad will need to be as enticing as possible. The clips are selected scenes edited to 30 to 60 seconds and transferred to ¾-inch tape to be supplied to television stations. By providing the same scene clips to all television shows that will review or talk about the film, you ensure a certain continuity in the marketing.

PRINTED MATERIALS

The printed materials include posters, ad slicks (artwork that will be used for newspaper advertising), press kits, photos, and transparencies (slides). Posters can be used sparingly (at theatre sites) or for what is called "wild posting," when posters are placed on construction sites, buildings, or any free space in the downtown area. Since this practice is not like buying advertising space, your posters may be covered by others a few hours after being posted. The ad slicks will reproduce the poster if it looks good in a small size. If not, something else will be created to be reproduced in the newspapers. Press kits should include a short (10 to 15 lines) and long synopsis (one to two full pages) of the film, a complete list of credits, biographies of principal cast and crew, as well as copies of any articles published during the production of the film. In addition to the press kit, a selection of black-and-white and colour photos as well as transparencies should be available for the press.

ADVERTISING

The distributor will use some or all of the following advertising media: newspapers, magazines, radio, television, subway stations, bus shelters, and outdoor advertising.

Newspapers are the major and essential media support used for films since audiences use their newspapers when choosing a movie to see. Again, the distributor will either advertise in all local papers or choose the appropriate ones. For examples, *The Toronto Sun* may not be the best vehicle for a three-hour, subtitled German film!

Magazines are seldom used, but although they are expensive, they can reach a large number of people. In this case the key is reaching the right target audience. For example Robert Altman's *Pret-à-porter* was advertised in ELLE *Quebec* magazine.

Radio is mostly used by the studios when the film has a very

popular sound track. Radio is, however, regularly used for promotion of a film, such as its premiere. The use of radio stations
will be discussed later in this chapter.

The most expensive but most effective way to advertise is
on television. Well-placed ads (that is, placed in the appropriate
time slot) can reach the largest number of people and, since
television is also a visual medium, they can have the biggest
impact. Of course the success of the ad placement will depend
on the effectiveness of the television ad.

Subway stations, bus shelters, and outdoor advertising are also
very expensive and only used for bigger-budget releases.

PROMOTING THE FILM

To attract people's attention in today's crowded market place,
strong publicity and imaginative and different promotions are
essential to the success of a film. Publicity is free and will be
obtained by having the media talk about the film. Promotions
can be free, but not necessarily, and are usually done in partnership with a third party (for example a radio station, newspaper, or beer company). The promotion efforts will start from
one to eight months before the release of the picture and are
only limited by the imagination and bank account of the distributor.

Usually, there will be a *premiere* (on the Tuesday or Wednesday
before the film's opening) organized with a radio station and a
newspaper. In return for free advertising, the distributor will
provide the station and paper (who then become co-presenters)
with free tickets for the premiere.

Arranging a tie-in between the opening of a film and a *special event* will inevitably attract additional publicity. For example, a film about family abuse can be shown at a charity gala to
benefit an organization for abused children. The distributor will
then work in concert with the organization, providing the film

free of charge in return for free publicity, and hopefully, good word of mouth. Free outdoor screenings have also become a popular event in the past few years. It is also possible to create an event. For example, for the release of *Shadow of the Wolf*, a film shot in the wild north, the distributor flew the press — along with the print, projectionist, and the necessary equipment for a screening, to northern Quebec, where there was a special screening for the Inuit community who played in the film. Although such events attract the media's attention, they in no way guarantee the success of a film.

A film may receive funds from a *sponsor*. The deals can vary from film to film, but basically, a sponsor (for example, a brewery) will provide some of the promotion budget in return for having its logo or trademark on the posters and trailers. Although this is more common in television, films too can benefit from sponsorship. The key is to approach the sponsor early, since corporate marketing commitments are usually planned months in advance.

The *promotional tools* that can be created are limitless: from T-shirts to buttons to baseball hats to place mats for restaurants. You should, however, be careful about your choice of gimmicks. Giving away T-shirts bearing a film's logo in the middle of winter may not be a very effective way to promote it! Besides the promotional items handed out at festivals, giveaways are primarily used as sales incentives for the video release.

MERCHANDISING

Merchandising is more specialized than simply creating giveaway items. It is done on a much larger scale by a third party specializing in producing items in a certain area such as music or books. In the case where the film lends itself to tie-ins, such as compact disks and cassettes of the soundtrack, the distributor will work with the music publisher to market the film more effectively. Some movies lend themselves to merchandising tie-ins, but unfortunately are usually very high-budget, wide-release films. It simply would not make sense to manufacture a toy resembling a film character if the movie is to be released only in Canada. Canadian films will more likely benefit from tie-ins with books and CDs.

FESTIVALS

Festivals in Canada and abroad often serve as a launching pad for a film. The Montreal, Toronto, and Vancouver Film Festivals are used to premiere Canadian films, and when these films are showcased in a high-profile section (such as competition in Montreal or a gala in Toronto), it is a good idea to release them immediately after the festival. In the case of festivals abroad, there are more factors to consider. Is the festival known in Canada? Did the film receive a major prize? At present, the only festival that can really support a release is the Cannes Film Festival, but there are sometimes exceptions to the rule. More details will be given regarding the festivals in the foreign sales section.

PUBLICITY

The publicist, either on contract or working in-house for the distributor, will try to obtain interviews for the director and cast with newspapers, magazines, and television and radio talk shows. The press will see the film before committing to do interviews, and of course it helps if they like the film and will give it a good review.

All this is free (apart from a few lunches), and it should be exploited to the maximum since it is the only way the public will get to know the filmmakers if they are previously unknown. Obviously, however, if the director or cast are already known to the public, it will be much easier to get journalists' attention.

It is also important to work with a publicist who has clout with the press, since there is so much competition. Several films are released every week and you have to compete with them for the available airtime and for space for articles. The publicity process can be repeated with the local press in each major city if the picture does not receive a pan-Canadian release.

A Brief Overview of Other Media

HOME VIDEO

The home video market has, in the past ten years, emerged as the most lucrative part of the distribution business. It has grown and matured (and will likely be replaced eventually by new media such as CD-ROM and pay-per-view). Home video has also become more sophisticated. A few years ago, distributors could release any action title with a good advertising campaign and be assured a certain revenue. Nowadays, consumers look for known values and higher quality. Of course, certain genres will still work better on video (kickboxing, gore, action), but in general, films that are a success on video were also a success theatrically.

The distributor will release the film for rental on video approximately six months after its theatrical release (or earlier, if the film was a flop). He or she will choose a street date for the picture's availability to the wholesaler, who in turn will sell the cassettes to retailers. A cut-off date will also be set, by which time the orders should all be made. This procedure will ensure that the distributor does not duplicate or stock more copies than will be actually be required. Additional orders may be placed after the cut-off date, but 80 to 90 per cent of all orders are received within a month of the availability date.

In the past few years, rental sales have gone down and the

"sell-through" market has emerged. Cassette are sold directly to consumers at a price that is usually under $20. Children's videos are the most popular sell-through product followed by theatrical box office hits and classics. How-to's and exercise tapes are also extremely popular. The cassettes are sold directly to the major chains (Kmarts, music stores, pharmacies, toy stores, Price Club, and so on). The key to a successful sell-through release is placement. Space in stores is limited and certain companies own the racks on which the cassettes are placed. The distributor will often have to go through those "rack-jobbers" to obtain good placement. Cross-promotions are also a very important part of the sell-through process. For example, a kids' video dealing with trucks could be sold with a toy truck.

The market is becoming so fragmented that a good distributor should also look for other ways to increase sales such as direct mail or direct response. Premium sales are also becoming more popular. Companies such as Avon, Petro Canada, or McDonalds will buy a large number of cassettes for "bounce-back offers" (buy one of our products and obtain a cassette for $5). Again, the product has to lend itself to such sales.

PAY-PER-VIEW

The pay-per-view window begins from 30 to 90 days after the video release date. There are currently two main pay-per-view services in Canada, but it is hard to predict how many will be operating five to ten years from now. Consumers with the right software at home call in to order a movie and are charged directly on their monthly cable bill. Under current regulations, the Canadian services will play at least one Canadian film per month and remit 66 per cent of the revenues to the seller. In the case of non-Canadian titles, the revenues are split between the cable company, the pay-per-view service, and the seller.

PAY TELEVISION AND CABLE

Pay television remains the primary market for theatrical feature films on television. The "pay window" begins 12 months after the initial release or 6 months after video. For Canadian films, the prices can vary, but there is still a premium paid for "Canadian content," since the services have to obtain a certain quota to maintain their licence. The distributor will negotiate a price per subscriber or a flat license fee. Prior to 1995, there were only three movie channels in Canada: The Movie Network in English Eastern Canada, Superchannel in Western Canada, and the French-language Premier Choix. Last year the Canadian Radio-television and Telecommunications Commission (CRTC) issued ten new licences, including Showcase, Moviepix, and Bravo. Although they are not exclusively movie channels, the emergence of those new channels will allow for more exposure for Canadian films on television, but it is too early to evaluate the impact the new channels will have.

NETWORK TELEVISION

The network television window starts 15 months after the beginning of the pay-TV window and is still potentially the most lucrative of all forms of television exhibition, since it can reach the largest number of viewers. In recent years, however, network television has moved away from purchasing theatrical feature films in favour of made-for-television movies and other types of shows. You should therefore not count on a network sale unless you or the distributor can get a commitment while the film is in production. While networks normally have a certain price range for feature films and currently pay a premium for Canadian content, it is still up to the distributor to negotiate the best possible price.

SYNDICATED TELEVISION

If your film is not sold to a network, then the syndication sale follows the pay-TV window. However, if the film *is* sold to a network, the syndication sale will follow its network window, which can be as long as five years. In recent years, the syndicated market has become smaller as the smaller independent stations merge into bigger broadcast groups. (For more about syndicated television, see Chapter 6.)

THE NON-THEATRICAL MARKET

The non-theatrical market window can occur at any time after the initial theatrical release, since it will not usually interfere with the commercial exploitation of the picture. It includes, to name only a few, airlines, schools, institutions, military organizations, ships, and government organizations. Rentals of 16 mm films have been almost completely replaced by rental of videocassettes in these markets. The potential for lucrative revenues in the non-theatrical market place can be quite high for certain types of films (for example, films that are based on a book that is required reading in schools), but in general a producer should not count on much.

FINDING DISTRIBUTION IN THE UNITED STATES

The number of Canadian films that obtain theatrical distribution in the United States is very limited. Here are the possible deals to look for:
- with an independent distributor;
- with a major;
- with a broadcaster;
- with a syndicator (or TV distributor); or
- with a video distributor.

The deal you will be able to get depends on the type of film you are selling. An "art film" will most likely be bought by an independent, while a video-driven title will have more chance of being purchased by a major for direct-to-video distribution.

Very *few* Canadian films receive theatrical distribution in the United States. In 1994, only three received very limited release (*Zero Patience, The Boys of St. Vincent,* and *Calendar*). A somewhat offbeat or art house film is more likely to receive interest from a theatrical distributor than a mainstream title. There have been years when more than three films were released in the United States, but there are no major successes to recall. Other examples of films that have been or will be released in the United States are *Love and Human Remains, Exotica, I Love a Man in Uniform, 32 Short Films About Glenn Gould, Shadow of the Wolf, Bethune, Highlander III, Highway 61,* and *Double Happiness.*

Exposure and success in important festivals and good critical reviews are the major factors that can help to sell a film in the United States. Major Canadian distributors will have existing relationships with independent U.S. distributors and can help negotiate the contract. Prices can vary from no advance to millions of dollars and are very hard to estimate without reference to a production.

SUMMARY

The most important thing to remember is that, despite everyone's efforts, your picture will most likely not make any money theatrically! A theatrical release will, however, in most cases enhance the value of the ancillary rights and, if the film is at least a critical success, will put the director and/or actors in a better bargaining position for their next picture.

Foreign Sales

The description of the Canadian theatrical marketplace —

dominated by American films with a dearth of available screens for independent product — would also fit almost any other country in the world. You can imagine, then, how hard it is to obtain theatrical releases for Canadian films abroad. The majority of Canadian films, even though they are released theatrically in Canada, will be sold directly to video distributors or television broadcasters around the world. However, there are now a few Canadian directors, such as Atom Egoyan and Denys Arcand, whose work is recognized by international distributors. In order to increase the number of favoured directors and films, Canadian films need to be exported and promoted with the same expertise required for domestic distribution.

Since we have already covered the basic principles of choosing a distributor, negotiating contracts, and the process of theatrical distribution, I will not elaborate on the same points, but rather point out the differences and add the new variables that come into play in the international market place.

WHAT YOUR DISTRIBUTOR CAN DO FOR YOU

As with Canadian distribution, getting a commitment from a distributor at script stage is important, since he or she can and should help with some or all of the following points:

- casting actors who are recognizable internationally and who will attract foreign distributors' interest;
- ensuring that all necessary materials needed for the campaign will be created;
- sending scripts to specific distributors to create awareness of and interest in the picture;
- placing ads in the appropriate trades to announce the film;
- approaching the major festivals, if appropriate.

Once the film is completed, the distributor should be:

- planning the marketing strategy regarding the festivals and markets;

- creating a new campaign if the Canadian one is inappropriate for the foreign market;
- advising foreign distributors that the picture is completed and negotiating the best possible deal in each territory.

CHOOSING A DISTRIBUTOR

While the foreign sales agent can be different from the Canadian distributor, it is often advantageous to use a distributor who can offer both Canadian and international distribution. It will certainly be more cost-efficient, since promotional material can be used by both departments, and because the Canadian festivals often have an impact on foreign sales, the decision about attendance should be made jointly. In Canada, there are very few foreign sales agent who export theatrical films. You can look abroad for a foreign sales agent, but there are some restrictions if your film was financed with the assistance of the Canadian funding agencies. You also then lose the financial help provided by these agencies for the marketing of your film.

Here are some other important points to consider:

- What types of films does the seller represent? In general, the seller will have contacts and relationships with international distributors who acquire the same types of films (for example, action genre) he or she represents.
- Does the seller attend all the important theatrical markets (briefly described later in this chapter)?
- Does the seller have the financial capabilities to market your film adequately? Attending the different international markets is very costly.

Of course the other criteria mentioned in the domestic section apply to choosing an international sales agent as well.

THE CONTRACT

The contract to be drawn between the producer and the

international distributor will basically be the same as for the domestic distribution contract except for:

- the territory, which will be defined as "The World" followed by territories that may be excluded from the deal (for example, the co-producing country in the case of a co-production).
- the distribution fee, which is usually a commission of 15 per cent to 30 per cent to the distributor (depending on the size of the advance);
- the definition of deductible expenses, since the expenses for international distribution differ slightly from domestic — there are other costs involved, such as travel, entertaining, and the cost of shipping cassettes and prints across the world.

THE MARKETS AND FESTIVALS

If your picture is selected for one of the major Canadian festivals and you think you should handle the sales on your own, you may want to reconsider after you've read this section, which covers the most important factors to consider when planning the international "release" of the picture.

Throughout the year, there are numerous international markets and festivals. If you chose to, you could be going from festival to festival all year long. However, there are only a few important ones, and they are also the venues that a distributor should be attending. Accepting invitations to small festivals without consulting someone who is knowledgeable may ruin your film's career, since the major festivals require some kind of exclusivity. You may find yourself disqualified from a major event for having attended a festival in a quaint little town in Normandy.

For a theatrical picture, the most important decision to make is when and where to premiere the film. Your distributor should be familiar with the strengths and weaknesses of the different venues and will be able to assist you in making that decision. For example, if your film is finished in July, is it wise to wait for the Cannes Film Festival the following May to premiere it? Do you want to take the chance of not being selected? Although it sounds very prestigious to be selected in Venice or Berlin, would this be the best choice for your film? Here are some questions to ask when making this decision:

- Will the film be completed in time to qualify for this festival?
- Does the film stand a chance of being selected for this festival?
- Does the film stand a chance of being honoured at this festival?
- What other films will be in competition?
- What are the costs involved in attending this festival?
- Is the festival well attended by the right distributors?
- What are the other options?

While opinions may differ on each festival, the advantages and disadvantages listed below are the ones that are generally accepted by the industry. *Markets* are generally attended strictly by buyers and sellers, and some producers, and are not open to the general public. Most *festivals* have a market component, but are also attended by filmmakers, press, and the general public.

MONTREAL INTERNATIONAL FILM FESTIVAL

When: Last week of August to Labour Day.
Market: Yes, principally attended by television buyers, producers, and sellers with films available for Canada.
Advantages: Competitive festival attended by international press; great launching pad for French-Canadian titles; relatively inexpensive place to promote a film well.
Disadvantages: If selected for the Panorama Canada section, your film is likely to go unnoticed, since the focus is on the compe-

tition, yet your film will now be disqualified from other major film festivals.

Venice International Film Festival

When: Early September.

Market: Yes, mostly attended by European sellers and buyers.

Advantages: Very prestigious competition — with the right "buzz," a film can be discovered here.

Disadvantages: Selection is usually very highbrow and not necessarily viewed as having commercial potential; very expensive to attend in order to obtain the necessary amount of publicity to get your film noticed; prizes won don't necessarily mean box office for North America; if your film is not noticed, it will be disqualified from other major film festivals.

Toronto International Film Festival

When: Second week of September.

Market: Not officially, but a very efficient informal meeting place.

Advantages: Non-competitive, so films in sections other than the Galas are noticed as well; relatively inexpensive place to promote a film well; great launching pad for films made in Toronto; well attended by all the American distributors.

Disadvantages: May harm the release of a film if not done immediately after the festival; if the film has been reviewed during the festival, it may be ignored when it's released; the film may get lost in the shuffle.

Mifed (Milan)

When: Last week of October.

Market: Yes, attended by all American and European sellers.

Advantages: Well attended by major buyers; efficient because offices and screening rooms are located in the same building;

since it is mostly a video-driven market, your picture may stand out as the only film with theatrical potential.
Disadvantages: Expensive to attend; geared towards video-driven product; bad screening facilities.

SUNDANCE (PARK CITY, UTAH)

When: Late January.
Market: Not officially, very relaxed business atmosphere.
Advantages: One of the best places to sell your film to the United States.
Disadvantages: Competition is reserved for American Independent Films so your film will be shown in a sidebar, which will get less attention.

BERLIN FILM FESTIVAL

When: Mid-February.
Market: Yes, although quite small, and easy to "work"; well attended by "specialty film distributors."
Advantages: Great venue to find a German distributor; very prestigious.
Disadvantages: Prizes won don't necessarily translate into box office for North America; if your film is not noticed, it will be disqualified from other major film festivals; takes place right before the AFM.

AMERICAN FILM MARKET (AFM) — LOS ANGELES

When: End of February.
Market: Very well attended by Latin American and Asian buyers.
Advantages: Very efficient and business oriented; relatively cheap to attend; great screening facilities; well attended by major buyers.
Disadvantages: Buyers will go from screening to screening and not necessarily screen the entire film; not a great market for non-English language pictures.

Cannes Film Festival

When: Mid-May.

Market: Yes, it runs parallel to the festival.

Advantages: Most prestigious of all festivals if your film is in selection; well covered by the international press; prizes won here have repercussions internationally; well attended by all major players in the industry.

Disadvantages: Extremely expensive to attend (travel, offices, and promotion); very large and crowded so it's easy to go unnoticed; if your film "bombs" in Cannes, it is *dead*.

The events listed above are the major ones geared towards theatrical and video features. There are also several television markets and festivals, which are covered in Chapter 6.

THE MATERIALS

For international distribution, in addition to the materials listed in the domestic release section, you will need to provide the following:

- *A PAL master.* The world video standards are PAL, NTSC and SECAM. SECAM is seldom used nowadays, so a PAL master is sufficient to service clients with screening cassettes or submasters. All European territories use PAL and so do most of the Asian countries.
- *Separate music and effects tracks.* Since the film will need to be dubbed in several languages, it is very important to have a complete and high-quality M & E track.
- *Promo reel.* This is a longer version of the trailer, and since it is geared at a buyer and not a consumer, it should reveal more of the film than a trailer does).

PRINTED MATERIALS

In addition to the press kits, flyers are usually created to facilitate selling the film. The flyer is usually a one-sheet with visuals (usually the campaign) and a short synopsis and cast and crew list on the reverse side. It can, of course, vary in its format and quality, depending on the budget. A textless transparency of the campaign should also be created so that foreign distributors can overlay the title and credits in their own language.

ADVERTISING, PROMOTION, AND PUBLICITY

Advertising for the international market is quite different from that for the domestic release. Ads should be taken in the industry trades (*Variety*, *Hollywood Reporter*, *Screen International*, and so on) and placed when the distributor will be selling the film actively at markets and festivals. Festival and market guides are another alternative for advertising, as are dailies published by the trades during the markets and festivals.

Whereas T-shirts, pins, hats, or buttons may not be the greatest *promotional* tools for the domestic release of a film, they are in great supply at festivals. In order to be noticed, they would have to be quite original, and worn by the right people. Cocktail parties to introduce a director or actor are also quite popular at festivals. Again, there are no limits to the stunts used by distributors in order to get their film noticed (such as an inflatable Arnold Schwarzenegger floating in water off Cannes!), only budget constraints.

The *publicity* for a film should begin while the film is in production to create awareness of it. The trades are once again the ideal medium, since they are read by all the potential buyers. When the film is actually presented at a major festival such as Cannes, Toronto, or Sundance, a good publicist is essential in order to obtain press coverage and to make sure the press screens your picture. A good review and coverage will definitely help sales.

THE DEAL

Sales are initiated and, ideally, concluded at the markets and festivals. A seller should be closing sales all year long, of course, but most sales and follow-ups are done at markets. For a theatrical film, the distributor will want to buy all rights, but it is sometimes possible to withhold television rights, which can be sold separately to a broadcaster. The seller should have relationships with distributors in each territory and be able to attract the right buyers to the screenings. However, in certain territories, it is not uncommon to go through a middleperson. Some films can be pre-sold, but it seldom happens for Canadian pictures since there are no elements — such as name directors and stars — that can help guarantee box office.

It is the seller's job to obtain the best possible deal for the picture in each territory. This doesn't necessarily mean the best advance, but rather the best *combination* of advance, distributor knowledge and reputation, and the back-end deal (the percentages given to producer and seller for theatrical, video, and television distribution).

The main deal terms will be negotiated and then it is the seller's job to provide a contract and follow up for payments, release dates, and reports. The deal terms outlined for the domestic release apply for the international market. However, since in certain countries, it will be very difficult to obtain overages (for example, in Bulgaria and India) it is wise to obtain a larger advance and do an outright deal with no back-end. Your seller will also become indispensable here because there are so many different laws regulating taxes, censorship, and imports in all the different territories that a producer will lose money and time if he or she wants to handle the sales.

SUMMARY

Remember that you should not be too discouraged if your

picture cannot be sold and released theatrically around the world. In order to achieve the best results (international recognition and revenues), it is imperative to choose a distributor who really wants to sell your film. It is hard to get a film noticed, but very easy to "kill a picture" if the marketing is not handled properly. Closing sales at the right time is vital, as is grabbing foreign distributors' interest when it's there. Films, unlike wine, do not get better with age; they're more like ice . . . they melt.

In closing, let me remind you that a relationship with a distributor should be based on trust and co-operation. Both of you should want what is best for the film and do your jobs accordingly. That way, you are ensuring your picture will be distributed in the best possible way and that, in turn, should make it easier for you to produce your next film.

8

Co-production

by W. Paterson Ferns

*P*at *Ferns is one of the pioneers of independent production in Canada, of co-production between Canada and Europe, and of Canadian productions on U.S. televison. He co-produced the first Canadian mini-series on U.S. network television as well as Canada's first movie and first mini-series on Masterpiece Theatre. Ferns was President of the Banff Television Festival during its rise to international prominence and is currently Executive Director of its Board of International Advisors. His celebrated Market Simulation is presented annually at Banff and has now been "exported" to the United States (NATPE), Europe (MIPCOM), and other venues. He is President of pat ferns productions limited in Toronto. Ferns is married with three children and lives on Air Canada.*

The Pros and Cons of Co-production

Co-production is a dirty word. Co-production is the future. Co-production is probably both and neither. According to its detractors, co-production means compromise, and compromise in creative matters is often a threat to quality. Its proponents argue that quality often costs money, and, with the fragmentation of audiences in television, the only way to sustain reasonable budgets is through co-operation, one reasonable form of co-operation being co-production. Since co-production can mean many things, it can be a confusing area to explore. But it is important to understand both the opportunity it offers and the real challenges it presents; to see its potential light *and* to recognize its dark side.

Canadians have become experts in co-production. We have had to, given the nature of our country and its proximity to the United States. Canada has the longest undefended border in the world, but one that technology (and free trade) is now rendering irrelevant. The microchip, the computer, the satellite, and optical fibre have created a digital revolution that has transformed communications. Canada was one of the first countries to experience this particular television revolution, and now Europe is having to deal with "open skies," the problems of border protection, and the predominance of one form of programming — American — over all others. In this sense, Canada is the future. English has become not only the language of international trade, but also, increasingly, of television programming; and the cheapest and most pervasive source of content to fill the new technologies of delivery comes from the United States. The key to the future of many countries is the existence of a political will to survive culturally, and in this co-production has a part to play.

Communications networks rapidly lead to trade in culture, and trade in culture raises basic fears about national sovereignty. Canadians have traditionally been skilled in trade, and in creating communications networks, but we have been less skilled in protecting the content of the trade along our communications networks. Frequently, *resources* have ended up being exported rather than manufactured goods with a Canadian imprint. At the same time, our domestic market has been dominated by imported manufactured goods that shaped our expectations and our tastes. In both film and television, we have exported our talent and imported American programming. For those in the cultural industries, the future has always been precarious. We have had to guard against being hewers of wood and drawers of water to ensure that we shaped our own destiny. Part of creating an alternative has been the development of co-production agreements with other countries.

The story that always gets a laugh at international conferences on co-production is to describe Canada itself as a co-production: either a collaboration of two founding peoples or a multi-part collaboration of many nationalities. Of course, the Fathers of Confederation could have structured an "ideal" co-production favouring American technology, British government, and French culture. Instead, we ended up with British technology, French government, and American culture. The point that strikes home in every country is the reference to American culture, for the United States has produced the most energetic and inadvertently expansionist popular culture the world has ever known: Coca Cola, Elvis Presley, McDonald's, Disneyland, Star Wars, and so on. But we should not find this depressing. Instead, we should remember that the appeal of American entertainment programming resides in its authenticity as an expression of an intact national culture. The challenge we face is how to compete with that culture and, in doing so, how to preserve our own.

Living next to this successful cultural giant, Canada has had to wrestle with problems of identity and industrial development more intensely than other countries have had to do. Some of the solutions we have come up with — including co-production — have become models on which the world can draw. The invasion of television signals from across our southern border and the dominance of our theatrical feature film distribution system by American interests (who view Canada as part of their *domestic* market) have made it difficult for us to tell our own stories and showcase our own talent. This predicament is now complicated by rapid technological change, which is further fragmenting the audience and making it difficult to compete with giant foreign corporations to reach more discriminating audiences.

Until the mid-1970s, the response of much Canadian talent was simply to head south to Hollywood. To stem this tide and to preserve a sense of a distinct culture, Canadians had to rely, on the one hand, upon protection and quotas for Canadian content and, on the other hand, subsidies, incentives, and tax breaks to enable an indigenous industry to grow. Compounding the problem was the fact that our small market could not sustain high-quality production entirely funded at home. So Canadian producers had to pack their bags and roam the international marketplace to find funding for those projects that would not be fully funded by domestic "public service" institutions such as the CBC and the National Film Board.

To bring some bargaining chips to the international table, Canadian producers had to demonstrate that there were instruments in Canada that would bring benefits to collaborative ventures. Among these instruments were co-venturing arrangements, co-production treaties, and twinning. Instead of exporting talent, Canadians decided to explore the virtue of being ourselves, telling our own stories. It is surprising to think that some of the strongest indigenous programs of the past two decades have in fact been co-productions. *Anne of Green Gables* involved partners in both the United States and Germany. *Glory Enough for All* was a British/Canadian co-production. *Heaven on Earth* was the first television twin, again involving British support. It was Canada's first appearance on *"Masterpiece Theatre."*

Before going further, it is important to understand some

principles of collaboration. Film and television are collaborative arts and co-production must be an extension of this collaboration. The producer's role is to harmonize different visions and different talents, to find different solutions to the constraints that are imposed. If it seems that compromise in co-production is inevitable, a good producer can minimize these dilutions of an original vision. A good co-production can preserve what is authentic.

The Regulatory Institutions

In this chapter, we are talking about productions that involve more than one producer. And we are talking about the agencies that regulate what qualifies as Canadian content, because that is vitally important to end users, especially broadcasters. The three key institutions we will describe are Telefilm Canada, the Canadian Audio-Visual Certification Office (CAVCO), and the Canadian Radio-television and Telecommunications Commission (CRTC). Telefilm Canada is a Crown corporation that provides various kinds of support to the independent production industry, which indirectly benefits both public and private broadcasters. CAVCO was created as part of a program of the Department of Canadian Heritage to encourage private investment as a contributor to the growth of a mature Canadian production industry. The primary role of the CRTC is to regulate broadcasting in Canada. All three institutions have an interest in co-production.

The official rationale for co-production is to enable Canadian producers and their foreign counterparts to pool their creative, artistic, technical, and financial resources in order to co-produce films and television programs that are considered national productions in each of the countries involved. As such, they may benefit from legislation and government assistance (direct grants and tax incentives) in both or all of the countries involved.

However, the financial assistance offered by each country is given specifically to the producer from that same country so that the relevant domestic agency is able to monitor the domestic benefits available to a co-production through the domestic producer.

TELEFILM CANADA'S ROLE

Telefilm Canada has a major role in co-production and this role is twofold. Its Co-productions Department is responsible for the certification of projects, working closely with CAVCO to ensure that all the relevant criteria are met. Telefilm Canada may also participate in co-productions through its Production and Development Department. The benefits that would be available from this department through its investments must be applied for and evaluated for a co-production just as they would be for a domestic application. In these cases, the percentage share that Telefilm Canada might contribute to a co-production would be a percentage of the Canadian share of the co-production rather than of the production as a whole. For example, in a Canadian production Telefilm might invest 30 per cent of the total budget; if that same production were a 50/50 co-production, the 30 per cent Telefilm contribution would be on 50 per cent of the budget (or 100 per cent of the Canadian side) and thus represent 15 per cent of the total budget.

In those co-productions in which Canada has a majority position, Telefilm Canada maintains its regular decision-making policies about how the production will meet its objectives regarding Canadian audiences, quality, originality, diversity, and so on. In minority Canadian co-productions, Telefilm Canada concentrates more on the benefits of reciprocity vis-à-vis each country, in the interest of maintaining stable relationships between Canadian and non-Canadian producers. Thus, if a minority Canadian co-production were targeted for a non-

Canadian partner's national audience, Telefilm Canada might still invest, if it felt that significant benefits would accrue to the Canadian production industry. Overall, Telefilm Canada attempts to maintain some reasonable balance in its international relations, so that Canadians participate both on a majority and a minority basis in foreign co-productions.

OFFICIAL TREATY CO-PRODUCTIONS

This brings us to the area of Official Treaty Co-productions. At the time of writing, Canada has film and television co-production agreements with Algeria, Argentina, Australia, Belgium, Bosnia-Herzegovina, China, the Commonwealth of Independent States, Croatia, the Czech Republic, France, Germany, Hong Kong, Hungary, Ireland, Israel, Italy, Mexico, Morocco, the Netherlands, New Zealand, Romania, Slovakia, Slovenia, Switzerland, and the United Kingdom — and there is also a film-only treaty with Spain. (Details on the existing Official Co-production Treaties are available on request from Telefilm Canada). Additionally, Canada has signed "mini-treaties" with France to encourage modest financial support for France/Canada co-production that might not otherwise meet the criteria of the Official Treaty. The purpose of the mini-treaties is to promote French-language production and to provide special financial assistance for qualifying cinema, television, and animation projects.

The Official Co-production Treaties tend to be somewhat more flexible than the points system (which will be described later in this chapter) that applies to domestic Canadian content production. However, the Treaties do try to balance creative, artistic, and technical contributions from each country. Ideally, these contributions should be in a proportion comparable to the financial participation of each co-producer. However, there are certain minimum requirements specified in each agreement that must be met. In many cases, the minority co-producer must bring at least 15 per cent of the money to the table and in some cases this minimum is as high as 30 per cent. Further, minority co-producers must spend at least these minimums on elements in their respective country or with their respective nationals. In addition to financial participation, there needs to be a sharing of markets and revenues so that equitable distribution arrangements and profit sharing are achieved.

The Official Treaties also provide the advantage of easy access for foreign creative, artistic, and technical personnel — and the temporary importation of their equipment. Without Treaty approval, work permits and carnets for equipment can take much time and effort. In order to reflect a balance, there is an expectation that when most of the shooting of a production takes place in one country, the post-production will be in the other country, or, if there is shooting in a third country, then the post-production will take place in the majority co-producer's territory. Again, the Official Treaties are reasonably flexible and reasonable, as long as the co-producers reflect the balances that are indicated by the financing structure. Shooting in third countries is not encouraged, but there may be compelling cases for it if the story takes place in a very particular geographic area. However, the purpose of the Official Treaties is *not* to promote shooting in third countries' studios, given that there are sound stages in Canada or in the co-producer's territory that could serve as well.

Animation always seems to require special arrangements and, in the case of Official Treaty Co-productions, all creative activities must be carried out in the two participating countries, although subcontracting to facilities in third countries of certain non-creative technical production is permitted, as long as this does not exceed 25 per cent of the total production costs.

Star performers also require special arrangements and the

use of a third-country performer is generally limited to one role in an Official Co-production. However, in Europe, there is a free flow of labour, and thus there can be considerable flexibility in the use of stars. The treaties do allow for "multipartite co-productions," which involve producers from more than two signatory countries. However, each country must meet the requirements of minimal participation set out in its respective Treaty.

TWINNING

There is an additional instrument permitted under the Official Treaties, which has been used on a limited basis. This is known as *twinning*. This involves the creation of a "production package" consisting of two productions of broadly comparable length and budget. The regulatory authorities look at the overall expenditure and use of talent for the package as a whole rather than on an individual production-by-production basis. Hence, for example, an essentially Canadian production and an essentially German production of identical budget could be packaged together, as long as the package achieves 50 per cent expenditure on Canadian elements and the same producers are involved in both productions. Thus, each of the projects may be able to keep its national character from a creative and technical point of view, but enjoy benefits in both countries.

The key requirements in twinning are that the same producers must be involved in both works; that there must be an overall balance in the cross-over investments (the German investment in the Canadian production and the Canadian investment in the German production), and that these must represent at least 20 per cent of the total production budget; that revenues must be shared on an equal basis; that each producer has ownership of marketing rights in his or her own country for *both* productions in the twinning package; and that both productions must be in the same program category and of similar duration. In the case of television productions, the same broadcaster must broadcast both productions in each country, and, while twinned projects may be produced consecutively, recognition is not given to the package until *both* productions have been completed. It is also required that the time between the completion of one production and the start of the other does not exceed one year.

WHERE DO YOU APPLY?

While applications for co-ventures (and non-Treaty twins) must be made to the CRTC, applications for Official Treaty Co-productions (and Treaty twins) must be made to Telefilm Canada. These applications must be made before the commencement of principal photography or key animation. Both co-producers must submit an application to the appropriate authorities in their respective countries. If a Canadian producer is also seeking other benefits, such as capital cost allowance or investment tax credit, an application must be made to the Canadian Audio-Visual Certification Office which recognizes the Official Treaties as administered by Telefilm Canada. If a producer's sole aim is to achieve Canadian content for broadcast purposes, then the application is to the CRTC. Its interests in Canadian content are confined to television.

For Canadian producers to have credibility in seeking partners, they need to bring to the international bargaining table money and/or benefits. The key benefit on the Canadian side of the equation is to be able to guarantee to domestic broadcasters that the production qualifies as Canadian content. In television, Canadian broadcasters will pay a premium for Canadian programming, because a certain level of Canadian content is required either by mandate or by regulation. If one meets these criteria of qualification, a production may also be eligible for federal or provincial funding benefits from such institutions as Telefilm Canada, the Ontario Film Development Corporation, BC Film, and so on. Additionally, there are various film investment programs, tax benefits, capital cost allowances, refundable tax credits, and so on, that are available to qualifying Canadian productions. This is our "currency" in international trading. So how do these benefits work — or more particularly, how does one qualify for them?

The CRTC's Role

WHERE DO YOU APPLY?

In television, the qualification for Canadian content status is granted by the Canadian Radio-television and Telecommunications Commission. Their Public Notice (dated April 15, 1984) for Recognition of Canadian Programs, sets forth the basic criteria that define what constitutes a Canadian program. The CRTC will provide a "C number" or an "SR number" (Special Recognition number) to those productions that qualify according to the terms of the Public Notice. There is essentially no difference between the two, although a "10-point" production could earn the broadcaster additional benefits. The CRTC also acknowledges that there are other ways to qualify, including the meeting of the criteria set down by the Canadian Audio-Visual Certification Office. The role of CAVCO is vital if you wish to access many of the tax benefits available federally, and, in some cases, meeting the CAVCO criteria is also required for acceptance by provincial agencies. The third method of qualification is provided by Telefilm Canada on behalf of the Government of Canada through the administration of Canada's Official Co-production Treaties. What are the key requirements in each of these methods of qualifying for Canadian content status?

HOW DO YOU QUALIFY?

All three organizations define a Canadian program as being one that is produced by a Canadian production company — and the role of the producer is vitally important. He or she must be the central decision maker. This role is subject to close scrutiny as the system has occasionally been abused by so-called "service productions." In these cases, a Canadian production manager may take the producer credit, though he or she has not really been in charge of the production, but is simply a "front" for (usually) an American production company.

In addition to having a Canadian producer, both the CRTC and CAVCO require that a production has to earn a minimum of six "points" based on key creative functions that must be performed by Canadians. By function, these points are awarded as follows: director (2 points), writer (2 points), leading performer (1 point), second leading performer (1 point), head of the art department (1 point), director of photography (1 point), music composer (1 point), and editor (1 point). The regulations also require that either the director *or* writer and at least one of the two leading performers *must* be Canadian. However, exemption is possible for a production in which both the writer and the director are non-Canadian or in which both leading performers are non-Canadian, *if* all the other key creative functions are filled by Canadians.

After the appropriate point qualification is met, there is also a formula covering expenditure, which requires that 75 per cent of total remuneration paid to individuals *other* than the producer and the key creative personnel as listed in the point categories must be spent on services provided by Canadians. Further, at least 75 per cent of processing and final preparation costs must be paid for services provided in Canada. If a film or television program meets all these criteria and is certified by the Canadian Audio-Visual Certification Office, it is then eligible for all the benefits available to the Canadian production industry. Whether or not the benefits will be received depends upon whether they are automatic or discretionary. For example, capital cost allowance, or tax credits, if one qualifies, are automatically available, whereas an investment by Telefilm Canada will depend upon their discretionary decision.

CO-VENTURES

What is the availability of Canadian content status for productions involving more than one producer and in which one or more producers is non-Canadian? The CRTC regulations make a distinction between *co-ventures* and *co-productions*. Co-ventures are described as international collaborations that are not included under the Official Treaties administered by Telefilm Canada. This includes ventures with a foreign country that does not have a film or television treaty with Canada, as well as ventures with co-producers in a "treaty country" when these ventures step outside the provisions of the Treaty. The key function in a co-venture is again that of the producer.

By way of example, one could co-venture, but not co-produce, with an American producer because Canada has no co-production treaty with the United States. Similarly, one could co-venture with a British or French partner if the greater flexibility (in some areas) of the co-venture arrangements is more appropriate to the project than to operate under the requirements of the Official Treaty. However, the Canadian producer is required by the CRTC's regulations to have no less than an equal measure of decision-making responsibility with his co-venture producer on all creative matters and must be responsible for the administration of not less than the Canadian element of the production budget. There are legal definitions of what is a Canadian production company.

The co-venture agreement between the Canadian company and its foreign partner must be filed with the CRTC, although these agreements are kept in confidence. Among the requirements to ensure that there is genuine collaboration is that the Canadian production company must have sole or co-signing authority on the production bank account. For co-ventures shot in Canada, the production bank account must be in Canada. For those shot partially in Canada, a Canadian bank account would be required for the portion of the production shot in Canada. And in the case of co-ventures shot entirely outside Canada, there must be a Canadian bank account for payment of the Canadian elements of the program. The Canadian production company has to have an equity position in the production and an entitlement to profit sharing. It must be at financial risk or have budgetary responsibility, and, for greater certainty, the CRTC's Public Notice spells out that the Canadian producer must have no less than an equal measure of approval over all elements of the production, regardless of the number of foreign persons fulfilling the functions of executive producer or producer. Thus, a production with four American executive producers and one Canadian producer in which a committee of five made decisions by majority vote would not meet the requirements of a Canadian co-venture. In essence, co-ventures with the United States must meet the same criteria as a wholly Canadian production, with the exception that there can be a sharing of producer responsibilities subject to the criteria listed above.

In the case of co-ventures involving a country with an Official Treaty with Canada and in which the co-producer is from a Commonwealth or Francophone country, it is possible to achieve Canadian content status from the CRTC through a Special Recognition number if the production attains five points; if at least 50 per cent of the total remuneration paid to individuals (other than the producer and the key creative personnel) is paid to Canadians; and if 50 per cent of post-production work is paid for services provided by Canadians.

This is a useful additional flexibility where a project will not qualify as a wholly Canadian production and does not want or have the ability to go through all the requirements of the Official Treaty in order to acquire access to certain Canadian benefits.

BENEFITS FOR FOREIGN PARTNERS
Thus far, we have concentrated on the Canadian benefits in a collaborative venture. We should remember that in a co-venture, and more particularly in an official co-production, there may be benefits to which the foreign partner has access that increase his or her ability to bring funds to the table. For example, if capital cost allowance financing is available in the Republic of Ireland, by using the Official Canada/Eire Co-production Treaty, one could have a production that enjoys Canadian content recognition and access to significant Canadian benefits as well as Irish, and hence, European content recognition and the benefits of an Irish tax shelter.

In co-production, the meeting of technical and administrative criteria is one thing. Achieving creative collaboration is another. In order to understand the tensions and difficulties in making co-production the best of all possible marriages, it is important to understand some history. In doing so, it is instructive to look at the difference between cinema and television.

A Little Background — Cinema vs. Television

Cinema was, from the outset, an international medium, as opposed to television, which was essentially national — news, weather, and sports. Now changing technologies have prompted concern about the internationalization of television.

Hollywood is the capital of world cinema. From its early days, it placed no restrictions on the nationality of filmmakers. Before the days of sound, there were no problems of language. But even with the advent of the talkies, there was no reluctance to use talent from around the world. Hollywood simply engaged the best. Cinema was a private-sector venture and its financing came from the box office. This led to the production of films that had universal themes and could be promoted by stars identifiable to the general public. Films popularized American myths and values and influenced filmmaking around the world. Some have said that U.S. dominance of world cinema came about because the United States *is* the world, a nation of immigrants from every corner of the globe.

Cinema has to reach such a broad range of tastes (not necessarily the lowest common denominator) that it has found a form of storytelling accessible to all. The size of the U.S. market allowed producers in many cases to recover all their costs of production from the U.S. market alone. This enabled them to "dump" their product on the rest of the world at minimal cost, providing them with a strong competitive advantage over domestic production or the exports of other countries.

By contrast, U.S. television has been a parochial and inward-looking industry until very recent times. It did not need productions from elsewhere and was happy with its own. Television production was funded by advertisers and was content to create domestic stars, be they news readers, sportscasters, or comedians. The domestic market was large enough that it did not need anyone else for financing. It proved to be an enormously successful medium for the great American public and it shaped their culture. If one explores the tastes of television audiences around the world, one will see a strong preference for domestic or national fare. Obviously, news, weather, and sports are national in scope. (Though there now are people who watch international weather on the Weather Channel — a comment on the rest of the programming!)

But while domestically produced entertainment is the most popular programming in every country (except, until recently, in English Canada), American programming always ranked second, while production from other countries came third. One of the strengths of American programming is its universality, but it also has high production value. And again production value often relates to production cost. For a long time in English Canada, the preference of the Canadian audience was almost exclusively for American programming, probably because audiences prefer high production value programming to low. But when provided, in recent years, with high-quality English Canadian production, they have turned to indigenous programming, just as people in other countries do.

In the United Kingdom, which is perhaps the most protected television market in Europe, there is little appetite for co-production. However, with increasing penetration of satellite channels and the coming of cable, we will see that protected marketplace become subject to more and more fragmentation and competition. When that happens, it will be hard to sustain the high costs of domestic drama and there will be a need to look to forms of collaboration to maintain a flow of entertainment to compete with easily purchased American drama.

It is possible to make an analogy between a world dominated by national television with the Renaissance world of the wealthy, aristocratic patron. One could say that it was ideal for the artist to have all the funding coming from one source, so that he or she did not have to waste time running around seeking commissions from a multitude of partners. But the ability of networks to fully fund their programs is weakening, and even U.S. networks are beginning to search for partners to make up their deficits. With the decline of the single "patron," co-production becomes more and more necessary.

Co-production's Future

In a more internationalized world and a more competitive

world, there will be a need for more deals in order to make quality production happen. But the more partners there are, the more complex the deals, and the more danger of dilution and compromise for creators. The challenge of co-production is how to protect the creator and not allow the deal to lead the creative process. This means that we must go back and ask ourselves: what business are we in? Essentially, we are in the storytelling business. If you have a really good story, it will probably cross borders and have universal resonance. Those are the stories that are suitable for co-production. But a story alone is not enough. You need a good script. And good scripts must have a sense of *authorship* — that is, the mark of the individual on them. Good scripts and good stories do not take place in some convenient mid-Atlantic spot or some vaguely European location. They need a sense of *place*. They need reality, not unreality. To achieve a sense of place and a sense of authorship, co-production partners need to agree on the story they wish to tell, agree on the writer they wish to tell it, set it in a real environment, and then let the talent they hire demonstrate their talent. The motto must be to have *as many executive producers as the deal needs, but only one producer to lead the creative endeavour.*

If American entertainment programming is Canada's — and the world's — principal competition, and if its strength resides in its cultural authenticity, then we must find a way for co-productions to have that same authenticity — or rather a different authenticity. We have to tell our own stories, not imitate theirs. We have to recognize, too, that quality is in part a function of quantity. While the United States may have the economies of scale, if we can get together to create co-productions with a sense of authorship, a sense of place, and a sense of identity, we may yet find that we can produce real programs that can compete around the world. In this way, co-production becomes the future rather than a compromise, a solution rather than a mish-mash of loosely connected deal points with a cobbled-together co-production almost as a by-product. Trade in culture is not easy and it does raise real concerns about national sovereignty. But if co-producers believe in freedom, in talent, and in the individual; if they can look beyond national borders and domestic limitations to put trust in the creative talent, there is a chance that co-production can become a vital element in a cultural survival strategy for all countries.

9

Publicity

by Kevin Tierney

*K*evin Tierney is vice-president of Productions La Fête. Following
studies at McGill and Concordia Universities in Canada, where he
received degrees in literature, education, and film, as well as University
College Dublin in Ireland, Mr. Tierney taught overseas in Algeria, Chad,
and China. Upon his return to Canada he continued his teaching career
at John Abbott College in English and film. At the same time, he
embarked on a parallel career as a freelance film publicist working on some
15 U.S. and Canadian feature films. From 1986 to 1988, he was vice-
president of David Novek Associates, a Montreal public relations company.

He began his production career in 1992, when he served as co-
producer of the thirteenth Tale for All, The Clean Machine, *and
since has gone on to produce, with Rock Demers, the five-and-a-half-
hour award-winning documentary series,* Pierre Elliott Trudeau:
Memoirs. *Once again with Productions La Fête, he is the producer
of* The Return of Tommy Tricker, *and is the executive producer of*
Song Spinner.

Introduction

Rather than speculate about whatever became of Fred and
Freda, the Goose Bay two-steppers on whom much of the

discussion of publicity was focused in the first edition of this book, it might be more profitable to define more clearly the terms of this chapter heading: publicity and promotion. To these I would add another: advertising. This interrelationship is what we call *marketing*, and is now itself the subject of an accompanying volume, entitled *Selling It*.

I think of *publicity* as being "controlled information," the kind of information whose purpose is not only to inform and make aware, but to enhance interest and invite curiosity. (If any of this begins to sound not unlike some contemporary journalism, the connection isn't coincidental — publicity and journalism are both spin doctors, and the only real difference may be the patients.) It is when publicity has succeeded that it faces its greatest challenge: controlling what it has created.

The film and television businesses may be the only places left that officially have posts for people called *publicists*, but that doesn't mean there are fewer of them outside of film and TV sets. On the contrary, PR people — or "media advisors" or media consultants, whatever the current appellation — have become even more firmly entrenched in the hierarchy of the celebrity-driven professions. They may be the first people a celebrity calls when in a jam, sometimes before lawyers and doctors.

Advertising is publicity that's been bought and paid for. Obviously if someone is paying for it, that same someone gets to control it. There are fewer variables with advertising than there are with publicity, but the risks are greater. Advertising costs lots and lots of money, and in spending all that money one not only receives the attention the ads create, but also creates the public perception that one is successful.

Promotion is the group of activities surrounding an event, person, or object that are created to bring more or different awareness to it. The activity could be a contest or a give-away, something that used to be thought of as a "publicity stunt."

Promotion, too, seeks to create awareness but is prepared to be more direct and less subtle, and is generally more closely tied to a specific goal or objective.

As I re-read *Making It* after so many years and thought about what has happened in Canada in the areas of publicity, promotion, and advertising in the past decade, two things appeared abundantly clear: we have learned fast and become quite skilled at advertising and promotion, but we still lag way behind in publicity.

Film and TV Publicity

Publicity is absolutely fundamental to the film and television business. It always has been, and there are no signs to indicate that any change is coming. It is an industry that feeds on self-promotion, and that has always sold itself as well as its products. Compare the independent production industry, for example, to other industries, such as banking or mining. Clearly, these businesses do not seek publicity. Apart from needing to communicate a certain amount of information to their private investors, and engaging the services of agencies to create advertising campaigns to attract consumers, their owners and managers and employees are happier out of the limelight.

Showbiz folk, on the other hand — as a wise old lady says in an Israeli movie I recently saw — think they should get applause for sleeping. Publicity in this business is not a choice that is made at a certain point in the process; it is a necessity. Those who have done well in the film and television businesses, and continue to do so, are those who grasped this concept early on and have made it work for them.

In Quebec, for example, Productions La Fête and Rock Demers have shown how a small company with a niche product and an eye to the international market can today boast sales of their films to more than 100 countries around the world.

Similarly, Roger Frappier has succeeded in overseeing the creation of films with both audience and critical appeal, whose returns both domestically and internationally have been greatly enhanced by well-structured and imaginative publicity campaigns.

Ten years ago this chapter began with a discussion of corporate public relations, which some people thought of as a side issue, slightly irrelevant to the discussion at hand. What we've seen in the last couple of years, however, is that companies with corporate publicity strategies now lead the way at the Montreal, Toronto, Vancouver, and even New York stock exchanges. Alliance, Nelvana, Cinar, Malofilm, and Atlantis, among others, are recognizable corporate names. Their increasing public profile has allowed them not simply to take bows and make long acceptance speeches at award ceremonies, but also to find new sources of financing to fuel their growth. Fred and Freda go public! What a concept.

Exactly the same situation exists on the level of specific projects. It isn't coincidental that the most successful films or series are made by people who understand that publicity is imperative. In concrete terms, this means:

- allotting sufficient funds in the production and distribution budgets in order to publicize adequately;
- sticking to those amounts when occasions for budget slashing and cutting arise, as they inevitably do;
- taking the same amount of care in hiring and developing publicity professionals as is given to any of the other vital departments.

In other words, just as much time, energy, faith, and support should go into the selection of a unit publicist as goes into the selection of the director of photography, costume designer, or business and legal affairs advisors.

The Purpose of Publicity

The basic purpose of film and TV publicity is to persuade as many people as possible to see a particular film or show. Everything else flows from that. In order to get them to watch, they have to be aware; in order for them to be aware, they have to be informed; in order for them to be informed, they need sources of information. With an overwhelming amount of information available to the public each day, the publicist's challenge is clear: make the information attractive.

The publicist manufactures the information and disseminates it. The further his or her reach, the better the odds that more people will take notice. Information, like everything else that is prepared for public consumption, must appeal to the consumer. Obviously there are things that are easier to make appealing than others, but that's not the publicist's decision. The professional publicist usually doesn't get to decide *what* he or she will have to communicate, but simply *how*.

There are, nevertheless, certain rules of thumb. Publicists really have only one thing going for them: credibility. It's not a self-replenishing commodity. Once lost, it may be gone forever. So the first principle is easy: don't lie. Publicists must find new ways to tell the truth or avoid the pitfalls by not offering an opinion. The second principle is: be available. Publicists can hardly ever create their own schedules. Instead, they have to be ready to adapt their schedules to accomodate either the client or the media.

By definition, a publicist must serve many masters: the producer, the distributor, the sales agent, the TV network, the corporate sponsor, the advertiser, and even certain individuals within these groups. All of them probably have their own agendas and all expect the publicist to deliver. On the other hand, there are the media and their needs, which they fully expect the publicist to cater to. The publicist is smack in the middle of all these interests and is sometimes forced to walk a fine line. Knowledge and credibility make it workable.

There is no difference, in principle, between creating publicity for feature films and creating it for television; nor is there any difference between publicizing a documentary and publicizing any other kind of movie. The basic objective is the same, even if the details change a bit. In all cases, the better you know your market (the audience and the media) and your client (the networks, producers, or distributors) the better you can do your job.

Who's on First

Ten years ago, publicity was thought to be the domain of the producer. In the interval, distributors, at the urging of such institutions as Telefilm Canada and their provincial counterparts, have come more and more to the fore, so much so that it might be tempting to switch all responsibility for publicity over to them. Once again, though, we have enough pertinent examples to conclude that success stories occur when producer and distributor work together from the outset of a production and, in concert, hire competent people to create an intelligent, rational, and well-planned publicity campaign for the productions they are involved in together.

For instance, opening *Jésus de Montréal* in Quebec theatres the same day the film made its debut in competition at the Cannes Film Festival gave tremendous impetus to the film's performance at the box office. Alliance wisely did just the opposite for *Exotica*, opting instead to use Cannes reaction to the film as the beginning of its build-up of critical momentum that would culminate at the Toronto International Film Festival four months later. The salient point is that both publicity campaigns were well planned, both had a sense of how to use publicity to create awareness in the audience their creators had targeted, and best of all, both worked beautifully.

Unfortunately, we still have many, if not more, examples of producers who ignore publicity needs at the budget stage and wake up to it too far into production to do anything about it. There are also distributors who sign letters to acquire films at the script stage and never reappear until the producer tells them the finished print is ready and it's time to write a cheque.

Well-planned campaigns work just as well in television, though in this medium the likely coupling is the producers and the networks working together. When the relationship works well (*Million Dollar Babies* and *Road to Avonlea* come immediately to mind), the level of awareness of these shows is tremendous, such that they have a real chance of breaking through into the public's sensibility. Why does such a different fate await other shows? Over-worked and/or under-imaginative network executives? Producers who have all too quickly or out of sheer necessity had to move on to other projects? Worst of all, perhaps, discouraging audience reaction and/or reviews? The legitimacy of the questions unfortunately bring with them no easy answers.

While obviously it is the publicist who is responsible for publicity, a strong case can be made that so, too, is everyone else, from the receptionist who answers the phone in the producer's office to the bureaucrat who moves along any piece of paper bearing the name of that project; from the producer to the distributor, from the director to the actors, from the writer to the editors. Banal though it may sound, each of these people not only has the opportunity to create and extend awareness of the projects they are involved in, but arguably each has the responsibility to do so. Why bother working on a production unless you think it's great? Creating public interest in what we in the film and television business do individually and collectively is something we can all take part in. Americans are particularly good at this. In fact, there are few people on the planet better at congratulating themselves for being themselves than American showbiz people. Which is, I suspect, why they have invented the greatest number of award shows in the world.

It is, in fact, people within the industry who often create or perpetuate what is called "the word": what supposed insiders are saying about a show's merit, and potential. It's amazing how many projects are stillborn as a result of some sort of "negative" perception that has already decided their fate before they appear on big or little screens.

Canada's own best example of this is probably *Bethune*. A case could be made that both the film and the miniseries are better pieces of work than a great many things produced in this country. But, for a number of reasons, neither were given much of a chance. The subject is probably worth a book of its own, and certainly cannot be detailed in this chapter, but in publicity terms the production could almost serve as a primer on what *not* to do. A three-part series in *The Toronto Star*, reporting from difficult locations in China, used every cliché in the journalist's handbook — "according to one crew member who chose not to be identified" and so on — to describe a catastrophe in the making. A cover story in *Maclean's* magazine only added to the original mythology. In the end, it was very clear that a mistake had been made in allowing journalists access to what was admittedly a difficult shoot.

Of course, this was not the only publicity surrounding the shoot or the later struggles for the dead doctor's cinematic soul, but nevertheless the *word* was out and it was not good. Some of that could have been better controlled by a full-time unit publicist. However, other circumstances truly were beyond anyone's control. When *Bethune* began shooting, China was still a "darling of the West." By the time *Bethune* was released, however, China's post-Tian An Men Square reputation had been tarnished. Suddenly, the audience for the film was significantly reduced, and nothing any publicist could do could change that.

Types of Publicity

The person or group responsible for the production is also responsible for ordering, buying, and paying for publicity, as is the person or group responsible for its distribution/diffusion/ selling of the project. As has already been stated, they should seek the best possible person to whom they will entrust publicity.

Today our maturing industry has people who specialize in *unit publicity*, which is production-oriented, and others whose speciality is *launch publicity*, which is a distribution function. Midsized and larger corporate structures in the film and television industry also have their own in-house publicity people. They have such titles as: vice-president of corporate communications, director of communications, communications coordinator, or communications manager, but their fundamental tasks are the same, as are many of the tools of their trade.

UNIT PUBLICITY

Unit publicity starts during preproduction of a film or series, when the show is being crewed, the cast is being signed, and the production is gearing up. It ends when the film has wrapped or finished shooting, and the publicist has handed over to the producer all of the materials he or she was engaged to generate, organize, or supervise during shooting. These materials include: biographies of principal cast and crew; a synopsis of the story that positions it to the media; and production notes or information relevant to the shooting of the movie or series.

LAUNCH PUBLICITY

Launch publicity should start almost as soon as production begins. It really kicks in, however, as soon as a date is decided upon by the producers, distributors, and exhibitors for the release of a film. At this stage, the publicist's responsibilities include: adapting and updating the press kit; finalizing poster and art work for ads; choosing black-and-white and colour photographs for inclusion in the press kits; organizing press screenings, interviews, and premieres; supervising and overseeing the production of trailers, sample episodes, and TV ads; and generally trying to get as much media coverage as possible for the opening of the film or the broadcasting of the show.

Both unit and launch publicity have specific, concise, short-term goals, and both are dealt with at length in the accompanying volume to this book, *Selling It* . I urge anyone interested in these topics to read the appropriate chapters in that book. There is also a quite extraordinary amount of work involved in doing all of the things that occur in between these two stages, assuring the continuity that is so necessary for successful publicity.

CORPORATE PUBLICITY

Corporate publicity has as its mandate the short-term, mid-term and long-term objectives of a company, either a production house or a distributor. It is much less specifically project-oriented. Instead, it is an ongoing, five-days-a-week, 12-months-a-year gig. If the corporate entity has gone public, even more hours often have to be found, so great is the increased demand for information required to feed hungry investors. But there's more.

For example, who prepares the preliminary materials used to find development funds, such as concepts, outlines, and their accompanying marketing plan? Who co-ordinates with advertising agencies and/or corporate sponsors who are involved or associated with certain promotional activities that occur during the making of the film, the theatrical release of the film, the release of that film on video, then on film and/or television, etc.? In-house publicity people.

Successful companies, like successful writers, directors, and actors, realized long ago that the film and television business is not about a single project; it's about a series of projects.

Long-term publicity goals pay off, as evidenced by the ever-growing identification of certain production and distribution company names with their areas of expertise: Nelvana and Cinar for animation; Sullivan Films for their *Green Gables* franchise; *Tales for All* as high-quality children's films; and the great strides Alliance has made as both a producer and exporter of top-quality Canadian television drama. These successes did not come overnight, nor are they the result of a single project and the attendant publicity hoopla surrounding it. Instead, they are based on well-grounded publicity strategies that set out to establish these companies, first across Canada, and then worldwide.

For some, their presence came via a particular type of programming, a certain style of presentation, or image. For others it came as the result of some very successful corporate partnering both in Canada and abroad. But in all these cases and others, the companies have benefited from a strong commitment to corporate publicity management of the sort that postulates the whole can and should be greater than the sum of its parts.

Tools

THE PRESS RELEASE

The publicist's most basic tools are words. The words lend themselves to all sorts of formats but none is as important or useful as the good old press release. This is usually not more than a page long, with a strong, succinct headline and a first paragraph worthy of being reprinted in a newspaper in its entirety. It always has more than one purpose, but must have at least one bit of something that is either *news* or at the very least is *newsworthy*.

It's amazing how many times I have seen entire press releases unashamedly reprinted, as though written by a journalist. This is yet another good reason for making them complete unto themselves. But at the same time, each news release should also be created to serve as part of the corporate image or trademark that is either being introduced, perpetuated, or enhanced.

A good press release is only as good as the mailing list it's sent to, which is not, despite its name, addressed only to the press. In fact, any number of publics can be addressed by either the same document or slight variations thereof. Audiences for press releases might include:
- investors — private, public, and other;
- government and financial institutions, including embassies, consulates, and delegations;
- special interest groups;
- company clients, suppliers, and partners; and
- potential clients and partners.

COMPANY NEWSLETTERS

Rather than try to pad press releases into weightier and lengthier pieces of fluff, good publicists who have the budgets to do so come up with company newsletters that function more like quarterly reports on a wide range of company activities. While daily newspapers probably wouldn't touch much of this information, judging it not to be "hard news," these newsletters are very effective ways of communicating with the kinds of groups outlined in the preceding list. They can also be effective in attracting the interest of magazine editors who work with long lead times, and may decide to do stories about companies, their principals, and their projects.

Successful newsletters are those that strike a good balance

between copy content and layout. While publicists do not necessarily have to be graphic artists, a flair for organizing material and finding interesting and reader-friendly ways to present the company's information (not to mention knowing how to edit their own and others' copy) are tremendous assets.

Similarly, a publicist can go a long way with some knowledge of how to use more sophisticated technologies, such as the making of corporate videos. Publicists don't actually make these, but they should know what needs to go in, and what to leave out, and when and to whom to show them.

THE IN-HOUSE PUBLICIST AS OVERSEER

Corporate publicity tends to have less to do with such standard forms of publicity as:

- stunts — staging an event to gain media attraction;
- gimmicks — creating hats, jackets, T-shirts, key chains, and other tchatchkes;
- press junkets — bringing selected members of the press to a location when the movie is shooting or arranging interviews with key cast members and the director when the movie is being launched;
- movie stills — working with the set photographer to assure proper coverage and the fabrication of particular elements that will later be used to create artwork for posters and so on.

However, the in-house publicist can and should play a role in all of these, for it is he or she who has the responsibility of the larger picture: the process of making and selling the production *and* fitting a single production into the company's overall corporate objectives. In effect, the corporate publicist's mandate is to oversee and supervise *all* of these elements, as well as merchandising and audience testing of both the show and its publicity in order to provide the continuity that is so vital between production and launch and between the production house, the distributor, the foreign sales agent, and the broadcaster.

The Process

Successful publicists are those who understand what is involved in the overall process of getting their "message" through to its intended audience. That "message" can take the form of a film or TV show or series; it can also be a corporate announcement, or a personality, or even a stock issue. It doesn't, in the end, really matter. What does matter is the clarity of what is to be communicated and the passion with which it's delivered.

There is also of course, knowledge, some of which comes from experience, but much of which must come from homework. How well do you know your product? How closely can you stay attuned to it during all of its various incarnations from idea to script to production to post-production. How clear are the *objectives* — the company's, the producer's? Is everyone involved on the same wavelength in terms of what they want to achieve? The publicist should be sure of this, as it is probably he or she who will be held accountable for failures. Successes, on the other hand, everyone likes to share in.

How well do you know the media? There's nothing people want more from a publicist than access to their well-filled rolodex. It's much easier to "pitch" stories to members of the media if you know them and know what they like to cover. It's also a big mistake to set up an interview between an important journalist and a producer or star or director whose previous work was skinned alive by the very same journalist.

How much do you know about the environment within which you are active? Reading trade magazines is essential, as is reading everything else that might be useful. Take inventory of what is available in the general press, trade press, and specialty publications.

Once you know what's out there, do a little investigating into their specific needs: do they have long or short lead times? What kind of photos do they tend to run — head shots, group shots, action stuff, colour or black-and-white, vertical or horizontal? This is all very basic *and* very important.

Always try to deliver what's asked for by the media, and if possible a little more. For example, a journalist is asking for information on something. You send it along and to sweeten the pot, you send with it a great picture that no one has ever used before. He or she gets it, throws it on the editor's desk along with the small article. It turns out to be a slow day or there's a screw-up somewhere and suddenly the paper needs a visual to fill up the space. Bingo! They run your shot and suddenly, for the cost of a printed photo, you've got probably five times more *free* coverage than you would have gotten without the picture. While it may not always work out that way, the more you plug away at it, the more chances you have to get lucky. On the other hand, don't try to get a TV magazine to put a horizontal photo on their cover when all they run are verticals. You're supposed to know this.

How well do you know the demographics of your audience — what they watch, what magazines or newspapers they read, what radio stations they listen to? Once again, all this information exists; it just has to be found, digested, then used. How well do you know the international markets where your productions sell? Their media and marketing needs?

In publicity, the old adage does not apply — what you don't know *will* hurt you.

A Note on the Publicist's Working Environment

If publicity is to be effective, there must be outlets for the message or the controlled information to reach the public. These outlets include daily and weekly newspapers, weekly and/or monthly news or popular magazines (or better still, fanzines), radio and television talk shows, and magazines shows that do profiles.

Although we continue to hear talk in Canada that "we" (that is, film and television professionals) aren't good at creating publicity and generally promoting ourselves, it's arguable that we would, in fact, have the ability to do it *if* we had more opportunity to practice and had somewhere to show off our efforts. Blame and accusation aside, the fact remains that there is little real public interest in the English-Canadian film industry: neither in the films themselves, nor in their makers, despite a few exceptions like Atom Egoyan, nor in their leading performers. Who and where are our stars? More important, how do we *make* stars?

In other places and situations, we would learn to know them from seeing them in the media outlined above. In Canada, these simply do not exist, or do so on a scale that can only be described as minuscule. An appearance on *Canada AM* would be great if it were one of five or ten appearances on a variety of TV shows, but if it's just that one as the entire media tour, it's unlikely to have much impact.

Meanwhile, shows like *"Entertainment Tonight"* and *"Letterman"* are watched by millions of Canadians and we dutifully go to see everything publicized and promoted on these shows. We read literally thousands of magazines from *Premiere* to *Time* to *Life* that regularly promote movies. But what is being promoted is somebody else's movies, somebody else's stars, and somebody else's mythology.

Sadly, it sometimes appears as though we have bought into it and embraced it as our own, becoming so subjugated that even proposing an alternative sounds like heresy. The worst example? Both major theatre chains in this country hand out *free* glossy promotional magazines filled with their controlled information about what movies we should be preparing to spend our money on to see next. They seldom have a word about Canadian movies.

To be a good publicist you need to be aware of what you're up against. The fact is that Canadian films account for approximately 3 per cent of the annual box office gross. That is not only the result of poor publicity or a lack of it. That figure is not a complaint, it's a *fact*.

In this, the age of publicity, the demands on the public's attention have never been greater. Is there a danger of overload in all of this publicity? Such a question is an inevitable off-shoot of the "Death Star/500-channel universe" with which we're being threatened. In some ways it's a reasonable enough question: how is it possible to publicize all of the programming that will fill those channels? How much "controlled information" can the public take in before their circuits break down?

Big numbers notwithstanding, it seems to me that people discover their own limits simultaneously with the discovery and evolution of their own interests. Publicity, like publishing or broadcasting and even movies, has not for a long time been addressed to *everyone*.

Successful publicity, like the message it has been created to carry, is addressed to a specific audience. Knowing who the appropriate audience is for any kind of cultural product is fundamental to making that product in the first place. If we don't know who is going to want to see what we're making, or, even more important, who is going to be ready to *pay* to see what we're making, my advice is don't make it. No amount of publicity in the world is going to make people like what we make. It can make them aware that the thing exists; its corollary functions of advertising and promotion can even get a certain number of them actually in the door, but if there aren't enough of them in the first place, and/or if those who do see it don't like it, we don't need publicity, we need to find either another subject or a new line of work.

It's a bit of a fool's game to make future predictions in an area as volatile as publicity. However, one thing is clear: the public appears to have an insatiable appetite for publicity. How else can we explain the number of books written about the Royal Family, books by movie stars or about them, books about Elvis Presley, and so on? The number of trade and specialty magazines devoted to promoting actors, musicians, and others? The existence not only of a phenomenon such as "*Entertainment Tonight*," but of an entire U.S. cable network, E!? The appetite seems sufficiently ravenous to allow even "boring old Canadians" a kick at the can. Can anybody explain why we will apparently always be fascinated by the Dionne quintuplets and the two world wars?

The key is to capture the attention of the public. Every day, creative and talented individuals find new ways to do just this. The smart ones also devise new ways to keep it.

10

PRODUCTION
AND THE
LAW

by DIANA CAFAZZO AND DOUGLAS BARRETT

*D*iana Cafazzo and Douglas Barrett are partners in the KNOWlaw
Group of the Toronto Law firm of McMillan Binch, specializing
in the area of media and entertainment law. As well as representing
clients in the broadcasting, music, publishing, live theatre, and computer industries, they act for many large and small film and television producers across Canada. They both contribute to "Binchmarks," the legal
column of Playback magazine, and lecture and teach about legal and
business affairs in the media and entertainment industries.

Making the Most Effective Use of Lawyers

There is an old joke about a lawyer falling overboard into the
shark-infested waters. Instead of devouring him, the sharks pick
him up and help him back into the boat. "Professional Courtesy,"
explains a veteran crew member to his neighbour.

This story exemplifies the discomfort and reluctance many
people feel about dealing with lawyers or making extensive use
of their services. The fact of the matter, however, is that most
independently produced film and television productions today
involve complex commercial transactions. The combination of

high budgets, multiple sources of financing, and conventional production risks contribute to a situation in which all participating parties wish to ensure that all the "legalities" are correct. The risks are too high to do otherwise.

THE NATURE OF LEGAL SERVICES

There are four basic types of service that a lawyer can be expected to perform for clients in the film and television industry. The lawyer should:

1. be able to provide advice on the fundamentals of commercial law and intellectual property law and on all aspects of developing, financing, producing, and distributing film and television productions;
2. be familiar with industry "standards" and able to negotiate fair and productive deals for clients;
3. be on reasonably good terms with the key decision makers in the industry and able to ensure that clients will be seen by these individuals; and
4. be capable of producing understandable and thorough legal documentation in an efficient and cost-effective manner.

Most observers would now agree that these services are likely to be performed more effectively by a lawyer specializing in the media and entertainment field.

In recent years, the number of Canadian lawyers practising largely or exclusively in these areas has increased. However, the group remains extremely small by comparison with other areas of practice, with only about two or three dozen individuals across the country and heavily concentrated in Toronto, Montreal, and Vancouver.

THE "RIGHT" LAWYER

Finding the right lawyer and establishing a successful working relationship can be a difficult and intimidating task. Perhaps the best approach is to contact other people active in the industry to find out which lawyer they use and how happy they are with the services provided. Ask about the lawyer's professional qualifications, accessibility and responsiveness, billing practices, and possibly most important — congeniality and helpfulness.

Create a short list of two or three candidates and take them out to lunch (one at a time, of course). This should eliminate the need to pay a consultation fee during your search. Tell the lawyer about yourself and your business plans; ask for a sales pitch on what the lawyer can do for you, particularly in relation to the four types of services outlined earlier; request specifics on dates, billing practices, and payment requirements; and try to make a realistic assessment of how important your business is going to be to the lawyer.

Remember that if you become a successful independent filmmaker or producer in today's industry, you are likely to have frequent need of legal services. You want to establish a relationship with a lawyer that will last for many years. There are several secrets to establishing such a relationship:

- the client and the lawyer must respect each other, work well together, and communicate fully to one another;
- the client must give clear instructions to the lawyer;
- the lawyer's assistance must be put to effective use by the client and produce practical and recognizable results;
- the client must believe he or she is receiving good value in return for the fees paid to the lawyer; and
- the lawyer must believe he or she is being fairly compensated.

CONTROLLING LEGAL COSTS

Knowing when and how to use a lawyer is an acquired skill. Because lawyers charge substantial fees, it is very easy to lose control of legal costs. Hourly fees vary from $75 to $125 for those recently called to the bar and from $200 to $300 or more for more senior counsel. Aside from the question of affordability, most clients feel they receive better value in the advice given by more experienced lawyers. Often, however, documentation may be more efficiently produced by supervised junior lawyers.

In order to control costs, it is important to carefully consider what you wish your lawyer to do for you and to prepare for the time you spend with him or her. On the other hand, if you treat the lawyer as if you can't wait to get out of the office or hang up the phone, you will lessen his or her willingness to be helpful. Here are some specific do's and don'ts:

- don't rely too heavily on your lawyer to teach you how to develop and carry on your business — rather, ask somebody else who is less expensive;
- don't ask or permit your lawyer to make your decisions for you; you — not your professional advisor — are the boss;
- don't take your lawyer to meetings at which his or her attendance is unnecessary;
- do ask for advice on the most advantageous terms and structure of a business deal before you begin negotiations or sign anything;
- do ask for regular reports if your lawyer is undertaking negotiations on your behalf;
- don't ask your lawyer to prepare documents that you can prepare yourself;
- do request your lawyer's comments on any documents drafted by you that could create contractual relations or liabilities;
- don't negotiate with someone else's lawyer without seeking the advice of your own;
- do ask your lawyer to keep you fully informed on an ongoing basis of the approximate cost of professional services you have incurred;
- do request itemized accounts and pay them reasonably promptly;

- don't hesitate to discuss fees, billing practices, and accounts in order to avoid any misunderstanding.

Following these rules will ensure that you get the most out of your relationship with your legal advisor.

Business Structures

There are several different legal structures in which to carry on the business of film and television production. Each has advantages and disadvantages; each is more or less appropriate for different types of business situations.

SOLE PROPRIETORSHIP

A sale proprietorship is a business that is owned and operated by one person. It is possible to register a name for such a business, and many people mistakenly believe that such registration gives the business the status of a "company." This is not the case.

In a proprietorship, all the contracts and other liabilities entered into or incurred by the business are the personal responsibility of the owner. The profits of the business are taxable income in the hands of the proprietor.

The obvious advantage of a proprietorship is cost: no formalities are needed to establish the business. The primary disadvantage is the personal exposure or liability of the proprietor to all creditors and claimants. Another, more subtle disadvantage, is the perception of the business community that a proprietorship is a marginal form of business, not to be taken seriously.

PARTNERSHIP AND JOINT VENTURE

A partnership is like a proprietorship, in that the business is operated on a personal basis, but there must be more than one owner. In a partnership, each partner is considered jointly and severally liable for the debts and obligations of *all* the partners. This means that a claimant can seek resource against *any one* partner for the obligations of the entire partnership. The affairs of the partnership are usually governed by an agreement that stipulates the share of profits and costs belonging to each partner and describes the manner in which the partnership shall be operated. Partnerships are also sometimes formed for tax reasons since, generally speaking, the income and losses of a partnership are taxed in the hands of the partners, not the partnership.

It is also possible to create a partnership of corporations. This is done most commonly when two or more corporations want to join together to work on a co-production. In this situation, the corporations will often form a partnership as a temporary structure that is used during the development phase. If the project successfully moves into production, the parties will often form a brand new corporation that actually carries on the production.

Sometimes when two or more individuals or corporations come together to work on a project, they refer to themselves as a "joint venture" rather than a partnership. In essence, they are trying to establish a structure in which they can produce and profit from a product that they work on together, but at the same time *not* be responsible for one another's debts and obligations. This is not an easy task however, as the partnership laws of the various provinces will, in any event, deem most of these joint ventures to be partnerships.

INCORPORATION

The corporation is the most common form of business structure. The difficult decision for most independent business people is knowing when to incorporate, since it can cost from $400 to $1000 in fees plus about $300 for disbursements, or out-of-pocket costs.

There are three possible reasons for incorporating:

1. your accountant tells you to do so for tax reasons;
2. you want to protect your personal assets from claims arising out of your business; and/or
3. you are making a long-term commitment to growth and believe it appropriate to incorporate at the outset.

In the first year of law school, students are taught that a corporation is a separate legal person, able to do everything that an individual can do except vote, marry, or join the army. Sometimes, however, the individual owner of a corporation finds it difficult to grasp the notion that his or her company is another "person." Yet this is the basis for the concept of limited liability.

It is easy to understand that a creditor or claimant should only be paid out of what you personally own, and should have no right to the assets of your family or friends. Similarly, a corporation is only responsible for its obligations up to the value of its own assets. Unless its owner or owners have specifically agreed to it in writing, it is very difficult for a creditor to claim against the owner's personal assets to fulfil the obligations of the corporation.

The owners of a corporation are its shareholders. Each year, the shareholders elect a board of directors to manage the operations of the company. The directors appoint officers to assume responsibility for day-to-day matters. Officers usually serve "at the pleasure of the board." This means that they can be removed at any time, subject to individual contractual arrangements to the contrary. At the end of the year, the directors report to the shareholders on the operation of the company, and new election of directors takes place.

This is how it works in theory. But what happens when the company is a business vehicle for only one or two people? Even though it sounds a little silly, the process is exactly the same — even where the shareholders, the directors, and the officers are all the same individuals. If you are the sole shareholder, director, and officer of a corporation, you will have to get used to wearing three hats. Sometimes you will take certain steps as a shareholder, sometimes as a director, and sometimes as the president of your company.

Most corporations active in the film and television industry are "private" corporations, in that they have relatively few shareholders and their shares are not available through one of Canada's stock exchanges. For the most part, shareholders in these companies actively participate in their business and the industry, rather than simply being passive investors. (There are some exceptions, of course, as some of Canada's largest production companies have recently "gone public".)

If the corporation has more than one shareholder, it is common for them to enter into a shareholders' agreement that is intended to limit their capacity to deal freely with their shares and to govern the management and operation of the corporation. Some of the specific matters covered by shareholders' agreements are:

- the number of shares to be issued to each shareholder;
- the number of directors to be nominated by each shareholder and the names of the first directors;
- the name of each of the officers;
- the role of each of the shareholders in the day-to-day operation of the company and the manner and scale of their remuneration;
- the right of the shareholders to sell their shares to a third party and the other shareholders' right of first refusal to purchase such shares;
- the right of the shareholders to force the sale of one shareholder's holding, the method of triggering such a forced sale, and the manner of determining the compensation to be paid for the shares;
- restrictions on how the shares will be voted in certain

circumstances;
- provisions for breaking unresolved disagreements among shareholders; and
- what to do on the death, incapacity, or marital breakdown of a shareholder.

There are, of course, many other possible provisions. Shareholders' agreements can be anywhere from a few pages to many dozens of pages in length. In order for such agreements to have any value to the signing parties, they must be specifically tailored to individual circumstances and fully understood. Never sign the 40-page form that a lawyer says is "standard" for all his or her companies.

A final point on the use of corporations in the film and television industry. It is now common practice for separate corporations to be established for each major project. Usually, the shares in these special-purpose corporations are owned by the corporation engaged in the overall promotion and supervision of film and television projects. This practice is advisable for three reasons:

1. it ensures that the general business assets of the parent corporation and its interests in other projects are not exposed to claims made against an individual project owned by the special purpose corporation.
2. it protects the interest of investors in the project from claims made in relation to other projects in which the parent corporation may be involved; and
3. it gives each project a clean slate, unencumbered by the banking and other commercial arrangements in which the parent corporation might be involved.

CHOOSING THE RIGHT NAME

Finally, a word about choosing a corporate name. There are three approaches:

1. you can use your own full or last name, provided you use additional differentiating language such as "Brando Television Productions Ltd.";
2. you can use a business-related combination name such as "Filmtel Productions Inc." provided somebody else hasn't beaten you to it or a name like it; or
3. you can use a unique name such as "Bombast Film Corporation" or "Argbarg Productions Incorporated".

Of the three approaches, the latter is preferable. The first approach makes sense only when the corporation has no other purpose than the provision of the services of its principal shareholder; the second approach frequently runs afoul of similar-sounding or similar-looking names already in use. Even if the name you choose is available for use, it might well have a tendency to get lost among all the other business-related names in current use. A unique name stands out and is far easier to protect. Any name you select must include "Limited," "Limitée," "Incorporated," "Incorporée," "Corporation," or the abbreviation "Ltd.," "Ltée," "Inc.," "Corp." or other variations permitted by the provincial or federal jurisdiction under which your corporation is formed. These are the words that signify that your business is incorporated, and they may not be used unless it is incorporated.

LIMITED PARTNERSHIP

The last form of business structure that can be used in the film and television production industry is the limited partnership. Each limited partnership has a general partner, which is usually a corporation responsible for the operation and management of the partnership, and one or more limited partners, who are usually individual passive investors. The primary advantage of a limited partnership is that it has all of the tax advantages of an ordinary partnership, but the liability of the investors is limited to the amount invested by each of them in the partnership.

Unlike a conventional partnership, a written agreement among the partners is a legal necessity. In the case of a limited partnership, the agreement tends to be longer and more sophisticated. This level of detail is generally necessary because the limited partners do not know each other and are delegating a great deal of power and authority over the affairs of the partnership to the corporate general partner. As always, the lower the capacity of the parties to trust one another, the greater the need for complex contractual provisions.

Limited partnerships are the vehicle of choice for tax shelter financing (more about this subject on p. 315), but are not otherwise widely used in the film and television business.

CO-PRODUCTIONS

Given the reality of financing film and television productions in Canada, many producers opt for doing certain projects as *co-productions*. This term actually has several meanings, but basically refers to a structure in which two or more entities (usually corporations) join together to produce a film or television production. Sometimes the entities reside in different provinces, and, in the case of international treaty co-productions, in different countries.

These entities join together as a partnership or a joint venture. If the project proceeds beyond the development phase and proceeds to production, the parties very often decide at that point to incorporate a corporation in which each will own shares.

Legal Implications in the Acquisition of Literary Property

COPYRIGHT

Copyright has always been considered a tricky and subtle area of the law in Canada. The Government of Canada is partway through a very long process of revising the *Copyright Act*, to modernize what is widely thought of as an antiquated approach to the protection of intellectual property.

The current law describes the types of works that are protected by copyright, including literary and dramatic works. The initial owner of the copyright in a work is the individual who is its author, unless the author wrote the work as part of his or her duties as an employee, in which case the owner is the employer.

Canada has a copyright registration system, but it does not require registration in order to obtain copyright protection. Such protection is obtained by the act of creation, and does not demand any further formality. Still, there are some benefits to be gained by registering the copyright in a work, so it's still advisable. For instance, it is far easier to obtain damages from a copyright infringer (as opposed to merely an injunction preventing further infringements) if the work was registered at the date of infringement. Since the Canadian registration system does not permit the physical deposit of the document in which copyright is claimed, many writers and others also send a copyright of their scripts to themselves by registered mail (and then store the envelopes away, unopened) or give them to another person to hold in order to provide some evidence that may help to identify the work in question.

Copyright itself includes the right to reproduce, publish, perform, or telecommunicate all or a substantial part of the protected work, and, more important, to prevent others from appropriating your work in any of these ways. The *Copyright Act* provides for an array of civil and summary remedies against those who infringe a person's copyright.

Generally speaking, the period during which copyright exists in Canada is the life of the author of the particular work, plus 50 years. It is axiomatic that no right may be granted for a longer period than it is held by the grantor. Therefore, contract provisions that grant various rights "in perpetuity" are, in fact, ineffective, in that they can't grant exclusivity beyond the applicable period of copyright. At the end of this period, the work falls into the public domain and may be used by anyone, without compensation to the author or his or her estate.

The aspect of copyright that many people find difficult to understand is its capacity to be divided and to be sold or licensed on a piece-by-piece basis. For example, the writer of a screenplay may license to a producer the right to make a single film for a television series, or may assign all film and television rights including sequel and remake rights. The right to publish a book based on the screenplay or to produce a stage play or a radio play are all separate rights capable of being sold or licensed on an individual basis, as are merchandising rights, the right to make interactive products, adaptation rights, translation rights, and so forth.

When a producer wishes to make a film based, for example, on a popular book, he or she must first acquire the necessary rights from the owner of the copyright in the book. With these rights in hand, the producer engages a writer to write a screenplay. The writer of the screenplay is the owner of the quite separate and distinct copyright in the screenplay, and the producer must again negotiate the acquisition of the necessary rights from the screenwriter. As you might expect, the higher the price paid by the producer, the more rights he or she would expect to obtain in return.

In the course of producing the film, the producer may engage a composer to create an original soundtrack. Since there is a separate copyright in the music, the producer must also negotiate for the relevant rights with the composer.

Once the film is completed, the film itself will have its own copyright, owned by the producer. Based on this right, the producer may then assign or license the commercial exploitation of the film around the world on a market-by-market basis. At one extreme, the film could simply be sold outright to a distributor; at the other, a distributor may only be given the right to arrange exhibition of the film on television stations in, say, British Columbia, after the film has been shown in theatres and on pay television in a specific order and for specified periods of time.

MORAL RIGHTS

Producers are also advised to obtain a "waiver of moral rights" from all individuals who create or provide copyrighted works for use in the production. An author's moral rights include:

1. the right of "integrity" — this right is infringed if the work is, to the prejudice of the honour of reputation of the author (*a*) distorted, mutilated or otherwise modified, or (*b*) used in association with a product, service, cause, or institution;

2. the right of "paternity" — this is the author's right, where reasonable in the circumstances, to be associated with the work as its author by name or pseudonym or, on the other hand, the right to remain anonymous.

Many broadcasters and distributors insist that the producer obtain a waiver of these moral rights, as they feel that their ability to safely modify or exploit the work of the author is potentially limited if the waiver is not obtained.

ADAPTATIONS

Frequently, film or television projects begin life with a producer's discovery of a marketable idea in a book or magazine. The producer decides to adapt the story and characters in the work into a format suitable for a film or television production. If the producer wishes to acquire or option the film and television rights in the work, he or she must first ascertain who holds those rights. Often this is not as easy as it sounds. If the work is a book, the rights holder might be the author or it might be the publisher of the book, depending on the provisions of the publishing agreement between the author and the publisher. If the work is a magazine article, the rights holder could be the author of the article or, if the author is an employee, the magazine itself.

Once the rights holder has been identified, negotiations can begin. Generally, the producer wants as many of the marketable rights in the literary property as possible, while the rights holder wishes to concede as few as possible. As in most bargaining situations, the price the producer is prepared to pay for the rights is usually the critical determining factor. In addition to a fixed acquisition price for the rights, the deal may include a royalty for the rights holder, in the form of a small percentage of the profits (often called "points") to be earned from the production.

At the very least, the producer should control the exclusive right to make the proposed film or television production and to distribute it in all types of media and exhibition, all types of television, videocassettes, and discs. In addition, agreements often grant the right to distribute the production in all media "now known or in the future developed." Beyond these minimum requirements, the producer could also acquire the right to make additional film and television productions based on the property, to make sequels to the initial film, to make productions in other languages, to adapt the property for the stage, to merchandise the characters, to create interactive products and so on.

OPTIONING A LITERARY PROPERTY

The structure most often used to acquire rights is an *option agreement*. As is the case with any other type of real or personal property, it is possible to acquire an option to purchase or license the various rights inherent in copyright. An option permits the payment of a relatively small amount of money, often 10 per cent or less of the ultimate purchase price, in return for the exclusive right to acquire the relevant rights at a future date. This allows a producer a period of time to determine at relatively low risk and cost whether a film or television property can become a viable project. During the period of the option, the producer is able to work on developing the property without fear that someone else might take advantage of this work by acquiring the rights.

To protect the interests of both parties, a written agreement is a necessity for optioning a literary property. The agreement will specify the nature of the property being optioned, the time period of the option, and the manner in which it is to be exercised. The agreement will also include the amount and manner of payment of both the option price and the acquisition price. Sometimes, the agreement will provide for the option price to be deducted from the acquisition price at the time the option is exercised. There may also be provision for the renewal of the option upon payment of a further amount of money.

It is obviously important for a producer to ensure that the option period is long enough to develop and finance a film or television program based on the optioned property. Because of the vagaries of the production industry and the requirements of many public funding agencies, an option period of at least two full years is recommended.

A producer actually acquires the optioned rights when the option is "exercised." A key element of the option agreement is the manner in which the exercise event occurs. If the option expires without the occurrence of the exercise event, no rights pass and the rights holder is free to negotiate with another party. If the exercise event occurs during the term of the option, the relevant rights are transferred to the optioning party under the terms of the option agreement. Because of its importance, the exercise event must be described quite precisely in the option agreement. Once the project is ready to go ahead, there must be no doubt about the producer's ability to obtain the necessary rights. Often the exercise event is the payment of the full purchase price of the rights; sometimes it is the occurrence of a particular stage in the production process, such as the first day of principal photography.

ENGAGING A SCREENWRITER

Once a producer has acquired, or possibly created, what are known as the underlying rights in a literary property, it is necessary to engage a writer to prepare the screenplay that is to be based on this work. In Canada, most successful film and television writers working in English belong to the Writers Guild of Canada (WGC). The Quebec-based French writers' guide is Société des auteurs, recherchistes, documentalistes et compositeurs (SARDEC).

The WGC is not a legal union in the true sense of the word, because it has not been certified by a labour relations board. Yet it negotiates "collective agreements" with most of the broadcasting organizations in Canada and with the various associations of independent producers. These negotiations occur more as an industry convention than a legal requirement. However, once the terms of these agreements are settled, the WGC uses its influence to ensure that the signatories and its own members adhere to them.

For independent film producers, the relevant writers' agreement is commonly known as the "WGC IPA." "IPA" stands for "Independent Production Agreement." (A copy of the WGC IPA can be obtained from the WGC in Toronto by calling 416-979-7907.) The essence of the WGC IPA is that, unlike the system in the United States, under which a writer receives residual payments depending on when and where a program is aired or exhibited, a writer under the WGC IPA is paid a royalty of 4 per cent of all revenues received by a producer from its worldwide exploitation in every medium ("Use Fee Royalties"). The writer receives two types of payments, which are advanced against

these royalties (that is, paid in advance of revenues being earned, but deducted later from the royalty owing):
1. the writer must receive a specified minimum payment for writing and submitting the script (the "Script Fee"); and
2. on the first day of principal photography, the writer must receive an "Advance on Use Fee Royalties," equal to the difference between the writing fees already paid and a specified percentage of the gross budget of the production.

Because both the Script Fee and Advance on use Fee Royalties are credited to 4 per cent Use Fee Royalty, a writer would not be entitled to share in revenues until most or all of the production budget has been recouped. In return for these minimum payments and royalty, a producer will acquire the rights to make a single film or television program from the screenplay and to exploit it in all media of communication throughout the world for the period of copyright in the screenplay. Under the provisions of the WGA IPA, a writer is required *not* to assign his or her copyright in the screenplay to the producer.

It almost goes without saying that a written agreement between the producer and the screenwriter is a necessity. It need not be long or complex, but it must ensure that the producer acquires adequate rights for the production and effective commercial distribution of the proposed film or television program.

WARRANTIES

When a producer enters into an investment, distribution, or exhibition agreement relating to a film or television production, the producer will be required to "warrant" or guarantee that the necessary production and distribution rights are held by the producer free and clear of any charge or encumbrance of any kind; and that the film, and hence the screenplay from which it is produced, will not infringe anyone's copyright, contain libellous statements about anyone, or invade anyone's right to privacy or publicity.

The effect of a warranty in any legal agreement is that the maker of the warranty is fully responsible for the consequences of the warranty's inaccuracy. For example, a producer warrants to a distributor that all necessary production and distribution rights have been acquired. This turns out to be incorrect, and the distributor is successfully sued for infringement of copyright. As a result of the warranty, the distributor could require the producer to pay for its entire loss, plus all its legal costs. In order to gain a measure of protection when making a warranty, a producer should ensure that the agreements with both the vendor of the underlying rights and with the screenwriter contain a similar warranty to the one that the producer will be required to give other parties.

A little-known provision of the WGC IPA stipulates that until the Advance On Use Fee Royalties, due on the first day of principal photography, is paid, no rights in the screenplay actually pass to the producer. Because of the contractual warranties (described above) that the producer is required to make, a failure to pay the applicable fee on the specified date can have very serious consequences indeed.

CHAIN OF TITLE

The various documents under which a producer acquires the rights to produce and distribute a film or television production are the fundamental base upon which the producer's own rights finally rest. If the documents are flawed, the copyright to the production is compromised. The documentation of every change in the assignment of these rights, from the author of the underlying work through the work's publisher to the screenwriter to the production company, is called the "chain of title." Quite often, tracing the chain of title can be an extremely complex task. Consider a situation in which a producer has purchased the rights to a number of books to be blended into a single story, has engaged a team of writers for the initial drafts of the screenplay, and has commissioned a number of rewrites. If the production is to be a musical, there is an additional lineage of rights belonging to the composer and lyricist and subsequently to those responsible for arranging and orchestrating the score.

When a well-informed investor, such as Telefilm Canada, is considering a particular investment, the first thing it requires is evidence that the chain of title safely delivers the relevant rights into the production entity that is seeking the investment.

A final comment about rights. Many producers arrange to have the relevant rights conveyed to their production corporations during the development stages of a project before the commencement of production. If this production company is an active business entity, it is likely to have a line of credit with a bank, and is almost certain to have executed a general security agreement in favour of the bank. Under the provisions of this type of agreement, the bank generally acquires a security interest over all program rights held by the company. A security interest is a form of encumbance that qualifies the title of the company to the program rights and hence its capacity to convey those rights to investors or distributors.

In order to avoid unnecessary complications in financing a production, it is therefore suggested that a separate corporation be established for each project designed to attract investor participation. The applicable rights or the project should be conveyed to this entity as soon as it is created, adding another step to the chain of title. Once this is done, the corporation must not make any banking arrangements unrelated to the specific project, including the giving of any form of guarantee to the active production company.

Legal Documentation

THE IMPORTANCE OF GOOD DOCUMENTATION

It is an intensely frustrating experience for many beginning producers to find out how much work is required to complete the documentation for an average film or television production. Just when they feel that all the pieces are in place and the real creative work can begin, the lawyers appear on the scene with all sorts of seemingly unreasonable demands.

These demands are often perceived as being excessive, an unnecessary reliance on technicalities and legalese. It must be understood, however, that when an inventor such as Telefilm Canada, or a major broadcaster or distributor, contributes hundreds of thousands of dollars to the budget of a production, it has an extremely strong interest in ensuring that it gets its money's worth in as risk free a manner as possible.

One of the unique qualities of a film or television production is that as a commercial transaction, it is merely an interlocking web of contractual elements dealing with property acquisition, financial packaging, and production and distribution, each layer built upon a previous contractual foundation. If the legal documentation for any layer is incomplete or improperly prepared, it creates a risk that threads its way right through the production.

Consider the implications of not controlling the relevant and underlying property rights, or of not receiving borrowed or invested funds on the day upon which they are required, or of losing the lead performer in mid-production, or of not being able to deliver a tape to the broadcaster in time for the scheduled airdate. Any of these events would have disastrous consequences, not only for the investors and distributors, but perhaps more importantly for the producer's own organization and reputation. While even the best legal agreements cannot ensure that these problems will never arise, they can substantially reduce the attendant risks by making absolutely clear who gets what, and who does what, at what times.

THE ROLE OF THE PRODUCER

Given the importance of contractual materials, the producer has a critical role in preparing the documents that will frame the production and ultimately bind it together. In the first instance, the producer must ensure that the documentation accurately reflects the arrangements negotiated for the production with all of the participating organizations and individuals. It is a terrible mistake for a producer to view the critical contracts as inconsequential technical forms. Any careful and professional producer will read, understand, and actively shape all of these materials.

Another critical matter requiring close attention is consistency among all of the contracts and agreements. It is amazing how often distribution agreements grant the same right to two different parties, or grant a right that the producer does not actually have. High-quality legal documentation is the lawyer's first responsibility; supervising and working with the lawyer is one of the producer's most important and least understood functions.

DEAL MEMORANDA

Because of the complexity of many legal agreements, producers often enter into deal memoranda or letter agreements, which briefly set out the matters that have been negotiated and agreed upon, and specify that a "full and formal" agreement will be prepared and executed at a later date. These documents are usually prepared and signed by the negotiating parties. Deal memoranda are very helpful in permitting business-like arrangements to be made quickly, effectively, and directly between the parties. They are also potentially very dangerous and must be used with great care.

Many producers believe that deal memoranda or letter agreements are not contractually binding. This is not the case; deal memoranda are no less enforceable than a hundred-page agreement. More often than not, they are never replaced by a "full and formal" agreement, despite the customary provision to the contrary. This is particularly likely if they contain a complete description of the transaction contemplated by the parties. For this reason, deal memoranda should never be entered into lightly. All contractually binding documents, no matter how simple or apparently inconsequential, should therefore be carefully reviewed with a producer's legal advisor before their execution.

Financing Arrangements

EQUITY INVESTMENT

In Chapter 4, there is a full discussion of the various mechanisms available in Canada for financing film and television productions. As a result, the comments here will be limited to a review of the basic legal concepts inherent in such arrangements.

The term *equity* is a synonym for ownership. In the context of a business corporation, equity is represented by the share capital of the company. In a film or television production, equity usually describes a direct, proportional interest in the copyright of the production.

The rights and obligations attached to the equity interest are found entirely in the legal agreement under the provisions of which the equity is acquired. When an investor signs the agreement and pays the purchase price of the equity interest, the relevant proportion of the copyright in the production is actually assigned and sold to the investor. Generally, an equity interest entitles an investor to receive a negotiated share of the revenues derived from the worldwide commercial exploitation of the production, both before and after the recoupment of its cost of production. (Sometimes the term "equity" is used colloquially to mean only an entitlement to a share of net profits, and not actually an ownership share of copyright).

If the investor is an individual, he or she is unlikely to have any creative role in the production or in monitoring production activities. However, if the investor is a broadcaster or Telefilm Canada, there is certain to be some form of continuing production monitoring, although the intensity of this activity will vary with the circumstances.

COMPLETION GUARANTEES

In order to protect the investor from any obligation for production cost overruns, the investment agreement should also protect the investor from any responsibility or requirement for contributing any more than his or her original investment. To ensure that funds are available to cover budget overruns, a producer will usually arrange for a *completion bond* from a *completion guarantor*. Once satisfied that the budget of a production is accurate and adequate and that all the required financing is in place, a guarantor will use its own funds to complete the production if the agreed-upon budget is exceeded. In order to protect itself, the guarantor closely supervises the production process to ensure that there is no drift away from an "on-budget" status. The guarantor reserves the right to step in and take over the production at any time if things are getting out of hand. If the guarantor is required to complete a production, it is entitled to recoup any costs it has incurred from the proceeds of distribution, once the production has returned its budgeted cost to the investors. The fee for a completion guarantee is usually calculated as a percentage of the cost of production.

ERRORS AND OMISSION INSURANCE

As has been indicated previously, the investment agreement will invariably contain an unqualified warranty by the producer that the investor is acquiring the interest in the copyright free and clear of all claims and encumbrances. Once the copyright has been sold to the investors, they assume some legal risk for infringement of copyright, libellous statements, and invasion of privacy (unless the investment vehicle is a limited partnership, in which case the investors are protected by their limited partnership status). In the event of a successful claim, of course, the investors would in turn claim reimbursement from the producer under the provisions of the warranty. However, this does not provide an adequate measure of protection.

To insure against the burden of copyright infringement, defamation, and invasion of privacy claims, a producer may obtain, along with the usual production coverage, an insurance policy covering what are known as *errors and omissions*. In order to obtain this coverage, however, a producer must satisfy the insurer that every possible prudent step has been taken to ensure that there will be no claims. Usually, the insurer requires that the producer answer a highly detailed questionnaire relating to the content of the proposed film or television production and obtain the services of a lawyer to help "vet" the project. If the insurer believes there is any appreciable risk, the coverage may not be offered or will be limited in some way.

TAX SHELTERS AND TAX CREDITS

In Canada, investment in a film or television production is made more attractive by provisions of the *Income Tax Act*. These provisions have been used to create what has been known as a *tax shelter*. Over the years, the tax shelter provisions for film and television production became progressively more complex and technical. As of 1995, the federal government decided to replace the tax shelter financing for film and TV projects with a 12 per cent refundable tax credit. This subject is discussed in more detail in Chapter 4.

PRE-SALES

Another frequently used technique for funding film and television productions is known as *pre-sale financing*. A pre-sale arrangement is one in which a broadcaster or distributor makes a commitment before production begins to pay a licence fee or distribution advance either during the course of production or upon delivery of the final product.

The licence fee would be paid in return for the right to air the production a specific number of times over a set period in a described territory. The distribution advance would be paid for the right to distribute the production in a described territory for a set period under specific terms and conditions covering the sharing of distribution revenues.

If the pre-sale commitment is payable on delivery, the producer might borrow against the broadcaster's or distributor's promise to pay. Alternatively, a producer might raise private investment for the entire cost of production and use the pre-sales undertaking as a form of committed return to make the investment more attractive.

Most productions that rely on pre-sales commitments as a financing technique arrange several of them for any given production. For example, a producer might obtain a licence fee from a Canadian broadcaster, an advance against distribution revenues from syndication (the licensing of programs to individual stations) in the United States, a licence fee from a Canadian or American pay television operation, and so on.

From a legal perspective, the most important aspect of any pre-sales commitment, aside from ensuring that it is a genuine commitment, is what is known as the grant of rights. Quite often, keeping the various grants separate and distinct can be tricky indeed. For instance, let us say that a Canadian broadcast network has purchased the right to air the production four times over three years; a Canadian regional broadcaster has the right to air it five times over a five-year period commencing after the network has had three runs; an American pay TV service has the exclusive right to air the production a number of times; and an American syndicator has the right to distribute the production once the pay-television "window" has elapsed. In this example, each of the exhibitors or distributors has acquired and paid for a specific right relating to a particular niche in the marketplace. The nature of the right is both inclusive and exclusive. That is to say, the right is not only defined by what the exhibitor or distributor can do, but also by what it cannot do. Each exhibitor or distributor, therefore, has as significant an interest in the clear definition of rights granted to all other exhibitors and distributors as in the definition of the rights it has been granted.

Because of the risks and complexities inherent in making a commitment to purchase a film or television production before production commences, pre-sale financing agreements have a tendency to be long and detailed, and to curtail the producer's control, both creative and financial. Those making the commitments usually wish to ensure that they have a sufficient number of contractual rights "in reserve" to take over the production if they believe it to be necessary.

Negotiating with exhibitors and distributors can be difficult and frustrating. More often than not, they insist that the producer sign a standard form agreement, which is heavily weighted against the producer. The only bright note is that when a producer signs such an agreement, he or she is in powerful company: all the best and most experienced Hollywood producers sign equally onerous agreements without flinching.

INTERIM FINANCING

Once a project's equity or pre-sale financing has been arranged, a producer may realize that the flow of funds resulting from these deals will not match the cash-flow requirements of the production. Usually, revenue from an equity investment or a major pre-sale will not be received until the latter stages of production or even until after the production has been completed.

In these circumstances, the producer must obtain a short-term loan to fund production activities. Telefilm and Rogers Telefund are two possible sources of such loans. Getting such loans from private banks is often very difficult, primarily because there is little accepted value in the collateral offered to the lender as security for the loan. Film and television productions do not have much in common with hard assets such as land or inventory, for which there is a readily ascertainable market.

In seeking interim financing, a producer may offer a lender one of the following types of security:
- the right to be repaid out of revenues from the exploitation of the production; or
- the right to be repaid out of the sale of equity units purchased by investors.

Private and institutional lenders are beginning to show renewed interest in the industry. At the moment, this interest is generally limited to projects undertaken by the more successful and financially sound producers. If these transactions prove to be profitable for lenders, however, financial institutions will likely become more receptive to producers' blandishments.

Some private organizations will still lend against an assignment of the revenues to be received from a sale of units to investors. However, most financial institutions will only "bank" a specific pre-sale agreement, which, for example, makes a commitment to pay a licence fee upon delivery of the completed production. The "bankability" of such pre-sale agreements depends very much upon the individual circumstances of each case. If the pre-sale agreement contains an excessive number of vague conditions concerning payment, the financial institution will either decline to accept it as security or heavily discount its value.

With the resurgent interest in the industry, there is also the possibility that certain institutions will lend against an assignment of revenues that have not yet been contracted for. However, this type of financial assistance will only be made available to producers with very strong track records, and only where the amount of the loan is quite small in comparison to the level of revenue that is virtually certain to be received.

No matter how enthusiastic financial institutions may become about participating in film and television projects, they will always seek as much security as possible for their loans. For this reason, producers dealing with them should expect a routine requirement that they provide corporate and possibly personal guarantees of the production's obligations to the financial institution.

Canadian Content Certification

As every Canadian producer knows, almost no market exists in Canada for his or her productions unless they have been certified as "Canadian" by a government agency. In addition to the predictable controversies and complexities surrounding the attempt to define a Canadian production, there is the added twist of having two (and some would say, three) separate certification systems. The two formal systems are operated by the Canadian Audio-Visual Certification Office (CAVCO) of the Department of Canadian Heritage of the Government of Canada and the Canadian Radio-television and Telecommunications Commission (CRTC).

THE CAVCO SYSTEM

The certification system operated by Heritage Canada is used primarily by those producers wishing to offer private investors units in a film or television production. This form of certification is necessary in order to take advantage of the tax shelter described in this book.

Essentially, certification is available to a production that:

- has a Canadian producer;
- achieves 6 out of a possible 10 "points" for key personnel;
- spends on Canadians 75 per cent of the remuneration paid to individuals other than the key personnel; and
- spends 75 per cent of all laboratory and processing costs in Canada.

The ten possible points for Canadian personnel are allotted as follows:

Director	2 points
Screenwriter	2 points
Highest paid actor	1 point
Second highest paid actor	1 point
Head of art department	1 point
Director of photography	1 point
Composer	1 point
Editor	1 point

There are other more detailed requirements, all of which should be carefully considered. For instance, either the director or screenwriter must be Canadian; and either the highest or second highest paid actor must also be Canadian.

CAVCO will also certify productions that are recognized under formal co-production treaties entered into between Canada and a number of other countries (excluding the United

States). Note though, that it is Telefilm Canada, on behalf of the Department of Canadian Heritage, that administers compliance with these treaties. A producer wishing certification of a co-production must first apply to Telefilm Canada for approval of the co-production, and then apply to the Department of Heritage for final certification.

For more information regarding the Department of Heritage certification system, you should write to:

Canadian Audio-Visual Certification Office
365 Laurier Avenue West
15th Floor
Ottawa, Ontario
K1P 5K2

THE CRTC SYSTEM

The certification system operated by the CRTC is used for productions that will appear on licensed Canadian television broadcast services. These broadcasters must all meet Canadian content quotas, thus making programs that qualify as "Canadian" somewhat more attractive than they might otherwise be. When a broadcaster appears before the CRTC to have its licence renewed, it must report how many hours of Canadian programming it provides. In addition, the CRTC has special rules for local station productions, sports programming, music videos, and dubbed programs.

The CRTC recognizes for its own purposes the certification issues by CAVCO under the rules described above. However, because of certain differences between the two systems, CAVCO does not recognize CRTC certification. Therefore, any television production that is made using private investment must be certified by CAVCO as well as the CRTC.

The basic CRTC system is the same as the CAVCO system,

relying on the identical calculation of points and expenditure requirements. The difference between the two systems lies in the CRTC's willingness to certify where:

- a program is produced under a "co-venture" arrangement satisfactory to the CRTC; or
- a television series complies as a whole with the requirements, even where some episodes do not; or
- a program package produced by a co-venture meets the overall requirements an average.

A co-venture can be certified where the Canadian and foreign production companies have equal approval over all elements of the production, where both have an equity interest in and financial responsibility for the production, and where both have co-signing authority over the production bank account. Co-ventures must attain 5 Canadian points and expend 50 per cent of total remuneration and processing costs on Canadians if the co-venture is made with a producer from a Commonwealth or French-language country. Other co-ventures are required to meet the same points and expenditure requirements as domestic productions.

The CRTC allows licensed television services a 150 per cent program credit for a drama that achieves 10 out of 10 Canadian points and is carried in prime time. (This means, for example, that a one-hour program scoring 10 out of 10 could be credited to the network in question as one-and-a-half hours of Canadian programming.)

The CRTC certification system is described in Public Notice 1984–94. CRTC Public Notice 1988-105 describes specific rules for animated films. For copies, you should write to Public Affairs, CRTC, Ottawa, Ontario, L1A 0N2.

The so-called "third" certification system is that operated by Telefilm Canada. While Telefilm accepts the certification requirements of both Heritage Canada and the CRTC, it sees itself as having a mandate to ensure that the productions it invests in are as Canadian as possible. For this reason, Telefilm often uses its considerable clout to ensure that the minimum Canadian content requirements are not just met, but exceeded. A few producers feel that this amounts to a separate, and largely unspecified, certification system. The fact is, however, that Telefilm is merely exercising its discretion to give its greatest support to predominantly Canadian projects.

Summary

If there are any points worth re-emphasizing concerning the business of film and television production and the law, they are these:

- Independent production in Canada is now a sophisticated and complex commercial enterprise. As one step in addressing this reality, producers should establish a good working relationship with a capable lawyer;
- Producers must be knowledgeable about all the matters discussed in this chapter and, indeed, in this book;
- Producers should understand the details of all the agreements they enter into for the financing and production of a film or television project; and
- Producers should insist on thorough and professional documentation for all major agreements and should personally supervise the preparation of this material.

11

THE WRAP

by SEATON MCLEAN

S eaton McLean is president of Atlantis Films Limited and is a principal shareholder and executive vice-president of Atlantis Communications Inc., Canada's leading independent producer specializing in
television programs.

He has produced for Canadian and American networks, with his
award-winning programming (Oscar, Geminis, Emmy, Cable Aces)
selling around the world. Recent series titles include: "Tekwar,"
"African Skies," "The Ray Bradbury Theatre," "Maniac
Mansion," "Twilight Zone," and many made-for-television movies.

The Business of Film and Television Production in Canada . . . the
title says it all. Not the "Art" of Film and Television in Canada,
nor the "Technique", nor the "Guide" — nope, the business.
That's what this book is about and that's what independent
production in this country has become: a business and a big
one, at that. Before the early eighties, most of the notable television drama production in Canada took place at either the
CBC or the NFB. That is not to say there weren't exceptions, like
"The Forest Rangers," "Adventures in Rainbow Country," "The

New Avengers," or *"Matt and Jenny,"* but they were few and far between.

The Canadian feature film industry only really came into existence in the late sixties and early seventies and was largely driven by government subsidies. Quebec films connected with their public in a way that has remained elusive for the rest of the country. Many incentives were tried to spark production at this time, some of which were frankly disastrous initiatives. The capital cost allowance of the late seventies resulted in a lot of bad films being made for the wrong reasons.

Now, most of the dramatic production in Canada is being independently produced and, just as significantly, this production is taking place in every region of the country. Television shows of the mid-eighties, like *"Night Heat," "Airwaves," "E.N.G.," "The Edison Twins," "Degrassi Street,"* and *"Danger Bay,"* paved the way for shows like *"Due South," "Road to Avonlea," "North of Sixty," "Tek War," "Ready or Not," "Madison," "Destiny Ridge,"* and *"The Odyssey."* Meanwhile the CBC, hit by budget cuts every year for the past ten years, is producing one in-house drama series (*"Side Effects"*) and few if any television movies. The NFB, also nailed by deep budget cuts in recent years, is preoccupied simply with trying to maintain its existence and fend off the eventuality of being relegated to training school status.

The hard lessons learnt as a result of the CCA experiment resulted in policy decisions that laid the groundwork for the emergence of a generation of young filmmakers. The key decision was to throw as much energy into developing a viable television industry, which inevitably spilled over into increased film production. Expectations were also altered and it was decided to slowly build the careers of filmmakers who could balance between the marketplace and personal expression. Directors like Denys Arcand, Atom Egoyan, Jean-Claude Lauzon,

Bruce Macdonald, and Patricia Rozema produced critically acclaimed work that also returned money. It helped that some of these films were low budget, so the risk factor on investment was minimal.

What is occurring in the industry today is the direct result of federal government policy and initiatives started over a decade ago. In July of 1983, the Canadian Broadcast Program Development Fund was established and the Canadian Film Development Corporation became Telefilm Canada. Funded to the tune of $65 million for an initial five-year term (it subsequently became permanent), Telefilm's mandate was to help create and foster a viable independent film and television industry. In addition to Telefilm, agencies were also funded by many provincial governments to assist regional production through investments and tax rebate programs. Not coincidentally, all of this government support and money was being pumped into the independent sector while the CBC and NFB budgets were, and still are, being cut to the bone. This situation will probably not change in the short term: say, the next five to ten years. In the long term it will probably be economics, and the battle between the defenders of support for Canadian culture and the free-market American lobbyists, that will determine whether the government can stay involved in the film and television business it has been so effective in helping to create.

Timing, as always, will be everything. As healthy as the production industry is today, one has to wonder what would happen if Canadian content regulations regarding broadcasting and government financial support were abolished tomorrow. Could a nation of 28 million people sustain an industry our size if it weren't subsidized? Could Canadian broadcasters afford to pay five or six times their present licence fees for homegrown production? Could even the publicly traded production companies that have sprung up in the last two years continue to exist in an unregulated environment? Would the industry, in order to exist, simply become a branch plant servicing Hollywood productions? Although vibrant, our industry is still in its formative stage, still learning, still growing, and, if we want to see its potential fully realized, still in need of support.

In 1985, Peter Pearson, then executive director of Telefilm Canada, was quoted in *Saturday Night* magazine, for a story on "The New Wave of Young Canadian Producers," as saying "They're the first generation who are going to stay here in Canada, who find it exciting to work in a Canadian content. They don't reach for the American star or the established director to make things work. They're young, intelligent, wilful, 200 per cent confident, and they're rooted in this country." Well, all that was true and is still true today. However, those "young wilful" producers are now ten years older, and ten years more experienced. More and more they *are* "reaching for that American star to make things work." This is the price that must be paid if Canadian producers, in the "business" of making films and television shows, are going to compete in a marketplace that is dominated by Hollywood. Indeed, nowhere else on the planet is this more true than in Canada. Our movie theatres' box office is factored into the large U.S. studios' "domestic" figures when calculating a film's take each week. Our airwaves are practically a mirror-image of those of the U.S.; a simulcast is the brass ring for Canadian broadcasters. Outside of Quebec, Canada doesn't have a distinct culture, a distinct language, or a geographic distance to protect itself from the marketing machine that is Hollywood.

The harsh realities are that, first, to get a film or television series produced you need a lot of cash; and second, if you add up all the places there are in Canada to get it, it usually isn't enough. So to finance your production you have to get a presale outside of Canada, the United States being the most obvious choice because of the items mentioned: proximity, language, and culture. If you are able to secure a U.S. commitment, however, you will have given something up — probably casting — to get it. The downside is that Canadian actors don't get the plum roles; the upside is that your film or television show will now probably attract a bigger audience in Canada and its sales potential abroad has just increased. One might argue that this makes good business sense.

Just as it has entrenched itself in movies and home video, marquee value will become more and more important to getting a broadcaster's commitment. If you buy into the scenario of a 500-channel universe, then this is even more true. Stars are one of the few ways, especially for TV movies, to ensure that your show will be produced. As budgets for U.S. feature films continue to skyrocket, fewer will be made, leaving a lot of good, recognizable actors looking for television work, and they'll get it. This in turn will mean that our ability to compete with these shows will be reduced unless we can attract the same level of marquee talent to our shows: that is, meet their price tag. And *this* in turn means that the budgets of these television shows will go up, making us more reliant on a U.S. pre-sale to get the show financed. Looks like a vicious circle, doesn't it?

Luckily marquee value can extend beyond casting to subject matter: people will always watch if the subject intrigues them. But, one way or the other, you must make your production stand above the crowd, because the crowd is getting bigger and bigger.

Recently someone asked me if it was easier or harder to start a production company today than it was 17 years ago. My first response was that it was probably harder then. After all, there were nowhere near the support mechanisms that there are now in the industry; nowhere near the outlets for produced films or shows; nowhere near the talent, both in front of and behind the camera; nowhere near the dollars that are now coursing through the veins of the business. Yes, definitely harder, I responded. Later I thought about it some more and realized that I might have been wrong. After all, there weren't the gate-keepers protecting the entranceways to the industry. Hell, there wasn't really an industry! It was cheaper, and if you screwed up, no one noticed. In short, there were a lot fewer distractions while you concentrated on getting the job done. No, upon reflection, it was probably easier to get into the business 17 years ago. Fortunately, I thought about it some more and realized "what a stupid question!" The correct answer to that stupid question is that it is *never* easy: not now, not 17 years ago. As the saying goes, if it were easy, everyone would be doing it! However, having said that, here are some facts of life that the Canadian producer takes for granted in 1995:

- Telefilm
- OFDC (Ontario Film Development Corporation)
- CIDO (Canadian Manitoba Cultural Industries Development Office)
- AMPDC (Alberta Motion Picture Development Corporation)
- B.C. Film (British Columbia Film)
- SASKFILM (Saskatchewan Film Development Corporation)
- SODEC (Société de développement des entreprises culturelles de Québec)
- OFIP (Ontario Film Investment Program)
- Rogers Telefund
- Maclean Hunter Television Fund
- Shaw Children's Programming Initiative
- FUND (Foundation to Underwrite New Drama)
- Canadian Film Centre
- Seven new specialty channels
- Cable Production Fund
- Half a dozen publicly traded production companies
  All but Telefilm did not exist before 1985.

Many tools are available to fledgling producers today, to aid them in learning and practising their craft, than there were ten years ago; trade forums, symposiums, trainee programs, guest lecturers, and workshops. The workbench is littered with every conceivable device a person might need to become a producer. The only thing that is missing is the manual. Bad news, there isn't one — not even the wonderful book that you now hold in your hands. Sure, there's a heap of good information that will make your life easier, but it won't make you a producer. *Tenacity* is a word that always springs to my mind when describing what it takes to become a producer. Sure, it helps to be creative, to be ingenious, to have good communication skills, but kid, if ya' ain't got tenacity, forget it! You have to be tenacious to get any film or television show made. It can take years and you'll suffer plenty of abuse along the way.

Access is another word that will figure prominently in the producing vocabulary of the future: access to stories and rights, access to talent, access to broadcasters, and access to funding. Last November, I was on a panel at the Vancouver Trade Forum. The subject was "How to Start a Successful Film Company." The moderator asked how many of the roughly 200 people in the audience were producers. More than two-thirds of the hands went up! The moderator then asked how many of those producers were with a company or entity that had more than three people working in it. Only half a dozen hands remained up. That's a big problem, because there isn't enough room in Vancouver (or Western Canada, for that matter), for 175 individual producers. Besides, producing is all about collaboration and teamwork.

The most obvious success stories in Canadian producing involve individuals who collaborated under one name or banner. The National Film Board, Nelvana, Alliance, Cinar, Credo, Atlantis, Salter Street, Paragon, Playing With Time, Rhombus, Insight, Great North, and Forefront among others. By and large it will be with these companies that those 175 producers will be, and arguably should be, working to transform their ideas into reality. These are the companies that have the all-important track record, have the connections to the broadcasters, and have access to financing and talent. They also have a big appetite for new ideas, ideas that can become films or television shows. Luckily, everyone can have a good idea now and then.

Canada's film and television industry is evolving more and more toward an American studio model: smaller companies or individual producers working under the umbrella of larger, well-funded, and probably vertically integrated companies. These "core" companies, among other things, provide an important service to the broadcasters and funding agencies: namely, screening. A producer will often be told to go and solicit the interest or involvement of one of these "core" companies before looking to the broadcaster or funding agency for a commitment. These companies will evaluate the viability of a project both within and beyond the Canadian marketplace, evaluate the professionalism of the producer, and be willing to play the role of mentor and intermediary if the project is greenlighted. This is not a bad thing: it is simply part of the maturing or evolution of the industry. The smaller producer gains valuable information and experience from working with the larger company; the broadcaster and funding agencies are more confident that the film or show will be delivered as promised; and the larger company fulfils its need for new ideas in which broadcasters have already expressed an interest.

This evolution was hastened by the fact that several of the larger and more established companies went public over the last year-and-a-half. For the first time in Canada's history, there are film and television production companies that are well capitalized. It will be these companies that will take a risk position in a producer's project; fund the development of a producer's idea; seek out international co-production possibilities for a producer's idea; and share the burden of financing a production with a broadcaster. They'll also, by the way, want to share the credit and control the distribution of the producer's idea once it becomes more than an idea. But of course there's always a price tag to getting your project made. And that is, after all, what it is all about: getting your project made.

Don't be sidetracked or distracted by the 500-channel universe, or the satellite versus cable debate, or whether interactive, CD-ROM, or pay-per-view is the wave of the future. And under no circumstances get into that Information Highway/Internet discussion! Remember, whatever the medium or delivery system, software is the message. The only thing that has changed, because of technology, is audience choice. You now have many more outlets for your ideas and many more chances to get your show made. At last count, there were approximately 80 different advertiser-supported or pay cable networks in the United States, and another half-dozen in Canada, all of them needing programming.

These new channels also afford a huge opportunity to up-and-coming producers (much as basic cable did when it started out in the United States) to cut your teeth and hone your skills. Because they don't have the same advertising revenue as the networks, they can't afford to pay huge licence fees, making them open to exploring cheaper alternatives, including the producer who has less of a track record and, just as important, less of an overhead. These channels, for the most part, work the niches and leave the "broad" casting to the networks. In even a 250-channel universe, niches are going to become more and more significant.

One need to look no further than the history of the magazine industry to see the course that television broadcasting is on; it's called narrowcasting. As the cost of publishing decreased with the introduction of new technology and the population increased as a result of the baby boom, publishers could cater to more specific tastes and deliver more specific demographics to their advertisers. What had been a hit-and-miss relationship through the large, broad-appeal magazines became a direct dialogue.

Gut instinct used to be the producer's secret weapon, but that is no longer the case. Things have gotten too complicated for any one person's gut to divine anything. We need to be aware of what the market is looking for, and what people are watching or not watching. Everyone is now aware of ratings. The Nielsen ratings are reported in the paper a couple of days after a show airs. There is more pressure to perform, to "get numbers." It's only going to get worse as the audience pie keeps shrinking for the traditional broadcasters. In Canada, it used to be that if you got a series on-air it was pretty well guaranteed to be renewed. There were plenty of viewers to go around for the few channels that existed, and it was easier for broadcasters to go with what they already had than to come up with something new. Could a "*Tommy Hunter Show*" or a "*Front Page Challenge*" or a "*Beachcombers*" ever exist on-air for a decade or more if they were being introduced to the marketplace now?

Meanwhile, although English-Canadian films enjoy critical attention internationally and domestically, the film industry as such remains a fragile enterprise and commercial success is still elusive. Many film companies earn their bread and butter through television production but use film as a prestige item. The risks are still enormous and the returns minimal. Quebec, which used to have a loyal audience for its local productions, has seen this audience drift away. Many of its filmmakers are also shooting in English in an attempt to break into the international marketplace.

In the highly competitive environment we work in, the priority must be to grab an audience, and once you have it, to keep it. We have to focus test our ideas more, get feedback on them, and be willing to alter them if our research tells us to. We have to become better entrepreneurs, marketers, and promoters to get our shows or films noticed. We have to know our audience, and be able to spot changing trends in the marketplace. A good idea is no longer enough: it's how you pitch it, sell it, produce it, then market it that makes for a successful film or television show.

This chapter benefited from the film industry expertise of Piers Handling, director of the Toronto International Film Festival Group.

Glossary

Above-the-line costs In a production budget, the amounts to be spent on "the principal creative elements," such as story and script, producer, director, and lead performers.

Adaptation A screenplay based on another work, most commonly a novel, short story, or stage play.

ADR See **Automatic dialogue replacement**.

Answer print The colour-corrected print made from the master negative with the final mix soundtrack, used for checking the technical quality of the film before the release prints are made.

Art director The person responsible for creating the "look" of the production, which can include supervision of the visual elements such as locations, sets, props, wardrobe, makeup, and hair. If there is no production designer, the art director is head of the Art Department. See also **Production designer**.

Assistant director See **First Assistant director**.

Automatic dialogue replacement (ADR) A simpler, more modern version of looping. See also **Looping**.

Bank financing See **Interim Financing**

Barter deal A three-way financing arrangement, whereby a corporate sponsor may invest in a production in return for free commercial time from the broadcaster who will be airing the production.

Below-the-line costs In a production budget, all the amounts to be spent on the production of the film that are not included in above-the-line costs, including cast (other than leading performers), crew, travel/living expenses, laboratory, legal and accounting fees, insurance, financing expenses, and post-production expenses.

Board See **Production board.**

Breakdown A scene-by-scene analysis of the script, identifying and listing locations, studio sets, characters, character/days, etc. Every department within the production will create its own breakdown to suit its own responsibilities.

Budget The detailed financial plan for the production, which dictates all details of how the production will be achieved.

Buyout Prepayment to performers for the right to exhibit or broadcast the production in which they appeared, in specified markets and for specified lengths of time.

Call sheet A form, distributed at the end of each day, listing all the scenes to be shot, all the cast, crew, extras, props, and extraordinary equipment required, and all the basic logistical needs for the following day.

Caps Payment schedules that put a cap, or limit, on the amount of money to be paid to cast or crew.

Capital Cost Allowance This was a tax deferral program administered by the Canadian Audio-Visual Certification Office of the Department of Heritage, designed to encourage private investment in Canadian productions. A private investor financing a production that was certified Canadian was entitled to deduct 300 per cent of his or her investment from personal income tax, over a period of two years. This was replaced by the Federal Tax Credit in 1995. See also **Certified Canadian Production** and **Federal Tax Credits**.

Cash-flow projection A timetable derived from the budget and production schedule that indicates the points at which income will be needed to cover anticipated cash outflow.

Casting director A person who advises on the selection of actors for roles in a production.

Certified Canadian production A production approved by the Canadian Audio-Visual Certification Office of the Department of Heritage to qualify as a Canadian production under the terms of the Capital Cost Allowance Program. See also **Capital Cost Allowance** and **Federal Tax Credits**.

Chain of title A series of documents attesting to every change in ownership of the property.

Cinematographer See **Director of photography**.

Completion guarantor The person or company who contracts to deliver a finished production at no additional cost to its investors, should it go over budget. The guarantor's fee is normally 1 to 6 percent of the budget.

Contingency (fund) An extra allowance added to the production budget to cover unexpected expenses. The contingency normally is at least 10 per cent of the above-the-line and below-the-line expenses to satisfy the completion guarantor.

Continuity The matching of actions, costumes, and other details from take to take, which to some degree is the responsibility of everyone on the set, but is the special responsibility of the script supervisor. See also **Script supervisor**.

Contra deal A financing arrangement whereby suppliers

provide services, props, etc. to the production, in return for the prominent placement of their products in the production or a promotional listing in the credits of the production.

Copyright The right to reproduce, publish, perform, or broadcast all or a substantial portion of a protected work. The owner of the copyright in the work is the author, unless the work was produced as part of the duties of an employee, in which case the owner is the employer. In Canada, the period of copyright is the life of the author plus 50 years. See also **Public domain**.

Cost report A document prepared weekly during production and monthly during post-production (usually by the production manager and the accountant), showing how much has been spent, how much remains, and the predicted final outlay in each budget category.

Co-production The term commonly used for any production that qualifies as an official co-production under the terms of treaty agreements signed between Canada and several foreign countries. Official co-production status provides the production with all the benefits of an indigenous production in both co-producing countries. See also **Co-ventures**.

Co-venture A production undertaken with a partner in a country that does not have a co-production treaty with Canada.

Craft services Members of the crew who make sure that coffee, snacks, etc., are continuously available on the set.

Cross-collateralization In a distribution deal, an arrangement whereby losses or unrecouped advances from the distribution of a film or TV program in a particular market or media will be recouped by the distributor from revenue received from other media or territories.

Dailies See **Rushes**.

Daily production report A detailed report on each day's shooting, including number of hours worked, number of scenes and pages shot, footage used, footage printed, and the personnel and equipment involved.

Day-out-of-days A calendar cross-plot that groups scenes and actors for the most efficient expenditure of time and money.

Deal memorandum Contractually binding document, setting out in summary form the terms that the negotiating parties have agreed upon. Usually followed by a "full and formal" agreement at a later date. Also called letter of agreement.

Deferral An arrangement by which director, cast, crew, suppliers, etc., may agree to wait for all or part of their money until a later, defined time usually after the production begins to generate revenues.

Development The work necessary — which may include acquiring the property, writing script drafts, budgeting, packaging of stars, director, and other creative personnel — to get a project to the point where it receives production financing. This is the stage in the production process when money is hardest to raise and most at risk.

Development financing The financing needed at the first stage of a film or television project, when the property is acquired, the screenplay completed, preliminary budget prepared, and some key creative personnel obtained. See also **Development** and **Production financing**.

Director The person with overall creative control of the production, which includes having input into casting and script, and translating the script into film or video form by choosing the images and moulding the performances.

Director of photography (dop) The camera and lighting supervisor on a production, overseeing the work of the camera crew. Also known as the cinematographer.

Distributor A person or company holding the rights to market and distribute films or videos to such markets as theatrical, free TV, pay TV, video clubs, airlines, etc.

Editor The person responsible for piecing together the various elements that have been filmed and recorded, to form a coherent whole.

Electronic press kit (epk) A video package distributed to news media to publicize a theatrical feature film. It usually contains interviews with stars and director, movie clips, sound bites, and behind-the-scenes footage edited to be easily adapted to TV formats.

Equity investment An investment arrangement by which the investor gains an ownership interest in an asset. (For the purposes of this book, the asset would be a film or television program.)

Errors and omissions (e&o) Insurance for a film covering the producer's legal liability for alleged unauthorized use of titles, ideas, characters, plots; invasion of privacy; libel; slander; defamation of character; etc.

Exhibitor The owner or operator of a movie theatre.

Fact sheet A short reference sheet in a television press kit, listing length of program, network for which it was made, concept for the program or series, cast, and technical credits.

Federal Tax Credits A replacement for the federal Capital

Cost Allowance program, intended to provide rebates to "qualified taxable Canadian corporations" for investment in Canadian productions that meet CAVCO (the Canadian Audio-visual Certification Office of the department of Heritage) certification requirements. See also **Capital Cost Allowance**, **Certified Canadian production**.

FINANCING See **Development financing**, **Production financing**, and **Interim financing**.

FINE CUT The final edited picture cut of a film.

FIRST ASSISTANT DIRECTOR (1ST AD) The director's right hand. During preproduction, the 1st AD will plan the shooting of each scene with the director; do the breakdown of the script; and prepare the board and day-out-of-days. On the set, the 1st AD transmits the director's orders to the crew and cast to the point when the director says, "Action."

FLATS Payment arrangements that provide cast or crew with a flat daily rate, no matter how many hours they work.

FOLEY A system for creating synchronized sound effects during post-production.

FREE TV Television service broadcast without charge to viewers; includes commercial (advertiser-supported) TV and public (mainly government-supported) TV. Also known as conventional TV.

GAFFER The head of lighting and electrical departments on the set.

GRIP See **Key grip**.

GROSS DEAL A type of distribution deal in which the gross receipts are shared between the distributor and the producer from first dollar, with no deductions other than the distributor's advance, if there has been one. See also **Net deal.**

Guarantee A sum of money that is payable regardless of a film's performance in the marketplace. The minimum amount of revenue offered for the right to exploit a movie. Guarantees can be paid in advance, on signing a contract, or at a specific date thereafter.

Interim financing Short-term funding arranged by the producer to bridge periods when cash flowing in will not cover predicted cash outflow. Also called **bank financing**.

International track See **Music and Effects track.**

Joint venture See **Co-venture**.

Key art The design concept used to identify a film or television program for packaging and marketing purposes, including such items as script cover design, advertising and promotional material, company logo, and title design.

Key grip The head of the grip department, in charge of moving cameras and lights, laying track for dollying, etc.

Licence Fee A payment made by a broadcaster in return for the right to broadcast a program on a specified number of occasions over a specified length of time.

Limited partnership A partnership in which the liability of each partner is limited to the amount invested in the partnership.

Location Any site where the production may shoot that is not in a studio.

Location manager The person responsible for finding, negotiating for, securing, and administering locations for a production.

Looping The recording of dialogue to replace original dialogue that is unusable because of noise, accent, or performance done to match previously filmed lip movements of the performer. See also **ADR**.

"Majors" The key Hollywood-based studios that produce and distribute major motion pictures, such as Columbia, 20th Century Fox, Warner Bros., and Paramount.

Music and effects track (M/E track) A film's sound track excluding the dialogue, needed for dubbing the film into a foreign language. Also called an international track.

Music cue sheet A list of all pieces of music in a production, stating length, composer, publisher, affiliation (Performing Rights Organization — PRO or Composers. Authors and Publishers Association of Canada — CAPAC), and usage (feature or background).

Mixing The combining of sound tracks — dialogue, music, and sound effects — to produce a single, balanced sound track.

Negative cutter The person who cuts the original negative (the film exposed in the camera) to match the fine cut of the workprint.

Net deal A type of distribution deal in which the gross receipts are shared between distributor and producer after deduction of distributor's fee, agreed-upon distribution expenses, and advances to the producer, if any. See also **Gross deal.**

Non-linear editing Refers to random access, computer-based, digital video editing, which allows for free movement and manipulation of audio and visual information.

Offering memorandum A legal document regulated by the Security Act, similar to, but more flexible than, a prospectus, commonly used in Ontario to sell shares in a production when is an exemption from the prospectus requirement. With an offering memorandum, the producer may approach no more than 75 potential investors and sell to no more than 50 of them.

Option (on a literary property) The payment of a (usually) relatively small sum of money in return for the exclusive purchase rights to the property within a specified time period.

Pairing See **Twinning**.

Partnership A business with at least two owners, who share proceeds according to an agreement. Each partner is liable for the debts and obligations of all the partners in the business. See **Limited partnership**.

"Pay or play" A "pay or play" obligation is a contract commitment to use (and pay for) the services of an individual, and to pay for these services even in the event that you do not use them.

Pay-tv A TV service paid for by viewers and carried on a network.

Playdates Dates when a film is scheduled to be exhibited in theatres.

"Points" Percentage participation in the profits of a production. Points may be defined in many ways, and must therefore be clearly specified when they are being negotiated.

Post-production The work done on a film after principal photography is completed: generally the editing, sound, music, mixing, and final lab work leading to the final answer print.

Post-production transcript A written copy of every line of dialogue and narration in a production, used by foreign buyers to subtitle or version (dub) the production in other languages.

Pre-sale A sale made to a distributor or broadcaster before the project has begun production.

Press kit A package of materials designed for the media, prepared under the supervision of the unit publicist. The kit contains photos; plot synopsis; bios of feature players, producer, director and screenwriter; column notes, and feature stories.

Principal photography The shooting of all scenes requiring the body of the crew and any of the leading performers.

Pre-production (prep) All aspects of preparation for production that take place after production financing has been confirmed but before shooting begins. See also **Development, Production, Post-production**.

Production board (the board) A graphic representation of all the scenes and characters in the production, arranged according to the sequence in which they will be filmed, and coded for interior/exterior and day/night. The information is displayed on flexible, removable strips. Increasingly, the board is being replaced by software packages that can output this information.

Production co-ordinator The production manager's right hand, usually with specific responsibility for communication changes in script and schedules and for organizing and disseminating logistical information.

Production designer The creative head of the Art Department, responsible, with the director, for the overall look, mood, and style of what will be shot.

Production financing The financing needed for completion and delivery of a project, including the pre-production, production, and post-production phases. See also **Development financing** and **Interim financing.**

Production manager (PM) The person who oversees all business and logistical arrangements for a production.

Production notes Detailed documentation ("the making of...") of the shooting of film, prepared by the unit publicist.

Production stills Photographs taken by the set photographer during the course of shooting a film or television program.

Profit All revenues generated by a production from all sources after deduction of all the costs associated with production, distribution, and exhibition.

Property The written description of a specific creative concept, stressing its unique characteristics. A story property would include a detailed description of characters, plot, and other distinguishing details.

Proprietorship See **Sole proprietorship.**

Prospectus A very detailed legal document regulated by the Securities Act in force in each province, which provides full financial information about a production as well as details about the business and everyone involved, used to sell shares in a production to the public.

Public domain Works in the public domain are unprotected by copyright. See also **Copyright.**

Publicist A specialist in co-ordinating and presenting information about a client in such a way that media attention is directed toward the client. See also **Unit publicist.**

Release print The print of a film ready for distribution and exhibition.

Rough cut An arbitrary stage of picture cut that falls somewhere between the first assembly and the fine cut. See also **Fine Cut.**

Rushes The positive film or video rendering of a particular day's shooting, usually screened the following day; also called dailies.

Sales agent Sales person who represents a producer or production company and its productions, usually on a commission basis.

Screenplay The script written for a film.

Screenwriter The person who writes screenplays and treatments for films.

Script The detailed written version of a film or television program, including dialogue and narration, and brief descriptions of characters, settings, action, and sound effects. The final version of a script is called the shooting script.

Script supervisor The person on the set who is responsible for checking that details match from one shot to the next, noting any changes in script and dialogue, and noting the director's choice of takes.

Second unit The backup crew on a production, which shoots additional footage that requires no dialogue or closeups.

Set photographer The person who takes photographs on the set (known as production stills) during the time the film is being shot, to be used for publicity and promotion.

Shot list A list of all the shots to be made for a production, on a scene-by-scene, location-by-location basis, prepared by the director with input from other personnel.

Simulcast The simultaneous broadcasting of a program by two or more broadcasters.

Sole proprietorship An unincorporated business owned and operated by one person, who receives all profits from the business and is liable for all of its debts and obligations.

Star Performer who is sufficiently well known that he/she is perceived to bring an economic benefit to any production in which he/she appears in a leading role.

Story property See **Property**.

Storyboard A graphic depiction of the sequence of shots and action, as planned before shooting the production.

Syndication sales Sales of TV programs or films made on a station-by-station basis.

Theatre circuit The chain of theatres belonging to a particular exhibition company.

Timing Colour collection of the negative in the laboratory.

Trailer A commercial for a film exhibited in movie theatres before or during the run of a film. Most trailers include scenes from the coming attraction edited to create the greatest interest in it.

Treatment A narrative synopsis of a screenplay, including descriptions of the characters, the plot in which they are involved, and perhaps some dialogue.

Twinning The contractual linking of two productions, one Canadian and one foreign, so that each is eligible for the support given to indigenous productions in its country of origin, and any financing secured can be cross-collateralized across the two productions. Also called **pairing**.

Unit publicist The person responsible for co-ordinating and disseminating information to the media about a film in production. See also **Publicist**.

Video-assist A small video camera attached to the film camera, which allows the director to see exactly what is being shot.

Weather cover Optional plans for the day's shooting schedule, so that interior scenes can be shot if poor weather makes the originally planned location impossible to use.

"Window" A period of time during which a purchaser of rights (e.g., theatrical, free TV, pay TV) receives the exclusive right to exhibit the production.

Work print A copy struck from the negative after processing, to be used by the editor to cut the film, and later by the negative cutter to match the original negative to the fine cut of the work print.

Wrap End of shooting, either on a given day, or at a given location, or of the entire production.

Wrap release A press release prepared by the unit publicist, noting that shooting has been completed.

Bibliography

Armer, Alan A. *Directing Television and Film*. Second edition. Belmont, CA: Wadsworth Publishing Company, 1990.

Benzion, Schmuel, and Rene S. Ash, eds. *The Producer's Masterguide*. New York: Producer's Masterguide, 611 Broadway. Exhaustive guide to film and video production in U.S., Canada, and Great Britain, updated annually.

Blum, Richard A. *Television Writing: From Concept to Contract*. Boston: Focal Press, 1984. Guide to film and television writing and marketing a script in the U.S. Covers public, cable, and network television.

*Blumenthal, Howard J. and Goodenough, Oliver R. *This Business of Television*. New York: Billboard Books, 1991.

*Bronfield, Stewart. *How to Produce a Film*. Englewood Cliffs, NJ: Prentice-Hall, 1984. Assumes no previous knowledge — stresses technical aspects of filmmaking.

Canadian Journal of Film Studies. Three times per year. Scholarly film criticism.

*Carrière, Louise. *Femmes et Cinéma Québécois*. Montréal: Boréal Express, 1983. Critical discussion of women filmmakers in Quebec. Includes an index to directors, producers, and films.

Changing Focus: The Future for Women in the Canadian Film and Television Industry. Toronto: Toronto Women in Film & Television, 1991.

Cineaction. Three times per year. Published by a collective; radical film criticism and theory.

Ciné-Bulles. French language film criticism.

Cones, John W. *Film Finance and Distribution: A Dictionary of Terms.* Los Angeles: Silman-James, 1992.

CSC *News.* Ten times per year. Published by the Canadian Society of Cinematographers to promote and foster the cause of cinematography and the interests of the Canadian film and video community.

★Desjardins, Claude. *Qui Fait Quoi — Répertoire.* Montreal: Qui Fait Quoi Inc. Magazine annual that includes film and industry listings for Quebec. Includes selected Toronto listings. Updated annually.

DGC *National News.* Irregular. Published by the Directors Guild of Canada.

Directory of Canadian Film, Television and Video Industry. Ottawa: Telefilm Canada. Updated annually.

Drabinsky, Garth H. *Motion Pictures and the Arts in Canada: The Business and the Law.* Toronto: McGraw-Hill Ryerson, 1976. Business and legal aspects of the motion picture industry in Canada as it was in the mid-seventies.

Focus Toronto. Formerly *The Toronto Film and Video Guide.* Toronto: Shuter-Springhurst. The directory of film, video, and multi-image facilities, personnel and current rates. Updated annually. Similar guides are available for Montreal, and Western Canada.

Frame by Frame. Toronto: Frame by Frame Publications. A guidebook to Toronto-based film, television, radio, and recording industries, listing production companies, production facilities, production services, freelance personnel, agencies, and consultants, and much more. Updated annually.

Gilbert, Taylor. *Producers, Distributors and Exhibitors of Motion Picture Films and Television Productions: Survey of Corporate and Financial Reporting.* Toronto: Peat Marwick Thorne, 1993.

Goldberg, Fred. *Motion Picture Marketing and Distribution: Getting Movies into a Theatre Near You.* Boston: Focal Press, 1991.

Goodell, Gregory. *Independent Feature Film Production: A Complete Guide from Concept to Distribution.* New York: St. Martin's Press, 1982. Guide to independent film production. Includes sample budgets, references, and sources useful to the filmmaker.

Harcourt, Amanda, Neil Howlett, Sally Davies, and Naomi Moscovic. *The Independent Producer: Film and Television.* London: Faber and Faber, 1986. Comprehensive guide to independent production, stressing the U.K. situation, including sample business forms and appendix of useful addresses.

*Hardin, Herschel. *Closed Circuits: The Sellout of Canadian Television.* Vancouver: Douglas and McIntyre, 1985. A highly critical examination of the CRTC and its role in the development of Canadian television.

Harris, Lesley. *Canadian Copyright Law.* Whitby, ON: McGraw-Hill Ryerson, 1992. Copyright law for the layman. Includes information on film and video.

Horwin, Michael. *Careers in Film and Video Production.* Boston: Focal Press, 1990.

International Festivals and Markets. Montreal: Telefilm Canada, 1993. Lists festivals and markets for film and television worldwide.

International Motion Picture Alamanac. New York: Quigley Publishing Company. Updated annually. Well-established directory with an American focus. Small Canadian section edited by Patricia Thompson.

International Television & Video Almanac. New York: Quigley Publishing Company. Updated annually. Well-established directory with an American focus. Small Canadian section edited by Patrica Thompson.

Katz, Steven D. *Film Directing Shot by Shot: Visualizing from Concept to Screen.* Studio City, CA: Michael Wiese Productions, 1991.

Katz, Steven D. *Film Directing-Cinematic Motion: A Workshop for Staging Scenes.* Studio City: CA: Michael Wiese Productions, 1992.

Kemps International Film and Television Yearbook. London: The Kemps Group. International production listings, stressing the British film industry. Includes a section on Canada. Updated annually.

Konigsberg, Ira. *The Complete Film Dictionary.* Toronto: Penguin Books, 1987.

La Revue de la Cinémathèque. Six times per year. News and comment from Cinémathèque québécoise.

Lazarus, Paul. *The Film Producer: A Handbook For Producing.* New York: St. Martin's Press, 1992.

LIFT. Irregular. Liaison of Independent Filmmakers of Toronto; a non profit co-op that supports and encourages independent filmmaking through the exchange of information and access to equipment and facilities. LIFT has a program of workshops and monthly screenings. It provides access to information regarding funding, sources, festivals, grant deadlines, and other related material.

Litwak, Mark. *Contracts for the Film Television Industry.* Los Angeles: Silman-James Press, 1994.

Litwak, Mark. *Dealmaking Film Television.* Los Angeles: Silman-James Press, 1994.

LoBrutto, Vincent. *By Design: Interviews with Film and Production Designers.* Westport, CT: Praeger, 1992.

Location Update. Monthly trade journal for locations and production.

Lukas, Christopher. *Directing for Film and Television: A Guide to the Craft.* New York: Doubleday, 1985. Guidebook specifically aimed at the novice director, covering all stages of production.

Magder, Ted. *Canada's Hollywood: The Canadian State and Feature Films.* Toronto: University of Toronto Press, 1993.

★Maltin, Leonard, ed. *The Whole Film Sourcebook.* New York: New American Library, 1983. Useful directory of film schools, film festivals, unions, distributors, and exhibitors, mainly in the U.S., with related industry information.

Mehring, Margaret. *The Screenplay: A Blend of Form and Content.* Boston: Focal Press, 1990.

Miller, Pat. P. *Script Supervision and Film Continuity.* Boston: Focal Press, 1990. Detailed guide covering all aspects of film continuity through each stage of production.

Morris, Peter. *The Film Companion.* Toronto: Irwin, 1984. Critical guide to selected Canadian producers, directors, writers, and films.

★Naylor Ensign, Lynn and Robyn Eileen Knapton, eds. *The*

Complete Dictionary of Television and Film. New York: Stein and Day, 1985. Defines over 3000 works and phrases in use in the film and video industries.

Newcomb, Horace and Robert S. Alley. *The Producer's Medium: Conversations with Creators of American T.V.* Oxford: Oxford University Press, 1983. Interviews with major U.S. television producers.

Nightingale Report. Weekly trade report. Lists events including festivals, markets, film, and video workshops.

*Oakey, Virginia. *Dictionary of Film and Television Terms.* New York: Harper and Row, 1983. Contains 3000 technical, artistic, and business terms in use in film and video.

Pendakur, Manjunath. *Canadian Dreams: The Making and Marketing of Independent Films.* Toronto: Douglas & McIntyre, 1993.

*Pincus, Edward and Steven Ascher. *Filmmaker's Handbook.* New York: New American Library, 1984. Introductory guide to filmmaking in the U.S. — emphasis on technical aspects.

Pintoff, Ernest. *The Complete Guide to American Film Schools and Cinema and Television Courses.* New York: Penguin Books, 1994. A good directory, but American in focus.

Playback. Bi-monthly trade journal covering the Canadian broadcasting and film industries. Playback Online @ Brunico Internet web site: http://bulldog.ca/brunico/

Posner, Michael. *Canadian Dreams: The Making and Marketing of Independent Films.* Toronto: Douglas & McIntyre, 1993.

POV Point of View. Irregular. The art of business of independent film.

Qui Fait Quoi/Entertainment Coast to Coast. Montreal: Qui Fait Quoi Inc. Covers the Canadian entertainment industries. Ten monthly magazines, 12 monthly newsletters, and an annual directory.

Rabinger, Michael. *Directing: Film Techniques and Aesthetics.* Boston: Focal Press, 1989.

Randall, John. *Feature Films on a Low Budget.* Boston: Focal Press, 1991.

Reel West Digest. Vancouver: Reel West Productions. A directory of film, video, audiovisual, photography, and graphic production in Western Canada. Updated annually.

Reverse Shot. Three times per year. Criticism and comment from the Pacific Cinematheque.

Richards, Ron. *A Director's Method for Film and Television.* Boston: Focal Press, 1991.

Roberts, Kenneth H. and Win Sharples Jr. *A Primer for Filmmaking: A Complete Guide to 16 mm and 35 mm Film Production.* Indianapolis, IN: Bobbs-Merril Educational Publications, 1984. Guide to all aspects of 16 mm and 35 mm filmmaking, aimed at professionals and serious students.

Rosen, David. *Off-Hollywood: The Making and Marketing of Independent Films.* New York: Grove Weidenfeld, 1990. Based on a study originally commissioned by The Sundance Institute and Independent Feature Project.

Rosenthal, Alan. *Writing, Directing and Producing Documentary Films.* Carbondale: Southern Illinois University Press, 1990.

Rowlands, Avril. *Continuity in Film and Video: A Handbook for Directors, Script Supervisors and PAs.* 2nd edition. Boston: Focal

Press, 1989.

Rubin, Steven Jay. *Reel Exposure: How to Publicize and Promote Today's Motion Pictures.* Shelter Island: Broadway Press, 1991.

★Sapan, Joshua. *Making It in Cable T.V.: Career Opportunities in Today's Fastest Growing Media Industry.* New York: Putnam Publishing Group, 1984. Vocational guide to cable television in the U.S.

Schihl, Robert. *Single Camera Video: From Concept to Edited Master.* Boston: Focal Press, 1989.

Seger, Linda and Whetmore, Edward Jay. *From Script to Screen: The Collaborative Art of Filmmaking.* New York: Henry Holt and Company, 1994.

Séquences. Six times per year. French language film criticism.

★Silver, Alain and Elizabeth Ward. *The Film Director's Team: A Practical Guide to Organizing and Managing Film and Television Production.* New York: Arco Publishing Inc., 1983. Recommended practical guide, stressing the role of the assistant director and production manager. Glossary.

Singleton, Ralph. *Film Scheduling: Or How Long Will It Take to Shoot Your Movie?* Beverly Hills, CA: Lone Eagle Publishing, 1984. Guide to professional film scheduling. Includes production board and sample breakdown sheets. By the same author: *The Film Scheduling/Film Budgeting Workbook* and *Movie Production and Budget Forms...Instantly!*

Singleton, Ralph. *Film Scheduling Film Budgeting Workbook.* Santa Monica: Lone Eagle, 1989.

Squire, Jason E., ed. *The Movie Business Book.* New York:

Simon Schuster, 1983. Each chapter is written by a different U.S. film industry insider, and the stress is on the Hollywood studio system. Several sample forms.

Steven, Peter. *Brink of Reality: New Canadian Documentary Film and Video.* Toronto: Between The Lines, 1993.

Strategy. Canadian marketing newspaper. Published every two weeks.

Take One. Three times per year. Canadian English language film criticism.

The Guide. Toronto: Canadian Film and Television Production Association. Updated annually. A Canadian location and production guide.

Thompson, Patricia, ed. *Film Canada Yearbook.* Toronto: Cinecommunications. Indispensable guide to production, distribution, and exhibition of films across Canada. Fully indexed, updated annually.

Topalovich, Maria. *A Pictorial History of the Canadian Film Awards.* Toronto: Stoddart/Academy of Canadian Cinema, 1984. Canadian film awards from 1949 to 1984. Includes brief history of Canadian film industry. Illustrated.

Tromberg, Sheldon. *Making Money, Making Movies: The Independent Movie Maker's Handbook.* New York: New Viewpoints/Vision Books, 1980. General guide to screenwriting, production, distribution, and exhibition for independent filmmakers in the U.S.

24 Images. Six times per year. Québécois French language criticism.

Who's Who in Canadian Film and Television – Qui est qui au cinéma et à la télévision au Canada. Academy of Canadian Cinema and Television. Wilfred Laurier University Press, Waterloo, ON, 1991.

Wiese, Michael. *Independent Film and Videomaker's Guide.* Westport CT: Michael Wiese Productions, 1984. Detailed introductory guide to the production, distribution, and marketing of independent films and videos. By the same author: *Film and Video Budgets*, a comprehensive guide to cost effectiveness in film and video production. Includes sample budgets.

Wiese, Michael. *Home Video: Producing for the Home Market.* Westport CT: Michael Wiese Productions, 1986.

Wiese, Michael. *Film and Video Financing.* Westport CT: Michael Wiese Productions, 1991.

Wiese, Michael. *Producer to Producer: The Best of Michael Wiese in Videography Magazine.* Westport CT: Michael Wiese Productions, 1993.

Wolfe, Morris. *Jolts: The T.V. Wasteland and the Canadian Oasis.* Toronto: James Lorimer, 1985. A positive discussion of the state of Canadian television.

Wyatt, Justin. *High Concept: Movies and Marketing in Hollywood.* Austin: University of Texas, 1994.

★Yeldell, Eric B. *The Motion Picture and Television Business.* Beverly Hills: Entertainment Business Publishing Co., 1987.

This bibliography was updated by the Film Reference Library, a division of the Toronto International Film Festival Group.

Unless otherwise indicated, all the material in the bibliography is available at the Library.

★*Not available at the Film Reference Library.*

Index